PRAIS

"Pushes mortality to the very edge with broncos, sharks, and drugs, coming together to create a disturbing picture of American life."
JOEANN HART, AUTHOR OF *ARROYO CIRCLE*

"These imaginative essays and stories, told in varying perspectives, are pulled together by the impulse to test our limits... All ask the same question: how much is too much? Kadish looks in unwavering honesty at the heartbreaking consequences of one wrong move."
CHERYL PAPPAS, AUTHOR OF *THE CLARITY OF HUNGER*

Enjoy The
Book

Joanna Kadish

ABOUT THE AUTHOR

Joanna Kadish edited newsletters on finance for Grant Thornton and the American Institute of Certified Public Accountants before her children were born. After that, she became a freelance contributor for the New Jersey Regional Section of *The New York Times* and several regional newspapers and magazines, including *The Cleveland Plain Dealer, Asbury Park Press, Seattle Magazine* and *Seattle Business Magazine*, among other publications. She published stories and essays in numerous literary magazines and won first place in *Adelaide Literary* Award 2019 Contest, and she was a finalist in the creative nonfiction category in the Spring 2019 *Pinch* Literary Awards, as well as a finalist in the Black Coffee & Vinyl Presents: Ice Cultures project, summer of 2018, and Cutthroat 2023 and 2016 Rick DeMarinis Short Fiction Contest. She has written a couple of novels, *Charting a Marriage* and *Swing Set*. She has an MFA in Creative Writing from Bennington Writing Seminars in Vermont and an undergraduate degree in literature and philosophy from UC Berkeley.

FLIRTING WITH EXTINCTION

COLLECTED ESSAYS & STORIES

JOANNA KADISH

www.vineleavespress.com

For Nick and Amalie

AUTHOR'S NOTE

Things have been kept as factual as possible and many names have been changed to protect individual identities. Many place names have also been changed, but not all of them, and for no reason, depending on the whim of the author.

PREFACE

This collection of short creative nonfiction and fiction examines debris of our throw-away culture and personal experience combining memoir and journalism to explore sex, motherhood, and death. And it addresses why I clawed my way back to a semblance of life as it is lived in a state of perpetual sadness while others have fallen around me like the proverbial dominos, first my paternal grandmother whom I loved dearly, and walked with often as a child watching her forget everything as her dementia grew more evident, followed by my father, who very much wanted to live long enough to see the dawning of the computer age, and his sister, my aunt who was lovely to me, followed by my teenaged twin boys. It also attempts to explain the stubbornness of the life-force that propels me forward to tell my stories and theirs, and why is it that there remains a gaping hole in my still-beating heart that no amount of time can heal or assuage.

Several essays examine the detritus of a marriage after a series of frenzied family camping trips, stints of frantic endurance cycling, baseball, and finally, partner swapping: all these stratagems employed to keep a husband's attention from wandering and keep him focused on keeping the marriage and family afloat—all of it in the end proving useless. We as a married couple kept repeating the same tired lines while everything around us fizzled and burned, and our children proved unable to extricate themselves from difficult situations; intervention only made it worse.

Listening one day to the crude undercurrent of his joking voice belittling my sense of humor (he said he could see the smoke issue from my ears), the realization came to me that my efforts were not perceived as equal. Even as I struggled to keep a part-time job while caring for our three young children, there was his belief that everything he perceived to be true was the complete truth and my perceptions were not valid, or misguided, and were to be disregarded as false. Over it all, what issued out of his sonorous voice was truly a gift from the gods, especially when narrating the jokes of the famous comedians: Jackie Mason, Lenny Bruce, or Seinfeld. I could not praise his genitals (like he did) as the family jewels, at least nothing extraordinary, more like ho-hum, unlike his radio announcer's voice, which does sound like sour grapes, but that part I kept private, no commenting on size as it is nothing that a person has control over. But in his defense, he does try hard to please the woman he's with, and that counts for a lot.

I fell apart at my father's death, the way he slipped from me. The specter of longtime married love gone awry is juxtaposed with stories about my feeble attempts to wrest my sons away from a vapid culture of sex and drugs. The pain of seeing them choose death like a feral song (is that not the way of all addiction?) and of being helpless to prevent what I saw happening.

The true story: Opioids have ripped my family apart, taken my beautiful sons who had so much to offer the world. They had a lot of friends and were extremely social. They both played guitar well and one had a gift for storytelling. Several of the stories are fictional—I wrote them in one of the boy's voices, the one who discovered his twin dead while—a twist of fate—he was left very much alive, left to deal with the pain of not having the one person he relied on for everything spiritual, a reason to live. His story is not unique. Many kids in their suburban high school were exposed to fentanyl; some of them got addicted; all were youth primarily from upper-middle-class families, a majority of them male with a wealth of opportunities open to them. And I know the problem is increasing. My kids' alma mater constantly holds monthly informational meetings for parents about it, and I hear from the grapevine what parents are doing to intervene, mainly sending them to lockdown schools.

It's not just kids in school and their parents, it's vast scores of people who are addicted to something and who are generally interested in the subject of addiction. My father was an alcoholic, and for a while when I was young and working for corporations, I drank too much. Is our culture to blame? Why is addiction to heavy drugs, in particular fentanyl, increasing in schools and elsewhere? Addicts generally cannot see a way out, not on their own. Plenty of rehab counselors would love to know how to beat the oppressive nature of fentanyl addiction, and can point to marginal success rates, with high recidivism. This collection of stories deals with the pain of losing beautiful, intelligent boys to this awful plague sweeping America. I would love to reach these people to help find answers. My deathwork, as Philip Rieff might have termed it, deals with the anguish of attempting to understand and explain the series of misfortunes sprinkling my life like confetti. How did I manage to lose everything I cherish?

ANATOMY OF A FIREFIGHTER

There's a picture of me at three cutting my hair with kitchen shears, hoping to look like my brother, leaving me with stubby hair bordered by bald spots, leading to haircuts for all my dolls. I paraded their shorn heads around the house. We lived east of Los Angeles on the edge of the Sonoran Desert, where the biggest excitement tended to be the kid-sized tumbleweeds that rolled over the landscape. Around us orange groves next to wide-open fields filled with dry grass where horses grazed. The land was teaming with the horny toads I liked to pet, their little horns tickling the skin of my fingertips. And the Gila monster, a large lizard about eighteen inches long, patterned not quite like tiger stripes, but with that same feel, orange mixing with the black, allowing the creature to disappear into the brush lighting fast.

My brother Marc suggested that we burn my shorn dolls. I agreed. Sparks from the burning plastic flew into the dry grass, the fetid stench scattered by contrary winds, sounding like hundreds of tiny fire-crackers going off. My father trained a garden hose full blast but the water dissolved into the fire's waiting maw. Marc and I threw pails of water at it, while my mother called the fire department, and I marveled at her depiction of hell as a large fire that continually consumes the hapless inhabitants, a Dante's Inferno.

I wouldn't have cared to start fires on my own, but Marc just started Boy Scouts and wanted to practice his fire-building skills. He taught me how to build one with dry kindling and balled up newspaper, and to detect the vinegary smell of burning wood before flames could spread like a sooty fogbank over the land.

One day when I was six, we found refuge in a dry creek bed full of rocks, brown weeds, and scrub. Marc thought it a good place to build a campfire. We put rocks around a cleared out area and placed twigs in the middle of it. Marc knew from Boy Scouts to form a teepee from the twigs. He rubbed two sticks together and created a flame in seconds. As the flame took hold, I settled on some rocks to enjoy the flaming beauty. But the fire quickly went out of control and my heart beat madly, almost to the point of dizziness, trying to scrabble out of the way. The flames were insatiable, consuming all the weeds and dry bush in their path. We hadn't thought to clear a wide enough swath around our campfire.

Marc sustained second-degree burns trying to stomp the fire out with his sneakers. I talked him into abandoning the fire and running back to the house for help. My father called the fire department, while my mother applied burn medicine and cool water to soothe our blistered skin. There's nothing worse than being burned—the pain lasts for weeks, sometimes months, and the skin can easily scar. To this day, Marc has a number of burn scars from that time. But to his credit, my brother was not easily deterred. I watched him develop his firefighting skills, learning how to starve fires to death, a skill that demanded peak fitness, endurance, the training of an elite warrior.

Several years passed. One summer—I was a teenager then—a fire broke out in Old Cajon. My brother's Boy Scout troop joined the firefighters and I tagged along, unbeknown to my parents, helping remove trees, stumps, roots, leaves, grass and weeds, exposing the nakedness of the earth to onlookers. No one averted their eyes. They must have realized that Mother Earth had feelings, and that her modesty drives her to cover herself with plants. A wanton thing, reveling under the gaze of firefighters, she hoped to excite their lust before the unruly flames blinded them with their heat. Fires are an ornery lot; they leap around the hills like phantoms, especially on inclines, where they burn twice as fast, covering more ground than fires on flat ground. Fires typically burn at 1500-to-1800 Fahrenheit, hotter than any oven. I didn't feel the need to follow the men in their hazmat suits, and never yearned to get close to that gothic theater of embers. I stayed far back with the most conservative of onlookers. My respect for fire power was legion, having already experienced several harrowing encounters with the beast. In the words of William Faulkner, "The past is never dead. It's not even past."

Charred skeletons of buildings and cars dotted the area. A cargo train sat idle on tracks, abandoned by its engineer. Iridescent flames of red, gold and copper licked the skies, heading into that pincushion of fire engulfing Lone Pine Canyon, and choking on smoky air. Helicopters whirred in smoky darkness, and in the distance bulldozers razed wide swaths in an attempt to contain its fury.

Trees toppled over in cascading showers of flame, sounding like cracking bones shattering my eardrums. Soot clung to my exposed skin, and my entire body felt hot and sweaty. Likely I was breathing toxins. I wondered how Marc was doing and hoped to spot him emerge out of the ashy clouds. My greatest fear, for him to be caught in its grip, every nerve end screaming, skin boiling, and dragon breath trapped in his lungs. When he emerged from his hazmat suit, he looked exhausted, his eyes teary, and high-fived me and everyone else, his smile as big as the sky.

From then on, Marc was hooked. I moved far away to go to school, no longer a sojourner in the land of drought. His stories of daring move me, but I'm no longer there to share the sooty air. If it wasn't for my memories, I wouldn't believe that fire unchecked is unruly, unbearable, and without mercy, just like the ocean that strives to contain it.

CALAMITY JANE

One day I left my dolls to ride horses and got thrown a lot. The dirt was soft, and the horses forgiving on our ranch fronting the eastern side of the Gabilan Mountains. In a burst of hubris I claimed that not only could I ride a rodeo bronc, but I could convince one to stop bucking and do my bidding. I was invincible, having already broken a few horses, a process I found exhilarating. I didn't believe I was any less for being a girl, but I also felt I had to prove myself, and believed in the innate kindness of the horses I knew and assumed all horses were like that. It didn't seem like a stretch that I could break a wild'un.

"You're too chicken," said the brother who totaled a jeep.

"I'll take the dare," I said.

This happened many years before women entered professional bronc riding, long before I saw Billi Halverson somersault off the back of a bucking bronc, cracking several vertebrae (which the film crew repeated in slow motion several times for the viewers who love the grizzly stuff, like me, looking to re-experience ancient injuries) in *Cowgirls,* a reality show on Ride TV. *Cowgirls* follows a handful of female bronc riders, mostly twenty somethings, in rodeos across the West, showcasing the leaping, bucking, twisting action of the horses, and close-ups of gorgeous women with bruised or broken legs and arms, faces planted in the dirt.

Later I learned that Halverson, a former bull rider in her early forties, now pursuing a career as a bronc rider, spent the remainder of the year recuperating in a neck and back brace. This was after she fractured her spine in several places and had a fiberglass and steel exoskeleton put in place while her spine healed. She left bull riding after repeated breaks to her arm, saying that she no longer has the kind of grip and arm strength that it takes to win—apparently there's less pull on the arm in bronc riding. Today she lives the chronic, daily pain all rough stock riders accept as part of the job. Which begs the question: why risk your health this way?

There's something about the frenzied bucking of a live animal that can't be duplicated by a machine, the possibility of besting a semi-wild animal, pitting one's puny self against a twelve-hundred-pound fury—a primal something akin to being doped up on meth except that it's naturally derived and makes the senses feel totally alive in a way that a drug can't. It's like glacier climbing, in that a wrong move could be fatal. and it rattles the body to a greater degree than the best white-knuckle technology can do, subjecting a person to varying degrees of gravitational forces in unfamiliar directions. And there's the danger of emerging crippled for life, a big draw for some.

Smashing one's body is commonplace in bronc riding, but usually it's the men sustaining the injuries. Last season Jesse Berry, a man, was stepped on by a bronc, requiring a total rebuild of his face. (His eye sockets were rebuilt from one of his ribs.) "I've had buddies of mine say they'd never get on again if they'd been hurt like that," Berry said to *Rodeo News*. "I thought long and hard while I was healing, but in the end, the call of good bucking horses was just stronger than anything else." He is echoed by Sarah Brown, nineteen, who started riding rough stock in 2017 and is a member of the Texas Bronc Riders ladies' team; she dislocated her jaw and crushed her back, but she's not letting that stop her. For me, the rare times I rode rough stock, I'd get thrown and the pain was momentary, a bruised arm or sore back, and the knowledge that I might not survive seemed less of a possibility, as I did everything in my power to survive. And even though I knew intellectually that it could happen, I could not conceive of dying. So I continued feeding my fascination, play-acting doing dangerous things and getting away with it, i.e. not dying; merely having an injury that can heal seemed totally worth the exhilaration of the moment, knowing that each time I made myself do it, the less scared I would be, and the more skilled I would become.

I was not alone in thinking myself protected by the gods. Before 1929, a lot of women competed in bronc riding, and many lived to tell the tale. And then Bonnie McCarroll, thirty-four, was dragged under the horse, her head hitting the hardpack with every buck. She died soon after. From then on, women were excluded from that event. Bronc riding is said to be the toughest sport in rodeo to master due to technical skills needed for success and is especially hard on the body. Women's bareback bronc riding was added as a special event at the Grand National Rodeo in San Francisco in 1979, but not women's saddle bronc riding. The people running the show thought it was too dangerous with a saddle. In 1991, National Finals Rodeo, the most prestigious rodeo in the country, finally allowed women back in, both for saddle and bareback. But they had to compete with the men, and only two women wanted to do this, lured perhaps by average earnings of up to $100,000 for individual event grand champions in the national finals.

That's been the state of affairs until July 2016 when the Texas Bronc Riders Association launched as a ladies' division, offering a team atmosphere with slumber parties, special training from top bronc riders, and one-on-one mentoring— and now that they've created a reality TV show out of it, *Cowgirls*, women are trying out for the sport in droves.

Seeing these bronc riders smash themselves to smithereens with such stoicism on Ride TV took me back to my childhood, when I was twelve years old some forty years ago, and I dreamt of becoming bronc rider. Back then, I never thought there was a chance of it happening— no women were doing it—but I held on to that dream anyway. Living on three hundred acres in cowboy country along the eastern side of the Gabilan Mountains, off California Highway 25 in the central part of the state had a lot to with it.

I blame my interest in bronc riding on these mountains. John Steinbeck in *East of Eden* called the Gabilans "light gay mountains full of fun and loveliness and a kind of invitation," folding around me like "the lap of a beloved mother". As Steinbeck put it, "beckoning mountains with a brown grass love."

Gabilan means 'sparrow hawk' in Spanish, to commemorate one of the many species prevalent on this short coastal range that runs along in California's central valley. The land looks solid, but it borders the San Andreas Fault, prone to seismic shifts in the earth's surface, and entire hills could be swallowed up, according to legend around these parts.

It was a magical place to grow up in. Mostly squirrels and yellow-bellied marmots owned the land and the occasional coyote, red fox and deer, the air dense with the scent of buck brush, peppergrass, wildflowers, and oak. In the spring, a carpet of poppies, wild mustard, buttercups and violets, lupines, harebells, and Indian paintbrush lingered through the dry hot summer until they mummified to the colors of an autumn bouquet.

=

First I had to get permission from my father. He liked to hang out on the patio in the evenings when not dealing with emergencies at the hospital, drinking and telling stories, or watching shadows lengthen and the sky turn black. Friends would stop by, their voices soft like the susurration of leaves, their laughter like the creak of tree limbs being nudged apart by wind. They were big in the shoulder, their hands roughened by physical work, eyes locked in perpetual squints, filling the air with a potent mix of leather and sweat. After the men had broken out the whiskey and their laughter had mellowed, I told my father my proposal.

"I can buy a rodeo reject for a hundred bucks, maybe less," I said. "I'll gentle him and sell for five hundred, maybe more."

I had saved the money from my work in a neighbor's orchards picking apricots for the past few summers.

18

"*À sua saúde*," Louie Cabral cried, lifting his glass of whiskey, his smile creasing like a dried-up creek bed, tributaries circling his eyes and mouth.

I was floating on air, endorphins pinging. Louie said he'd help, one of the bravest men I had ever seen on top a horse (my father was another), and not much taller than me, legs bowed, and fingers bent from gripping reins, and his right shoulder posed higher than the other. His Portuguese ancestry made it easy for him to tan; he was as dark as the insides of a walnut hull. Going by the moniker "The Wildest Roman Rider" on the rodeo circuit, Louie knew how to coax three-horse tandems to jump a flaming hurdle, and five-horse tandems over jumps of varying difficulty and always with his feet planted on two of the horses. He was also the original stagecoach driver for Wells Fargo Bank advertising and commercials, performed as a stunt rider for Westerns, and was said to be the only man who could jump three horses over a car, an Evel Knievel on horseback. My father met Louie on the operating table and told me that Louie had broken every bone in his body at least twice. I shrugged that off, thinking nothing of a broken bone, having never broken any.

My father's face flushed a bright glow. He clapped me on the back. "You're quite a girl," he said. He said a woman should be able to do anything she wanted.

I was the only one in the family who read philosophy for fun (my father was a philosophy major as an undergrad) and he tried for the millionth time to convince me to be a physician like him, but I was derailed by my poor aptitude for math, so why go down that path? And as the only girl in a family of seven brothers and finding being the only girl burdensome, having to deal with brothers who liked to tease, to stop their silly jokes, calling me chicken and so on, I wanted to do something so big, so godawful, they would be struck dumb with respect and adoration. Around the time my little sister finally arrived, I was too old to be pals, and fortunately at her arrival, Momma hired people to help with the cooking and cleaning. All of us kids continued to pitch in the running of my father's working cattle ranch, but I was the only one who worked with Louie, the only one crazy enough to get banged up repeatedly on a horse and enjoy it.

My father talked about how glorious we had it and mused about summers spent in the Grand Tetons on the Montana border with his cousin Kirk and a couple of fly rods, eating fresh trout when they could catch it, dried fruit and beef jerky when they couldn't. He knew how to cut and rope cows, drank like no tomorrow, and filled our ears with old cowboy songs, his smile as big as the wide-open sky.

"I can smell the bacon, just a' sizzling in the pan, and in the early morning, drinking coffee from a can..."

And he hummed the rest, the words he couldn't remember, and it changed all the time—sometimes he sang about ropin' cattle, other times it would be about sleepin' under the stars on the great plains with nothing but scrub and sky between a man and his god, because you see my father always did believe in a god, only his was a lot more flexible and relaxed than most folks.

It was a family tradition when we hit our teens to do something out of the ordinary, inspired by my father's stories of derring-do as a teenager. One brother drove a jeep with faulty brakes down a steep mountain road. The driver suffered a broken jaw and his passengers escaped with minor bruises, saved by the roll bar, but the jeep was totaled. Another brother swam dangerous undertows around Big Sur, not far from where we lived, with no injury but tired to the bone. And yet another brother shimmied a huge evergreen to the top and halfway down, fell, breaking his arm.

The day of the auction, my father came to the fairgrounds with me. Louie said he'd come, but my father thought we'd be fine without him. Neither one of us thought a rodeo bronc would be any different from any other wild horse. We were simply going on the fact that these horses were being sold for practically nothing. I didn't expect much in the looks department, but this one first struck me as especially ugly: a knock-kneed gelding with a neck too spindly to support his big head and thuggish face. But then I looked into his fevered eyes and realized his beauty, a by-product of the danger he exuded, a force that drew me like a magnet. Red dust boiled around his constantly churning hoofs. I'd heard wild horses glorified as otherworldly creatures, almost preternatural, and that mythical aura appealed to me. I didn't question the logic of why they were selling this horse when the rodeo people said, "to make room for a new crop of horses," although I should have figured their explanation had more holes than the night sky has stars, never mind the hard currency burning a hole in my pocket.

At home Louie took one look at him and said, "That cayuse has a wild streak alright. I'd be careful around him." He was a man of few words.

Louie trained Quarter Horses, bred from Andalusian, the Spanish war horse, and English Thoroughbred, able to outrun any other breed in a quarter mile race (Thoroughbreds need more time to reach their top speed), turn in a tight circle, and stop from a hard run to a stand-still. My father had a stable of a dozen such horses, gifts from patients. One of them, a palomino gelding out of the Thoroughbred considered one of the most influential founding sires of the Quarter Horse breed, clocked speeds up to fifty-five miles per hour in his heyday. But that was before we got him. He was given to my father after he developed a bum knee.

We kids liked to play cowboys and Indians. The Indians got to ride bareback, riding with minimal equipment, depending only on agility and instincts. I'd slide sideways off the horse's spine in a delicate balance, hovering over the horse's ribs so I wasn't visible from one side as I had seen pictures of the Indians do to avoid being shot by cavalry, holding on to the mane to stabilize my body. I did this because I thought it cool, and to avoid the moss hanging from the knurled oak trees like delicate lace. An early memory: my father bouncing all of us at the same time crowding the length of his leg, sometimes riding his ankle, and giggling uncontrollably, especially when he bounced his leg rough and high. When he got tired, he'd shoo us off, and we'd wrestle each other down, jumping on the piled-up bodies.

I had several years' experience under Louie's direction training cowponies through the entire process of accepting commands from a rider, learning to bear the saddle pad and the corset of the surcingle, and on through the process of wearing an empty saddle and then the bit. When the saddle came again, with me on top of it, the horses bucked, emitting piercing cries that would make the other horses dance with anxiety, but they always let me ride them, some sooner than others. On their backs the sun shining like a blowtorch made it possible for me to see further and cover more territory, like Steinbeck said, "A man on a horse is spiritually, as well as physically, bigger than a man on foot." It's hard for a person who has never spent time around horses to understand what this does to your soul.

It took three men to get the bronc into the horse trailer. The bronc turned out to be a trickster, dodging and feinting; I liked that about him. As contrary as it may seem, I was attracted to animals that displayed an indomitable spirit incapable of yielding easily, where the winning would be hard fought. I liked the challenge of making them my friend and doing so successfully offered me a way to compete with my brothers on my own terms. I did not want to be perceived as the only one shying from challenging opportunities. An eagle flew above me, and I thought it a good omen, shrugging off the bronc's outsized show of force. My first order of business was to demonstrate empathy and caring as Louie had taught me, but not without the tools at hand: the soft ropes, enclosures, and gates that locked. I knew to be judicious when applying those tools; no flicking a rope around the horse's head and being careful around the flank where he feels most vulnerable. I imagined I was a Kentauroi, a centaur, half man and half horse, and like the Greek philosopher Xenophon, who wrote about the concept of gentle training, I envisioned creating a synergistic relationship with the bronc, thinking his uneasiness would vanish with a gentle touch. Even tame horses can be easily spooked and can be dangerous to be around when they are. A horse might be called upon to employ his hoofs in an extreme situation, say, when confronted by a lion or bear. I would be shapeshifter, and steal into his conscious and rearrange the furniture, envisioning his transformation into my alter ego, my spirit embodied into horse.

Louie came by often to see how I was doing. Out of his mouth came teasing words, the laugh lines deepening like fissures in the desert, calling me "little sister," in his rough whiskey-soaked voice that reminded me of my father's cousins from Texas, big, fierce men with beards who came around to visit when they came out west, talking of rodeos and stampedes. Louie boasted that he taught me well. Like me, he thought plenty of treats would win the big baby over. He bolstered my belief in my powers as fledgling horse whisperer; neither one of us thought the animal's back story mattered.

Louie slapped me a high five. "So, what's the worst kind of sickness bronc riders can get?"

"I dunno, what?"

"Bronchitis, silly."

I learned it didn't matter what I had for him, alfalfa, oats, Omolene, or apples and cheese, every time I entered his corral he shivered at my approach and tried to bite with his vicious teeth. I knew to take care not to approach from the rear but only moved where he could see me, so he always knew where I was, a practice that usually helps calm skittish horses. I kept my fears to myself, thinking it was just a matter of time.

Next time I saw Louie, he had a few questions for me. "What's the definition of 'derange'?"

"Let me think."

"Times up. De place where the de cowboys ride."

"So what else can I do to get the bronc to love me?"

"Try pears, saltines, walnuts. Always works for me."

As soon as the horse finished his treat, he went on the attack. He kicked, he bit; he lashed out with everything he had. One of his kicks badly bruised my arm; anything he did to me, I'd suck it up. I had already boasted to everyone I knew that I was going to do this thing and I wasn't a quitter. I clung to the belief that I could change him, and that kindness would win out in the end. I told my father I needed the entire summer to gentle the cayuse, maybe longer; my arm slowed things down, but I didn't cry about it. Even so, my brothers taunted me unmercifully, calling me scaredy cat. I despaired as August drew to a close that I was not making inroads and thought about the cowboys cautioning that me to take care. "He kicks," one of them at the rodeo said ominously. Perhaps other bucking broncos were this intractable. I didn't know what other people's experiences were; I never thought to ask. Whatever happened to other people wouldn't matter anyway. My fate was sealed; I had to finish this thing.

My father asked how I was progressing with the bronc. "Has he stopped biting and kicking?"

"He can't kick when I have him trussed like a chicken."

"Be careful," my father said.

"You have two weeks until summer is over," one brother volunteered.

"I'll start riding him end of September," I said to get him off my back.

The morning I planned to ride the mustang turned out to be a scorcher typical for California's heartland. Louie was called away on an emergency; several of his horses broke through a fence, including a stallion, and were running loose in a neighbor's fields causing all kinds of havoc. I wasn't going put it off; I wanted to do this.

Up in the sky, a bird flew overhead in a lazy arc, distilling from the day a gesture of inviolate elegance.

"Condor," my father said.

With their huge wingspan, condors are the largest flying bird in the Western Hemisphere, their shrunken bald heads looking like a cannibal's prize: gray, yellow, or bright orange depending on age, easily identified by "Frill at the neck/Then the flutings of their Ionian/ Death-gowns," in the words of Sylvia Plath. We lived north of the Pinnacles, a mountainous area formed some twenty-three-million years ago as multiple volcanoes erupted, flowed, and slid over the land to form towering rock spires replete with rare talus caves and canyons with chaparral and oak, home to the California condor, an endangered species of New World vulture, the only surviving member of the genus *Gymnogyps*.

I could feel the flow of the bird's slender shape preying on my mind. Not that I felt that death was imminent. Believing in my own immortality, I reaffirmed that I was ready. In my day there was shame attached to a girl who shows fear.

Some twenty people had come to watch. Catcalling "Get'em cowboy, and "Show him who's boss."

The horse quivered when I cinched the saddle and his head shot up to the sky. He took on the walleyed look of a cornered animal. At the look of terror in his eyes, dread clogged my synapses. My father's face mirrored my own fears but the look of excitement on my brothers' faces reminded me that I would have to live with their contempt if I faltered, and that thought stopped me cold. Anything I said would be met with derision. There was no way out. I resolved to die with honor.

My father jumped away from the horse, and my knuckles turned white on the rope I held onto for dear life. I leaned back to stay centered; the plan was to avoid being flung forward. But I had never been on a creature that bucked like this one. He moved as if a tiger had landed on his back, sunfishing and windmilling, the likes of which I have never experienced before or since, and adopted a weird spiraling movement with his rear and front moving at different rates and in different directions. He swapped ends between jumps and came down ker-slam on four ramrod legs, head and fore legs twisting one way and the rump and hind legs another like he was on two invisible pogo sticks twirling at different speeds, something I was totally unprepared for.

I clung to the rope as if I was velcroed on, using my other arm to help balance my body some of the time, and other times I held onto the horn, though my back and neck felt as if I was being snapped in two. Then he jackknifed and swung his head down low. My main focus was to stay on, but he reared up so fast that I lost my balance and was thrown forward as if I was a rag doll. I heard the loud smack of my jaw hitting the top of his head. All this took place in a blink of an eye. The impact shattered my teeth and vibrated my skull, my mouth filling with sharp tooth fragments that crunched, gritty like sand. I hit the ground and rolled until I could crawl on my hands and knees, making haste to get out from under his hooves, scrambling for the fence.

Engorged with blood from yelling their spleens out, eyes lidded and balled, my brothers laughed and carried on, munching snacks and drinks. They reminded me of chickens with their long necks stretched, beaks poised to rip apart tender flesh.

A couple of the neighbor's boys, big hulking teenagers, backed the horse into the chute so they could remove the saddle and snaffle bit. My head spun as if I had gotten off a merry go round. I had never felt more elated, almost dizzy with pleasure, and curiously, there was no pain, even with the discovery of a soft mash of red flesh springing out of my gums where my bottom front teeth had been, my lips grimy from the dust of the corral that clung to the blood smearing my face. My father looked at my mouth and steered me to the car.

"I lasted the full eight seconds, maybe longer," I said, my words coming out in a garble. "Didn't I?" That's all I cared about, but I didn't think my father could understand me. No matter, I was confident that I would qualify for bronc riding.

"Get in the truck," my father said. "We don't have much time."

My father drove me to the county hospital where he worked as chief of surgery, saying we had to get my exposed roots covered before the pain set in. The condor stayed with us all the while, its body changing shapes, reminding me of my dependence on my father, who was always there to pick us up whenever any of us fell short. One of those times was when the entire family was on a weeklong fishing trip, and several of us had fished for hours in a remote river on the Montana border near where my father was born, trying every technique we had learned, but none of us could get any fish to bite. My father put on his rubber pants and waded out to the deep part where the rest of us had been afraid to venture, his rod flashing in a large arc behind him. My brothers and I followed him, but it didn't matter what any of us tried, we didn't have his technique. It took him half an hour to catch enough fish to feed us all.

"You're not riding that cayuse anymore," my father said.

"You won't get any argument from me."

In the emergency room, my father elbowed the resident physician out of the way and took over. My father's hands were soothing, soft as a bird's feathers. He usually refused to work on his own children from fear he would be too nervous to do it right, but this time he made an exception, placing a covering made from paraffin to protect the exposed roots. "I'll give you a little something so you can sleep tonight. I don't think aspirin will cut it."

I thought about my Spanish-speaking Anglo-Irish father with his advanced medical degree from Stanford working two nights a week at a free medical clinic in the valley for farmworkers, donating his time so they would have medical care. And even though I knew these things, I had no understanding of the sacrifices that he made for us and others. He doled out the painkillers, counseling me to only take them at night so I could sleep.

Louie stopped by. "I'll see what I can do with that critter," he said and vanished into the haze.

Only recently did I learn from watching *Cowgirls* how woefully unprepared I had been all those many years ago. I called Daryl McElroy, president of the Texas Bronc Riders Association, to find out what kind of precautions the contestants took to minimize the risks. I learned that the bronc riders go through an intensive three-day training camp and practice on the less challenging bucking horses—ones who aren't badass enough for pro circuit. They wear mouth guards and have safety vests, though few of them wear their vests. McElroy blames that oversight on superstition, saying "bronc riders are like baseball players, they have to do things a certain way or they don't feel prepared." And there's always an ambulance waiting and doctors on call.

My father grew up at a time when people didn't wear safety gear to ride a horse. The horsemen in those days relied on daredevilry and cunning. And it seems today, from what I've heard from these lady riders, things aren't much different.

My father didn't think of mouthguards as a requirement for riding horses. But neither one of us knew what it meant to ride a bronc. In hindsight, if I had worn a mouth guard, I might have had a different outcome. But I was lucky that my father had a lot of connections in the medical community and lined me up with a dentist who specialized in mouth reconstruction. He had me on a diet of jazz and nitrous oxide.

Five of my teeth were totally shattered beyond any hope of repair, requiring two implants to anchor a bridge; most of my other teeth were chipped so badly they required crowns. It was too big a job for the town dentist, so my mother had to drive me into San Francisco to see a specialist. I learned that every single tooth is a little organ, and the same blood and lymphatic fluid flows through my heart and all the other organs and systems in my body and flows through my teeth as well. A complex system of nerves connects my teeth to my brain, and every tooth is connected to one of the channels of life-force energy, the acupuncture meridians.

Reconstruction took a few years to complete. The pulp composed of nerves and blood vessels is fragile, and like our brains, easily damaged. Sometimes the internal damage takes a long time to manifest. Many of my surviving teeth needed root canals some ten to fifteen years after the initial trauma. During those years the pain felt like a series of jackhammers to the head, particularly when a root died, which happened every few months or so. It was not the kind of pain that an aspirin can mask fully, yet I deliberately chose not to take anything stronger for it. I couldn't overcome my father's aversion to painkillers; it was a mental thing. But when you allow pain to seep in like that, the entire brain is absorbed, tipping over into a keening that the body starts to wear like a custom-fitted garment. The worse was the nightmarish dreams. I had to wear a mouth guard, which I wear to this day, to prevent dislocating my teeth.

And there was the mental and emotional damage, the kind not easily erased. Every time I rode a horse, I could feel every tremor and tic that passed thought the horse's body and I would yank the reins in a spasm, and then realize there was no danger—but how to deal with the instantaneous and instinctual hyper-attenuated fear of tiny, winged creatures hovering around my horse's ears sending me in a panic?

I was walking outside sometime later and heard Louie call out, "Calamity Jane," the name he called me after my accident. He came around the corner of the barn sitting on a buggy pulled by a team of horses. I instantly recognized the rodeo bronc and thought I detected a sneer crossing his lips, his nose wrinkling in disgust, or perhaps it was mirth that convulsed him.

"I tried breaking the bastard, just like you did," Louie said, "and all I got for my troubles was this busted rib." He gently tapped his side. "Hurts like hell. Some horses can't be gentled. This here horse's one of them."

Just seeing the bronc filled my heart to overflowing, all my feelings jumbled. I was glad Louie couldn't break the bronc. But I was chagrined that I had tried such a foolhardy thing. I wanted to kick in the scaffolding, go back in time, and tell everyone that not everything is all that it seems. My brain might as well have been a tongue, my heart a knuckle. I could only squawk at the injustice of it all, my eyes fogging up though my tears. High above, a formation of grey-brown pelicans inked the deep blue, rising until they were just a sliver in the sky.

"I didn't realize it would affect you like this, or I wouldn't have bought him over today," Louie said.

"I'm over it." I lied and tried to stop sniffling, but inside, my blood ran cold.

"I'm putting your bronc to work for a new show," he said. "He tries anything; the other horses give him hell."

"Good." I wanted him to suffer.

Louie refused to let me slink away; he reminded me I was more than the circumstances in my body. He said I could create new dreams and counseled me to listen to that special sense I had developed for the untamable. He pleaded with me to stay the course and promised he'd work with me if I took on a newly broke horse that he'd bought in Boise. He said the horse had been too beautiful to pass up. But she came with caveats: a two-year-old filly prone to kicking and biting. I reminded Louie that I knew this problem.

She was the most gorgeous Appaloosa I had ever seen. With her beautifully dished Arab face, so delicate I could swoon, and her coloring, bay with white irregular spotting over half of her body. When she saw me, she slammed her rear hooves into a wooden backstop with thunderous force. My heart slammed with equal force into my throat, and I choked so violently I felt lightheaded. With Louie there, no way was I going to let my problem with horses get the better of me. I stood firm, although my legs felt as if they wanted to crumple. The Appaloosa grunted and snorted like a medieval dragon, expelling foggy plumes from her nostrils, her hot breath condensing in the crisp morning air. I stood stock still, shivering uncontrollably, watching the filly surge forward and bluff-charge, but she didn't come near. My weakness passed like a ghost in the night and my breath quieted. Then she galloped in circles around me. I didn't flinch. My spine grew rigid, and with arms raised and elbows bent, I held my palms open in a ninety-degree angle, a Buddhist pose. To my surprise, it worked. After a time, the horse stood still, blowing air. I inched toward her, extending my right hand, slowly stroking her neck, my breathing slowing to a yogi-like stillness. Her ears pivoted forward, and her panting ebbed. I spoke to her softly. She twitched her whiskered lips and uttered a sigh. I put my arms around her and lay my face against her neck. Soon I was riding the Appaloosa I named Starlight.

Starlight was more like a luxury craft, and the bronc akin to a fighter jet. With Starlight's assistance, I was learning to move past what happened to me in that corral that fateful day. Thinking I needed to commune again with the bronc—just me and him—I sought him out where he slumbered in a far pasture, calling to him from the fence. He looked at me, startled, kicking up his heels up as if he really wanted to clock me one, as if he was on an old tear holding onto ancient injuries baked into his unconsciousness, memories impossible to eradicate or make whole. I imagined when he saw me, it all came rushing back.

"I don't blame you," I said. The bronc turned his back on me. I spoke to his rear. The fence separated me from him and shrank my fear to a miniscule thing, a pale ghost of what it had been. A line out of Louise

Gluck's poem "Horse" popped in my head: "What is the animal/If not passage out of this life?" I gave Starlight a hunk of salami. The bronc turned around to face me, and I would have given the bronc some if he had moved closer to the fence, but he stood far back with a suspicious eye and watched the other horse eat, bobbing her head and smacking her lips.

ICE DUNKING

Unable to move, struck by a sudden jolt of fear, I stood as still as a tree stump, taking deep breaths of the hyper-oxygenated air on an Alaskan beach below Anchorage not long after the 2011 Tōhoku earthquake and tsunami. I couldn't get enough of the wild sweet smell, breathing so deeply of it I became lightheaded. Hovering above me in the deep blue bowl of a sky that crackled with star-filled light, a dark smudge: a bald eagle's wings poised flat as a board, spreading into a seemingly effortless glide. Around me all sides were rimmed by cold, metallic mountains of a bluish-green cast, glittery and snowcapped, dense with hybrid spruce, birch and alder running to the waterline. Trenches between mountains glittered with ice where active glaciers and ice fields flowed to meet Kachemak Bay.

Southern Alaskan waters looked ominous, a dark purple, with a lot of ripples and crosscurrents, hit by fractal wobbling coins of sunlight, blinding me so I had to avert my eyes. Stretch refrained from charging into the water like a wild dog released from captivity, something he might have done in the waters off Hawaii or the Caribbean.

He went in slowly. "Balmy," he said.

"Liar, liar, pants on fire."

"I heated it up for you."

Having swum all my life, practically since the time I could walk, I knew I could do this. I had never felt stronger or more capable, but it doesn't matter how often I dunk myself in ice water, each time I feel trepidation. By August, the air temperature off the coast of southern

Alaska dips from an average high of sixty-eight degrees, down to sixty. The water stays roughly the same, mid-fifties through September, about the same temperature as Bogeta Bay, an hour-and-a-half north of San Francisco, due to the ocean current moving up the coast, bringing warmth northward for a few months.

I immediately began to shiver. My reaction was not just from the cold, I feared. I brushed aside the things that could go wrong—a sudden squall, losing a fin—and instead I focused on the things I had to do well to make it through. Better not to think overly much about the dangers. Stretch worried about sharks with all the seals around. I thought it weird that he was voicing what I was thinking. I would never dream of being the one to bring it up to a man's attention, not unless there was immediate and pressing danger—I didn't grow up with nine brothers for nothing (by the time I graduated college, my parents added a few more males to the family tree. When questioned, my mother said she used the rhythm method, which is obviously unreliable at best. We all thought my mother was past childbearing age, but no). As a child, I had to show ingenuity and resilience—if I cried, I was hounded unmercifully, same with my brothers. My father never singled me out for special treatment. My mother did, but I invariably flouted her wishes and joined my brother's rough games, though I also liked flowery dresses.

My hesitation must have shown on my face. Stretch asked me if I wanted to back out. Part of me loved the edgy kind of exercise that not only required concentration, but also meant any misstep could end in my death. I thought about Moses parting the Red Sea and his advice to the people, saying "When you ... see ... forces larger than yours, have no fear of them, for ... your God ... is with you ... Do not be in fear, or in panic, or in dread of them." Maimonides, considered one of the greatest Jewish philosophers, explains that these verses do not prohibit feeling fear. Nor do they mean that we can rely on God to rescue us miraculously.

Sometimes I questioned how far I could take it, usually when right on the edge, at the point when I had to take a plunge and I had to acknowledge the perversity of my actions. There was no turning back.

My tremor turned to nausea. I had to ask myself for the umpteenth time why I was doing this crazy thing, wrestling my decision like an addict with her favorite drug.

After all, I was fit from lifting weights three times a week, swimming every day to strengthen my lungs, and whittled by a paleo diet. Not the kind of food a shark would like. Although the best cold-water swimmers have a lot of body fat, neither of us had much insulation on our bodies, one of the reasons we didn't attempt this swim in January.

Swimming way beyond the shore, I forgot sharks for a minute and took advantage of the tide pushing me along the craggy cliffs towards the horizon line, using it to guide me. Instead of avoiding the tides and currents, I wanted to use them to access the remote places where they might be unavoidable. To accomplish this, I used a dolphin kick technique perfected by Michael Phelps, a combination vertical and underwater kicking that allowed him to dominate the world swimming scene for the better part of a decade. When done at top speed, it brings humans a step closer to our ocean-bound kin, a seemingly perfect symbiosis of power and grace. This motion allowed me to achieve a singular feeling of utter bliss, half mermaid and half eel.

Coming up for air I spied glistening brown fur on a couple of serpentine-shaped otters, noses in the air and flipper-feet pointed up. Every now and then they barked ear-splitting sounds. Seals played nearby, and in the distance a humpback whale sliced out of the blue-black water, spraying wide like a garden hose, mitigating the shock of water in parts so frigid ice stuck to my eyelashes, and yet magically it seemed my discomfort was assuaged by the euphoria that flooded my entire being, and my ice cream headache receded. I knew the seals might attract sharks and I needed to keep an eye out, but sharks are super-fast; if one decided to attack, I couldn't outrun it. I had to face it down and that thought gave me the jitters.

My quest to swim with sharks started when I met Stretch. Having surfed and dived Caribbean waters long before he met me, he talked this up as something we had to do, recalling his encounters with sharks with the kind of reverence that mountain climbers regard Mount Everest.

Stretch regaled me with stories of their beauty, describing a special sort of energy flowing round them and the exhilaration he felt when a shark passed him by.

People have lost limbs enduring a shark's exploratory bites, and sometimes their lives. Sharks travel alone and have an average of three hundred teeth as sharp as knives, cutting through bone like paper. The odds are stacked against their prey; some sharks have fifteen rows of teeth in each jaw, while the bull shark has fifty rows of teeth. But, even so, it's possible the victims could have deflected the aggressor.

Stretch quelled my objections, saying, "At least they don't stalk their prey, despite what movies like *Jaws* would have you believe."

"I was at the beach other day and heard a man yell 'Help! Shark! Help!'"

"What did you do?'

"Nothing. I knew the shark wasn't going to help him."

I got him to laugh just as he promised to teach me how to outmaneuver any large fish that went after me. First off, he had me watch a video of a diver facing an oncoming shark that was obviously displaying signs of aggression. The posture I would have to take was decidedly aggressive and demanded I call on reserves I wasn't sure I had in my arsenal.

Stretch's mantra: go for the nose, eyes, and gills. I thought to myself: treachery abounds.

"I was attacked by a shark," he said.

"Did you punch him in the nose?" I asked.

"No, he just attacked me for no reason."

He was playing with me, but I was used to that with my brothers; they liked to kid around. I felt no inclination to play the victim and ask for special status as a woman. I knew advanced swimming techniques and told myself that if a dangerous situation presented itself, I would know what to do. Seals that fight back by attempting to injure one of the shark's eyes often escape.

I assured Stretch I knew to be vigilant, my eyes scanning for sharks, ready to raise the alarm, if need be, not relaxing my guard for one second. Eyes peeled for predators, lured by the rush of that perfect glassy wave, we swam the warm turquoise waters of Saint Lucia, the salt washing over limbs, eyes, and ears. Amid kisses from warming sunshine, we skimmed giddily euphoric on a liquid dance floor, though we stayed out of fishing areas and murky water, cover to the Orco, a kind of monster found in ancient fairytales that feeds on human flesh, and made a point of swimming or diving in clear water. I got to see sharks some distance away—and ignoring us, which I was ecstatic about. Seeing sharks in the flesh gave me an endorphin rush, a sensation something akin to drinking five cups of expresso, or seeing a zombie horror movie, with that anticipatory sense of narrowly averted danger.

But now I wanted to see one up close and personal, and suggested we could indulge my fondness for cold water swimming and at the same time, run into lots of wildlife, not to mention sharks. There's something exhilarating that happens to the brain when swimming in pure, icy water, the kind of cold that lights the brain cells on fire. Part of the joy may come from tightening of blood vessels, said by doctors to reduce inflammation and any pain that comes with it. One time in college, a few friends joined me skinny dipping in hot springs adjacent to a freezing cold pool in the Tahoe wilderness, jumping from one pool to the other in a dizzying two-step. After a few dips, the body can't distinguish between hot and cold, the nerve endings registering the extremes as the same, sending my spirits to the highest level possible without the aid of drugs, going with my desire to do things au naturale.

The kind of sharks we would likely see, the great whites, account for about one-half of all attacks on humans. Great whites are partially warm-blooded and can't stay motionless for long periods in the cold. They need occasional short bursts of speed in hunting to keep warm—it's a comforting thought that they have to keep moving and can't stalk their prey. (Generating their own heat allows them to see better and swim for long periods at high speeds.) If the potential dinner is too restive, the great white gives up easily (yay) and goes somewhere else. Hearing this made me feel good about our chances of surviving an encounter.

In Alaska and other northern coasts, there have been no unprovoked attacks for the past two hundred years, but that doesn't mean that one couldn't happen.

Right at that moment, I was chilled; even with fast swimming I knew my hands and feet would likely be numb when I got out. The number of times a person does this is not a predictor of ease with which it can be done again; each time takes courage. Open-water swimmers deal with tides, chop, and wind, along with drastic variations in air and water temperature. Depending on currents and tide, a five-mile swim can become a fifteen-mile swim. Add sharks to the mix and you have a crazy stew.

My first glacial melt happened when I was eight years old, in Montana mountain streams. This was after learning how to swim laps as a three-year-old in Southern California pools and finding that I was a creature of the deep, more agile in the water than on land, loving the cool of the water zapping the lethargy of the desert sun out of my bones.

Growing up, I spent many summers bathing in alpine ponds and glacial rivers in Montana and British Columbia. But I also learned that, as seductive as water can be, it can also be terrifying. One of my earliest memories, I don't know how old I was, perhaps four or five: My oldest brother pushed my head down before I could catch my breath numerous times. I kept gulping water, having tried unsuccessfully to spit it out when he let my head up for the briefness of seconds. I became lightheaded and giddy, filled with a nameless terror. The inability to breathe was overwhelming. He let go when I was about to pass out and nearly asphyxiated.

But I still couldn't breathe and choked for a time before I got my breath back. The violence of the assault shattered my nerves. My throat felt flayed as if it had been cut into by the sting of a whip. My father yelled at him when he saw me choking, and said he couldn't watch TV for a month, but that didn't change what happened to my psyche. I realized that my favorite activity had a dark side: water can be deadly. I could die if I was submerged long enough. And most shocking of all, I learned that it's not always true that someone would be there to save me.

While my breath struggled to return to normal, I scanned the beach. Everything was as it had been before. The earth continued its trip around the sun. Little kids ran into the water.

I almost died in that watery embrace in childhood, but I understood that water didn't bear a personal animus towards me. Water had been kind to me, buoying me up, allowing me to explore new frontiers; I believed in its magical ability to caress and heal. I was more afraid of my big brother, so I stuck close to my other brothers. The beauty of buddying up with the bros was that they also had to deal with the oldest sibling's bullying ways.

I continued to swim the ocean, having gained some understanding of the implicit dangers, where tides add a level of complexity not found in pools. There's the proliferation of life on a scale that seems other-worldly, like science fiction, but right under our noses. I've always been drawn to the life that is lived in the ocean: the origin of all life, the mover of kinetic energy, and like the wind, it takes on a circular motion as it transfers energy. And while we breathe air, if an air bubble gets into the blood stream it can cause respiratory failure, yet we need water to carry nutrients to cells.

Out in the middle of the bay, I knew that a shark could come along at any point in my journey and end it all. There was no force field protecting me, and that gave me an Atlas-like strength; it was as if I had been transported onto the backs of dolphins. I paid attention to body alignment and breathing, trying to stay calm, drawing all the oxygen I could haul into my nasal passages, my heart beating faster to pump more blood to my muscles, my cells working at maximum capacity to synthesize ATP. Working the larger muscles and elevating the heart rate burns more calories, generating internal heat. My senses were in such a state of high alert, I felt like my eyes bugged out of my head. I was certain I looked like a cartoon character or space alien. But looks don't matter when you know a wrong move could result in death, and that sense of foreboding spurred me along. Likely there isn't an open-water swimmer alive who hasn't at some point thought, "What is underneath me right now?" I imagined a great monster of the deep rising up underneath to take me, *schwomp,* in one great bite.

It could happen on the calmest day.

Stretch swam ahead; I followed in his wake. As if I wasn't already a nervous wreck, my agitation grew as I mulled over Stretch's story about meeting up with sharks, most notably, a bull shark, known for its nasty disposition, one of the most serious moments in his life, heart in throat, outmaneuvering this animal, mano-a-mano. Most of his encounters with hammerheads in Indochinese seas that came close enough to touch likely were simply curious, but he knew to move aggressively when the one of them approached and didn't simply pass him by. He pushed hard on animal's nose, as if to say in language the shark could understand, "Get away." The aggression paid off; the shark went elsewhere. But hammerheads have never been known to attack humans.

I played it safe and concentrated on the flow that comes from the fluidity of the water and the rhythmic movement of the body. I started doing the freestyle, less efficient than Phelps' technique, for a change of pace. Mindful of the shape of the lifting arm, the finger-tips dipping back in, and the paddling feet, I went into *Pratyahara* or sense withdrawal—the fifth element of yoga as described by the sage Patañjali in his *Yoga Sutras.* I was also mindful that the shape of the hand can look like a fish to a shark.

A pod of orcas swam by, apparently oblivious to our presence. The pod was more interested in dislodging a seal that had found itself on an ice floe, a terrifying and fascinating spectacle. The killer whales went underneath the floe and pushed it upwards, dislodging the web-footed, torpedo-shaped mammal, which then disappeared underwater for a brief time. Several times they did this, and each time, the seal flopped back onto the floe. This process kept being repeated, like a game of gotcha. Seeing the orcas, I tried to contain my excitement, and worked to perfect my yoga breath, making very stroke and tilt as aerodynamic and dolphin-like as possible, no jolting or jarring but a steady, smooth rhythm, rolling with the underlying chop of the water, keeping my hyper-attenuated eyes on the fish darting below, looking for sharks, knowing it was rarely possible to see them rising up, they're usually too fast, travelling up to forty miles per hour.

Something *loco* entered my brain. Trying to control my breathing, I told myself not to worry, having never heard of orcas attacking humans. Orcas have big brains and aren't as easily fooled as sharks, which are not known for their intellect. And I was certain of my life saving skills, particularly the tired swimmer carry. As a child, I practiced every chance I got, using my brothers as stand-ins for panicked victims, intent on becoming the best lifesaver the world had ever seen. I learned how to out-maneuver their flailing arms, and attack from the rear. When I taught swimmers back in the day, I told them that even the most inexperienced need not worry about drowning in calm water if they have the strength to float, and yet I couldn't shake my sense of imminent death. It was then that I realized this special sense—something I should thank my brother for, the one that nearly killed me—is what drives me to do this thing. Why? I wanted to tease this idea apart. Is it possible that I have a secret desire to finish what my brother started?

Regardless of what brought me there, I had to acknowledge that the only way to get out of my current predicament alive was to accept that death is possible—it happens to the best people. There are plenty of swimmers who take on challenges knowing they might die in the process. In 1810, the English poet, Lord Byron, who had a clubfoot but was a great swimmer, swam in the company of a friend who was a Royal Navy marine across the Hellespont, the narrow strait that separates Europe and the part of Asia that is now Turkey. Although the point at which the two men crossed was only a mile or so wide, the powerful currents that surged through the narrows forced them to swim nearly four miles before they eventually waded ashore. Lord Byron is said to have done it to honor the memory of Leander, the mythological Greek who swam these treacherous waters each night to meet up with his lover, Hero. I had no such claim, other than a stake in my standing as an athlete, and so I could boast about it to my brothers, with my boyfriend as witness.

The last five-hundred yards I lost the breathing rhythm that I had worked so hard to achieve. It fell apart, pummeled by relentless waves and the movement of icy currents through the warm ones, and the difference was stark. The frigid water stabbed me with ten thousand needles. My skin pulled tight. My muscles stiffened. Guided by the silt from glaciers and other runoff, the icy grit, I saw where the currents sheared against each other, the coldest I had ever been in. In contrast, the warmer currents felt like bath water, but it was murky, turgid; there was nothing friendly about it.

Suddenly a huge gray wall appeared, darker on top and fading to light gray, like an ombre fabric, except it was covered with a matrix of tiny, hard, tooth-like structures shaped like curved, grooved teeth. I saw that all the spines of the denticles pointed backwards towards the tail. The nerves up my spine jittered like the hind legs of crickets. It dawned on me that I was looking at a living animal's skin. As I observed the animal in its preeminence, I could see movement in the gills. Then an enormous blunt nose nudged me, pushing me forward. My heart stopped for the briefest of seconds and my breath ceased. It hit me that this was a shark. I suspected I was as good as dead. Right then an enormous eye came near, the cornea mostly black and the iris dark blue. Catching my breath, I gazed on what to me looked like the lidless eye of Sauron showing no fear, just curiosity, totally surreal, an absurdity. Its amorphous presence plunged me into a horrible ecstasy. I recognized that the shark was merely curious and not there to attack, but I was afraid, and my driving impulse made me push hard on the eye, for I remembered this is what I needed to do if I felt imperiled.

What Melville said in *Moby Dick* about Stubb's ease in killing the whale flashed in my consciousness, although I had no plan to kill: "When close to the whale, in the very death-lock of the fight, he handled his unpitying lance coolly and off-handedly, as a whistling tinker his hammer. He would hum over his old rigadig tunes while flank and flank with the most exasperated monster. Long usage had, for this Stubb, converted the jaws of death into an easy chair."

Even then I didn't lose my cool; like Stubb, my mind retained a laser sharp focus. I took care not to touch the beast the wrong way and knew instantly that it would feel relatively smooth if I moved my hand from head to tail, but rough the other way. The shark pulled back from me as if I had applied an electric current to it. I lost my calm and moved as if I had been the one stung, getting the shakes as if I had palsy, unable to contain the violence of my bleating heart crying weakly, plaintively, and looking for succor where there was none. Weird to see the animal move away in a rush of water, leaving chaos in its wake, and me choking and crippled by emotional upheaval, wanting badly for the boat to come and rescue me. I couldn't take my eyes off the point—now just a turbulent eddy—where the animal disappeared. It was up to me to gather my strength and move slowly, not too fast, moving as if I wasn't scared out of my skin, looking for Stretch and not seeing him, and thinking I was a wuss for wanting the boat.

An over-acuteness of the senses possessed me; I fell into a parallel universe. I was not gliding through the water or controlling my body movement very well; the cold was. My stomach seemed to hold only nauseating foam. I remembered how fluid my movements had been at one time. I tried to forget myself, and bring myself back to that time, but my limbs refused to obey. I used to think it was a bad thing, that my mind and body were somehow disintegrated, believing that I should do more yoga. But now I think it was beautiful how my body remembered to glide without making much movement, nothing to make the shark want to come back, moving like flotsam and jetsam with the tide. It took me a long time to understand that I would always come back, and there my body would be, waiting for me like a docked boat.

To be safe, unprotected immersion in water less than forty degrees must be kept to a maximum of five minutes. Any more than fifteen minutes and hypothermia will set in. I recalled learning that most people vasoconstrict to some degree, but then their capillaries dilate, and their core temp rapidly drops, which leads to severe, possibly fatal, hypothermia. The dilation causes 'an I'm a God'-like judgment, along with organ failure and death. Only Lynne Cox, owner of fifty-seven major open-water records, has been able to swim that kind of cold. Researchers still aren't completely sure what allows Cox's body to stave off that dilation phase, but after dozens of cold-water swims, they know she can survive longer than most.

Thinking of Cox in that freezing water made my heart quicken and my glide gave way to a choppy, frantic breaststroke. I became a rag doll, pushed underwater so many times that I became disoriented about which way was up. The violence of the current turned forceful; I would have exhausted myself trying to fight it. As it was, I couldn't surface for a while. Panic froze my synapses. In my despair, I believed I couldn't I make it, and yet I launched into Phelps' movement, knowing I might simply be swimming to the bottom without knowing and, flailing around, run out of air. But I couldn't fault myself for doing this swim. My feeling is that everything, even walking across the street, could result in death, and especially in water, an element that humans are not naturally equipped to handle. When we are submerged long enough, we die.

What would it be like to die? My early experience with near suffocation was fraught with agony. Nor did I believe there's a painless way to lose consciousness without painkillers. Nobody has been able to say what it's really like, though Dylan Thomas promised: "And death shall have no dominion". The idea of dying right then struck me as unreal and galvanized me to action. Suddenly, as if I had willed it, a reserve of energy was available to me, my energy boundless. I didn't know how this came to be, nor could I fathom the tiger heart that panted beneath me, but I respected its remorseless indifference and power. Right then, the shark was the least of my problems. I don't know how it was that I swam in in the right direction; I could barely feel my legs or arms, my skin not feeling any sensation, even the cold. But on my skin, my edges, there was a low hum. Could it be that Athena protected me, like the goddess did for Odysseus in his battle against the suitors? How else was I able to make the right choice? I saw the water grow lighter, from nearly black to a greenish purple, as I neared the surface where the sun penetrated. I resolved to make a sacrifice to Athena if I came out of this.

I popped up sucking up air. Stretch appeared next to me, looking star spangled. Everything seemed perforated with an inner light. I realized this is how to *be* in the moment, that this sensation was what the living animal body seeks: hyper-aware of existence and its precariousness. I was like a newborn child, looking at the world as if I had never seen it before. The realization at the forefront of my consciousness that all of this might have been snatched away in a twinkling bowled me over. I accepted how precious and tenuous my hold on life. This state of being doesn't happen often, where everything takes on a new glow.

"I almost died," I blubbered, my throat raw. "Did you see the shark?"

The thought hit me that what I saw was an undefinable shape that turned into something else, a shapeshifter, and could change again, and adrenaline flooded my body at the realization that nothing could be pinned down, everything was fluid. I kept turning around to see if a shark had come back and was watching me, behind me, turning corners on its way back to me. My heart quickened, my breath deepened, my blood rushed into a vortex. I didn't notice any of these sensations separately, but instead I sensed my insides had been thrown into a centrifuge that was spinning wildly, becoming hot. My eyes welled with tears.

"What happened?" Stretch said.

I recounted my story and listened to his encouraging words, saying I did the right thing, buoying me up and allowing me to call up the strength I needed. He let me draft off him until I could stagger onto the rocky shore a few feet from mossy forest at the mouth of China Poot Bay, 4.6 miles away from where we started. I felt my spirits return and I poured myself back into my body again, edge to edge, feeling how fleshy, how weighty I am, possessed of a heart and lungs, and muscles, but not much fat, all of it intact, thankfully not a shark's favorite meal.

It was roughly one o'clock. I coughed up seawater, my sinuses feeling tattered as if scored by the sharp rocks underfoot. My legs moved like wet noodles, my limbs felt weak, and my edges seemingly melted into the rest of me, as if I was a big pudding.

I couldn't navigate the rocks or stay clear of driftwood. I lay crippled, wrapped in a big fluffy towel until sensation slowly came back to my feet as pins and needles replaced the numbness, and cold blood from my skin and my feet and my hands spread to my core. I shivered for a half hour or so, and yet through it all I felt an idiotic kind of joy. I had done something crazy and edgy, and survived. Cold water swimming is decidedly an acquired taste, an adrenaline rush more addictive and exhilarating than anything I've ever done. I didn't want to get into the boat and look for the orcas and the shark. Stretch said I was lucky the shark only nudged me and didn't start biting right off. The animal likely would have leveled me with an exploratory bite if we had met up in the southern hemisphere where shark food is scarce. Listening to him, I couldn't move. My body housed a network of decisions that I had no control over; I was like the deer at the edge of the road, contemplating the unseen danger, as still as anything, powerless to move.

Then we went to Gore Point, one of the best beaches on the Kenai Peninsula, to find treasures like sports-logoed fly swatters lost overboard on cargo ships and mingled with seaweed and the incoming tide. We saw orange and black buoys dotting the black sand like giant horse pills, and the Japanese glass floats that are found in abundance around these parts. I stumbled on the perfect souvenir scattered among pieces of plastic foam and other assorted tsunami debris: a red fuel can with Japanese writing.

Stretch came up behind me and wrapped his arms around my shoulders. "So glad you weren't hurt."

"I keep pinching myself."

I flashed on the idea that chance, that fickle imposter, flips things this way and that way at random. I guess you could call that luck, my chance encounter with the shark. It felt to me as if I had been making a feeble attempt to find meaning in a meaningless universe.

Looking toward where tide rips collide, the rolling swells rearing up and steepening into whitecaps, I raised my water bottle filled with triple-filtered spring water to my lips and as I drank, the realization came to me that the most important thing is facing one's fears. A triumph over the self can be liberating and transformative, and in the words of Marcel Proust in *In Search of Lost Time*: "Our worst fears, like our greatest hopes, are not outside our powers, and we can come in the end to triumph over the former and to achieve the latter."

BETRAYAL

I walked in on them unaware. If I had known, I might have taken greater care to be quiet, or perhaps I might have simply peeked in and driven away without letting on that I saw them together *in flagrante delicto,* as my literature professor would have put it. But no, as luck would have it, I burst through the door, eager to tell Stefan the happy news. What I saw made me stop, my lips quivering from shock. Stefan's big frame was stretched out on the couch over the prone body of Phyllis, her shocking blue hair splayed against the bright roseate fabric like a peacock's tail. I couldn't believe what I was seeing. I stood rooted like a plant, unable to move. Phyllis scrambled as if a gun had been fired, launching into a sitting position, her trembling hands busily picking up her shirt where it lay in a jumble on one arm of the couch; her witch's eyes of burnt umber opened wide, stricken, boring into mine. Stefan jumped up and turned to face me.

As soon as I heard the word 'pregnant' drop from my mouth like a bloated insect, I wanted to take it back, soften the meaning, uncertain that I wanted to admit to my changed circumstance, not after what I saw. Crazy how I couldn't stop my overactive brain from spilling its contents: As though my mouth couldn't catch up to what my eyes had seen. We faced each other, him not speaking. I couldn't help myself, I had to say more. "I'm going to have a baby," I said, spilling my news as casually as water into glass. I felt as if I had broken something. "Oh, and by the way, without meaning to and without much effort, two people sleep together and in the process make a baby. *Quel Beaucoup!*"

His face was stony, the Rock of Gibraltar. Then he broke into a tight-lipped grin. "Good timing."

I half expected him to get angry and refuse to believe it could be his, or insist I have an abortion, plastering my hand with blood money. I shrank inside myself, wishing I could curl up like a bug, thinking that any discussion would be absurd. I still looked slender and felt no disturbance—why worry about it now, a baby seemed infinitesimal, nearly a year away. But I still didn't feel right; I watched their hasty departure in a haze, a heavy trepidation settling over me. Thoughts of impending doom dampened my spirits, fears not only for my own future, but for my unborn child.

The next day he called. He said he wanted to stay together. He asked if he could come back home.

"What about Phyllis?" I asked. "You two looked cozy together."

"She's married," he said. "She doesn't want a divorce."

"How do you see this working?"

"Phyllis and I've been friends forever, since college, as you know. And you've heard me say that she's the best investment advisor I've ever known. But we'd kill each other if we lived together. Both of us feel that way. I don't see her taking your place."

I told him crisply that we'd get together like we were going back to just dating and trying out our relationship for size, to see if we were a good fit. Until then, I wanted him to sleep elsewhere. In the weeks to come he couldn't have been more attentive, holding my door, offering to pay for things, letting me use his phone when mine died. He said repeatedly that he wanted to stay with me, baby or no baby. I could have an abortion for all he cared, it made no difference. He said he had made up his mind. I decided there was one last thing we had to do before making that final decision. I waited for the right moment to say this, and it came one night as we sat at a waterfront bar listening to seagulls and watching the pale tangerine and ochre cast by the setting sun diffuse across the sky. He said he loved me more than he had ever loved anyone, and still wanted to get married, but occasionally he needed to be with someone else for variety, someone with a totally different body, even their personality type had to be different. I told him we could discuss that later. Right now, we had another problem. We needed to spend time together with Phyllis and Mitchell. He paled when I said this, but I told him I'd play nice. Mitchell wouldn't be the wiser.

"I'm not looking to make a scene," I said.

"Tell me again why we should do this?" he asked.

"I need to satisfy my curiosity," I said. "I want to see if you can do it."

His normally ruddy face blanched; his skin looked stripped of all blood, white as bleached sand. "Oh," he said weakly, his voice questioning, the frown between his eyes deepening, and a faint motion, davening slightly like a religious person seeking divine intervention, facing east in the direction of Jerusalem. He even stopped his swaying and raised his hands, looking at me with such a face of despair that I quailed, and then he let them drop as if he had given up all hope, as if every ounce of his energy had completely deserted him. In a weak voice he said, yes, he would be happy to have dinner just the four of us, and he nodded in the affirmative, as if for extra emphasis.

The following Saturday, having decided on a restaurant, we came by to pick them up so we could drive there together. Early evening and the sun still shone brightly with no lessening of the humidity, making us sweaty and hot. Phyllis lived with Mitchell in a small clapboard cottage that wasn't visible from the road, hidden behind two large trees. At the door the smell of stale cigarettes and bitter coffee overpowered her perfume and left me reeling. Phyllis was only thirty, but from the way she held her body, one would have guessed she was much older. Stefan was the same age as Phyllis. I was a year older.

"You okay?" she asked, her voice barely there, sounding hesitant.

"Yes," I said as strongly as I could muster.

"Good," she said, turning to Stefan for a hug.

Mitchell shook my hand. He was a small, thin man with a goatee, wearing round John Lennon glasses, a wrinkly button-down denim shirt and tan chinos. His manner was subdued, quiet. He wasn't much of a conversationalist.

At dinner, everyone was cordial. Mitchell had no idea that anything was afoot. As the evening wore on, I noted the way Stefan and Phyllis looked at each other, and the way their voices changed when addressing the other, a purring quality that appeared in Stefan's tone and in Phyllis's, too, announced by the soft opening of lips, making me feel that Mitchell and I were the outsiders. My blood boiled.

"Mitchell and Phyllis," I said, looking around the table, a glass of wine in my hand. "I want to toast your marriage in the hopes that it lasts forever."

"And I toast the two of you, too," Phyllis said, sounding equally heartfelt.

I looked at her, at first with a kind of jealousy, and then with a blinding flash realized that of course they would have a special friendship. It was incumbent that I respected the special ties that bound them together. Stefan's grandfather had been beaten to death by German Nazis at a labor camp he had been thrown into a year before Kristallnacht for not having the proper papers. And made to work insane hours at the kind of manual labor that a Talmud scholar is not used to. His grandmother was not allowed to see the body. The coffin was nailed shut. Phyllis, too, had her own Holocaust connection, though it happened in Stalin's Russia with the Great Purge; after her activist uncle was sent to the gulag, her father escaped in the dead of night, headed to America. I strove to put aside my selfish absorption and understand that when people are persecuted for their religious affiliation, often unjustly, one had to make allowances. Stefan had many people in his life that he cared for and loved deeply, aside from myself. Though I did not want to be second best, the one he turned to when the other one was busy, or to whom he turned only for procreation, the baby maker, I resolved that I would open my heart and earn Phyllis's love as well, as much as humanly possible. Granted, our personalities might not mesh, but I resolved to give it a try. That called for a new understanding. And I was not one of those women who stayed with a man solely for his money; there had to be strong love and acceptance.

"I hope good things for us all and that we stay good friends," I said and sipped my wine, feeling my face flushing from the alcohol.

"Mazel Tov," Stefan said. "I second the motion. And just so you know, we're going to get married as soon as possible. Shotgun wedding." He raised his glass and downed it with a flourish.

HIGH WINDS

My father phoned to say he and my mother were fighting and she refused to come, so he was flying alone to meet Stefan's parents before the wedding. I said it was for the best and suggested he invite his girlfriend, Maria, knowing he hated traveling alone. He sounded surprised, hastening to say he liked the plan. Later that week when I picked up my father and his girlfriend at the airport, I told him I was prepared to tell Stefan's parents the truth. It was better to get things out in the open, even though I could barely think about it without feeling a cold wind blow through my heart. Stefan's parents were among the most conservative people I had ever met, but they were certainly more open and understanding than my own mother, and that was saying a lot. My father said I didn't really want to get married, or I wouldn't be so eager to unload this gem on my future in-laws. I told him they would find out sometime—maybe it was better that they learned what they were getting into before the wedding.

We had an hour before we had to be at the restaurant, just enough time to shower and change. His girlfriend decided to stay in bed and order room service, claiming jet lag, so my father and I came together to meet Stefan's parents, which seemed fitting. I had met his parents many times before; this meeting was for my father's benefit, to properly introduce them. The restaurant, near Midtown Manhattan in the meatpacking district, was a favorite of Stefan's. As we arrived, I saw Stefan and his parents standing in the lobby. Stefan looked impatient, saying we were late.

My father said to him, "Get used to it."

Tall and bony, Heinrich stood with his back bent, as if his muscles were too weak to support him. My father's comment about getting used to it seemed to unnerve him. Not his only was his expression off kilter, but his comportment looked all twisted and his clothes out of fashion, verging on the ridiculous. I felt a sob catch at the realization that my father, who had no sense of style and looked grubby wherever he went, no matter what the occasion, was being upstaged by Stefan's father. It made me think they might get along. I decided not to say a word about what I was seeing. What did it matter that his mustard colored, frayed nylon shirt made him look pasty and his threadbare gray pants that must have looked cheap years ago when he picked them up at JC Penny now looked like a disaster? My father moved forward to shake Heinrich's hand, introducing himself as Joe. I knew my father wouldn't care how Heinrich dressed; my father dressed with a similar lack of attention to detail, as if matters of dress did not concern him in the least. He loved to flout convention and wear comfortable clothing whatever the occasion, most of it selected from Macy's sales rack, so in that respect they were much the same. That day he wore a nice pair of slacks he picked up at Sears, but then he marred the effect by shoving one pant leg into the shaft of his work boot, while the other pant leg fell over the boot in a haphazard way, which could have been okay if his button-down shirt had not been wrinkled and the fabric stretched in parts that made the buttons look as if they were about ready to snap off.

I thought I saw a gleam in my father's eyes as he shook my future father-in-law's hand. Heinrich tried to smile, but his effort turned into a grimace, and he coughed in a burst of hard and guttural sounds as though he was spewing his guts out, a few spots of spittle landing on my father's shirt.

"It won't go away," he said with sickly look, standing with his thin shoulders curled in as if he would keel over any second. He made it clear that he only moved when he had to.

"That cigarette you were smoking outside the restaurant isn't helping matters," my father said, looking uncomfortable.

My father was overweight, but otherwise fully conscious of his health, never touching cigarettes, and mostly sticking to several glasses of red wine that he drank daily and whiskey for special occasions. As a young man, he had been a swimmer, hiker, and horseman, all of which he excelled at. They dressed much alike, yet Heinrich was everything my father was not: a colorless individual who never took risks (a career civil servant in the byzantine New York City administration) and always suffering some minor ailment, a cold or flu. There was always something marring his sangfroid. My father, a surgeon, was not keen on hypochondriacs, although they were his bread and butter: I tried to warn Heinrich, but he ignored my waving hand. My father's frown deepened, but Heinrich persisted. My father made it clear their sensibilities could not have been more different.

"I should be in bed," Heinrich said.

"I hope you're not smoking in bed," my father said.

Heinrich brushed off my father's comment; clamming up was his way of dealing. He had told me many times that the anti-smoking campaign by the Centers for Disease Control was all marketing hype, and the look he shot my father reflected that outlook. Was it possible for these two men, raised in different cultures and religions, to be understanding of each other and get along for the space of an hour or two? Hoping for a miracle and casting about to find something everyone might enjoy talking about, I changed the subject—to an equally troubling topic: politics.

"Besides the war, you have something else in common," I said, "both of you voted for Adlai Stevenson II against Eisenhower."

"Eisenhower won because Truman mangled everything," my father said. "Didn't matter what Stevenson campaigned on."

"Didn't help that McCarthy referred to Stevenson as 'Alger,'" Heinrich said.

Stefan's mother, Lois, asked why my mother had not come with my father to New York for the wedding. I told them my mother was recuperating at home in California from a long trip that left her stranded with no gas or money in the middle of a potato field in Iowa. She had driven off with my three brothers and sister without telling anyone, heading up to Canada to visit her mother whom she had not seen in years. My father had called my grandmother to see if she knew where my mother was, but my mother had not bothered to call any of her relatives in Quebec, other than her sister, or she would have learned that my maternal grandmother and grandfather had just boarded a plane to Paris. Why she did not call my mother puzzled me, but they were not always the best of friends, often fighting about something. My father had alerted the police, thinking my mother and siblings had been kidnapped. My mother called my father, hoping he would wire her money, and he persuaded to abandon her junk car and fly home. I tried to explain, but it didn't come out right; no one seemed to understand what I was saying.

"She's coming to the wedding?" Stefan asked.

"I don't know," I said. "I'm afraid to ask her. She's unpredictable."

"But she's your mother," Lois said, squaring her arms. She was a stout woman with a manly face unadorned by makeup and framed by a man's style of haircut. Her outrage was evident in her uplifted eyebrows, stern demeanor, and the lift of her hands as if she wanted to rap my fingers and tell me I would have to stay after school that day for my impertinence.

No one said anything—a few minutes of dead silence.

"Does she work?" Lois spoke in a forceful manner breaking the spell. She was an assistant teacher in one of Brooklyn's innumerable elementary schools. Her question left dangling in the air, was met by quiet all around.

I broke the force field. "She used to be a registered nurse," I said. "Now she's got four children at home; the other five are away at college or on their own." I had been on my own for five years and knew what it was to make my way in the world. I had conquered New York, but just barely, every day still surprised I still had a job that I was being paid for.

Lowering my voice and turning my head, so only Stefan could hear, I said, "She's a Jesus freak, as you know, but the rest of your family doesn't have a clue."

"My bubbe is xenophobic," Stefan said. "She hates everyone: Russians, Ukrainians, Poles, Germans, and French, anyone from any nation that capitulated." He smiled to show that he was above all that.

Months after we met and started hanging out together several days a week, I showed Stefan the letter my mother wrote me saying she heard from my father that I was dating a Jew. I had never confided this to her, knowing her extreme prejudice. Apparently, she heard about it from my father. My father also knew I had converted to Judaism, but I had yet to tell my mother, and I was hoping my father neglected to include this tidbit. She wrote to say that she would not mind a black man, but a Jew was out of the question. I never wrote her back; nothing I could say would make any sense to her.

At the time, Stefan had simply shaken his head, saying, "I can't wait to meet your mother," and, "and we'll get along well."

I explained to him that my mother was the type of bipolar who is never normal. That, on top of being a Bible-thumper, she was a Quebecois, a particularly backwards seventeenth century kind of Catholic, wearing the face of an unholy demonic extremist, more flagrant than most fundamentalist Christians. She never did take kindly to people who refuse to accept the pope's word as coming from God.

My fiancé said he could handle anyone, having worked in a mental hospital part-time while getting his college degree in psychology. There was plenty of distraction, so my fuzzy head was not apparent to all. I could not help but think my father might have inadvertently said something to my mother about the wedding and I imagined her showing up, thinking to do God's work, remembering her habit of blaming my father for every dashed dream, even the burnt toast and the rain. I shuddered over my wine and tried to shake my foreboding.

A few days before the wedding, when my father's family went out sightseeing, I finally got the courage to spill the one thing I had not revealed yet, knowing I couldn't get married with this nugget remaining hidden from Stefan's family. In front of his bubbe, Celia, I said, stumbling over my words, that my great-grandfather had immigrated from Luxembourg to America in the early 1900s, and fought in World War I when the US got involved. Luxembourg had been occupied by Germany in both wars, violating its neutrality. As I anticipated, when I mentioned this, all talk around the table ceased.

"But this was way before Hitler arrived on the scene," I finished lamely.

"Germans don't have a sense of humor," Celia said in a neutral tone, "Look how they dress."

"What do you mean?" I said.

"There aren't any significant German fashion designers," Celia said shortly. "Karl Lagerfeld is a joke, Robert Geller, and Philipp Plein, too. Germans lack imagination." Back in the 1950s, Celia owned a thriving high-fashion clothing store for women in Brooklyn.

Stefan laughed it off and claimed the rest of the family thought that what she had endured in Germany caused her to lose her sense of humor. "She's shell-shocked." He added that he had never seen her smile, no one in his family took her caustic comments seriously. I took his words at face value, hoping that she could see I meant to do whatever in my power to help my new tribe battle the scourge of antisemitism.

Fast forward to the day of the wedding when numerous friends worked on my makeup and hair and I lost myself in the mirrored reflection of my face transformed into a plaster cast, looking as though it belonged in a museum and not on my shoulders. The heavy makeup held my face in place, and I was loathe to crack the spell, though the obstacles to my achieving a state of calm were too numerous to count.

I heard a sharp voice at my elbow, and I thought it was my mother. I imagined her crying out that the Holocaust was part of God's plan, punishment for rejecting Jesus. For some people it is not enough that Jews call Jesus a great prophet, there is this strange notion of divinity that they must also have Jews believe—the idea of it made me feel a debilitating weight that sapped my energy, and my hands and my feet dragged me down like balloons made of lead.

In my mind's eye, I saw how she looked on the day I brought a boyfriend home in high school. She was standing on the porch with her hands on her hips in her ragged housedress, a frown crossing her beautiful face. Like an avenging angel, bent on cleansing his soul of filth, she hurled a barrage of platitudes like daggers to spear his quivering soul, telling him his religion was not good enough, that only hers would do. The boy stood there, staring at her in shock. I told her she belonged in the dark ages, and she grounded me for a week. I didn't pay attention; I snuck out thinking the worst she could do was scream at me. She did that all the time; regardless, though, I realized that it would have been best not to say anything. Nothing good would come of my incendiary talk. She was not going to hear me with an open mind—I would be greeted with a barrage of insults, and I was right. But being right does not create understanding; what was needed a spirit of enquiry and a scrambled montage of the evidence pointing to the discrepancy in her thinking, but I was not up to the task.

At the memory, I flinched, and the friend working on my hair said "Sorry." I did not explain that thinking of my mother caused my reaction. or explain that she said weird things like that when she forgot to take her medication, which was most of the time.

"Those pills," she whispered to me one day, "I don't take them. Your father is just trying to shut me up."

A half-hour before the wedding, my father said he would be on the cobblestone walkway that ran alongside the mansion we had rented for the occasion, but he was not there. I searched for him along the banks of the Hudson, the hem of my dress trailing in the dust, not sure I liked how my eccentric father presented himself. His gruff Wyoming ways did not sit well with me even as a child. I hated hearing him curse women drivers, and I didn't like the rough way he dressed, but even so, he was my father and showed me love in the only way he knew how, making sure I went to good schools and had plenty to eat, and learned how to ride a horse and rope a cow, which he considered essential skills. And whenever we talked of politics, the little ironies of life, he quoted the great philosophers, Hume and Burke, and historians such as Gibbon and Livy that he studied in his undergrad program in a fancy liberal arts college in Colorado, dropping quotes in nearly every conversation. Then there were the times we went, just him and me, to see Shakespeare plays at the repertory theater near Stanford University. In this way he taught me to value the great thinkers. I started reading Shakespeare, and then I felt driven to read as much of the western world's great literature as I could get my hands on.

I found my father standing by the still, black waters. It looked like irritation was oozing out of every pore. And I realized he is not enjoying the wait; he hated not having anything to do. I tried to put on a pleasant face. If he had not come, I would have felt terribly alone, without a support system, and painfully aware that Stefan invited his enormous extended family, while I chose to only invite the handful of relatives I knew well. My father said he was fine with a small group, so I decided to invite only my father's sister and her husband along with my three cousins on my father's side. I hadn't invited anyone from my mother's family in Canada; I met only a few of them when I was sixteen but never got to know them and couldn't even remember their names.

My father flashed me a half-baked smile, his eyes glazed and distracted, staring off into the distance. Maria patted her hair that had been curled and sprayed to a crisp, a bouffant style popular in the 1950s, and then twined her plump hands together around a small clutch as if she could not decide what to do with them. I was reminded that my father told me one time that I might want to consider styling my hair like Maria. I told him that times have changed, and girls don't want their hair to look like a helmet. He was reared in the time of Rosie the Riveter, an allegorical cultural icon of World War II, and he was used to seeing women's hair styled in a bouffant. Aunt Mary Jean worked for a summer in a factory making bullets, and ever since than she cut her hair short, curled it tight and teased it, even as she aged. Her freeze-dried efficiency represented my father's idea of female perfection. And it was better politics for me to say I would not be comfortable in a bouffant style. My best girlfriends styled my dirty blonde in loose curls, and I allowed them to apply hairspray. But no bouffant. My father looked past my hair, his eyes losing their focus. Lightly we touched, a perfunctory gesture, the sentiment familiar, albeit lukewarm.

Maria tried to say something, but I could not figure it out and looked to my father to explain. She had arrived in this country as a thirteen-year-old, immigrating with her mother from Italy, yet her English never seemed to improve. I bridled at my father's joviality as he excused her garbled speech and realized there was nothing I could do about my inability to understand her except learn Italian. I was stuck having to guess words that could morph into other forms like clouds chasing wind. My throat tightened, my head feeling as if my brain cells would flow away like helium balloons tied to the gates of the mansion we rented for the occasion. We started walking.

"Likely your mother isn't going to show," my father said in his gravelly whiskey-soaked voice. I lurched. "Though I wouldn't be surprised if she bursts in at the last minute; she's good at that kind of thing."

Peering through the veil's protective gauze, I tried to read the wall of expectant faces, but it was impossible to tell what people were thinking. I could barely get my feet moving; the cold wind sheared my nerves under the clear sky and ran up my legs, leaving them a shivering mass of mottled purplish flesh under the lace. The iridescence of the satin huppah trembled, occasionally expanding, and then snapping back like the sail on a sailboat in high winds. The gold fringe along its borders danced merrily from the crazy, shifting breeze. The four men holding the thin poles that supported the huppah staggered around in a vain attempt to keep the cloth steady. A couple of times, the entire apparatus dipped, hitting someone in the head before rising again on the mischievous April winds. The wind nearly wrested the poles out of the hands that held them. The tall heat lamps, blasting jets of heat our way, were no match for the changeling breeze. I struggled powerlessly against the wind's antics, snatching the heat pouring out of the heat lamps away as if I had done something to upset the ancient Greek god Aeolus, keeper of winds, making me worry out loud how I would survive this, my arms as chilled as if they were locked in a freezing block of ice, the bit of warmth from the lamps merely a tease.

Stefan's lips quivered and his hands shook in his attempt to lift the wedding band from its silk box. Into the meager frost-encrusted lawn the tiny ring fell, like everything in my life, lost in a haze of possibilities before its full enjoyment could be realized. The glittering gold eluded the pack of tuxedoed men in skullcaps swooping down, looking like a flock of blackbirds massing on a solitary worm. A little boy found it stuck like a pin under his socking foot. I was happy that the kid had taken off his shoes, although his mother did not look pleased.

The wind caught the rabbi's high tenor and hurled the melodic strains of Aramaic across the garden. One of the bridesmaids raised her white gloved hands to her face, causing the rabbi to stumble over his words. Scanning the crowd, I thought I saw my mother's face and I blanched, thinking she was just biding her time before storming the ramparts. She would make a stand and say that she was sent by Jesus to save our souls.

I could still hear her busting up a group of my friends drinking beer on the lawn at home: "Get down on your knees' sinners! Pray for your souls!" in her best tessitura voice, but then I realized with a start it was Maria I was looking at. How like each other they looked. The two women shared the same oval face and even features; they even affected the same style of dress. Maria lacked my mother's gift for speech, but she made up for it with her loving nature, her inclination to hug and kiss everyone. And Maria was an incredible cook. My father had gained weight since she had come into his life as his patient for heart trouble.

Maria, in her stiff dress, looked wan and cold among the women in heavy coats and furs holding onto their hairdos built to withstand the whimsical spring weather of New York, creating a cozy quilt of bright reds, somber blacks, and conservative neutrals as they posed gingerly on white foldout chairs, their ruby mouths puckering with their attempt to discern the ancient syllables. I looked around, thinking I must have missed something. A hush descended as the maid of honor lowered her shapely legs into a crouch so she could pick up the iris that fell from her limp hands.

The winds died down. I sighed audibly into the chill, overcome with relief that my mother was nowhere to be seen.

"Let this be a symbol of your marriage," Rabbi Shlomo said as he wrapped a napkin around a light bulb as an aid to an easier break. The breaking of the glass is usually followed by a "Mazel Tov!" accompanied by whistles and loud clapping, but in our case, people started to clap and suddenly stopped abruptly when the bridegroom's foot slipped as it did several times in a pantomime of a silent movie, until he smashed the glass, finally, on the third try.

"From this day forward, you'll never break her spirit," our comedian rabbi cried. "She'll always go shopping."

"I don't want to scare off any prospective bridegrooms, but there's an old Yiddish saying, 'A wife is like a little dove and a little devil, but a shrewish wife is a scourge.' By the same token 'Beating your wife with a paddle does not make the linen white.' In other words, the old saying goes 'Sweet talk makes the girls melt.' She'll come around if you're a mensch."

I laughed, but then the raging beast of fear snatched my mirth right out of my throat. I was pulled back into the merrymaking by the rowdy gang of young men who had come to see their good friend married. They forced me from obsessing over my mother by rudely pushing me into a chair and lifting it up high above their heads, and with the great, bestial strength of a mob, they hoisted me high above the heads of the people on the dance floor, their hands assuming a collective life apart from the individual below, making me feel like a small thing, a parakeet, perhaps, or a kitten. Stefan had been pulled up as well into a whirlwind of mighty hands, leaving him swaying like a crazily tilting rag doll, laughing and joking with the men dancing below in a collective paroxysm of joy. His face glowed, his eyes and mouth opening wide.

We reached for each other and held hands for the briefest of seconds before being pulled in opposite directions. My laughter sank in my chest, making a feeble chime as my stomach tightened from the back-and-forth tumbling. I felt like a carnival rider until the chairs righted themselves and we found each other's hands again, with boisterous handlers calling out one-liners as they marched us around the room accompanied by wild clapping and singing. I held onto the seat with my free hand, not daring to let go in that stormy ocean, each dip precarious to the point that I nearly toppled into the arms of a former lover. The men lowered the briar, and I jumped off that seasick voyage and headed straight for the champagne. But they were not done with their pleasure yet. The crowd grabbed my father and plunked his rotund body on the same chair I had so recently occupied. Under the folds of satiated man-flesh, he looked to be in his element: cheeks flushed, slightly drunk, and from the feverish glint in his eyes, it appeared the booze had not dulled his edge. He laughed, he cried, he joked with the men below as Stefan had done.

Scanning the crowd again, I saw my mother, her plump body sheathed in a tent dress. She had turned into a pillar of salt, her brow grooved into a berm as rigid as concrete. I was too far away to hear what was said to her, but whatever it was did not move her. Seeing her there, I remembered my mother's kindness to me as a young child, the days she allowed me to sit on her feet for hours as she washed dishes, and meantime giving me hugs whenever she paused to put things away. Back then I looked upon her face as if she were a goddess, her features sparkling with light and bringing gladness to my heart. When I hit puberty she seemed overnight to become overly shrill and difficult to listen to, or reason with. I recalled how embarrassed I had been on my graduation day from college when she called my father "The Wyoming Cowboy." And said to my friends: "It's the whiskey in his veins."

I raced around to her side of the room, ready for anything, but hoping for the best. As greeting, my mother demanded to sit with my father. Her voice through the years had lost its youthful lilt and sounded breathy, frog like, and came out as if issued with bellows. I wanted to remember her as she looked when I was young and saw her as more tolerant of other peoples' ways, and I told her that would be fine but first I asked her to wait where she was for a few minutes so I could arrange her seat for her. I hoped she would be willing, and she said she would. I went to my father and suggested I find a seat for Maria at another table. (My mother knew Maria by sight; my mother drove by Maria's house several times a day. If she spotted my father's car in Maria's driveway, she would shake her fist, roll down the window, and scream something ugly. For everyone's sanity, I refused to have them to sit at the same table.) With a horrific sense in my mind's eye of what was possible, I hustled Maria to a table across the room with friends from work, then came back to fetch my mother.

After a perfunctory hug, out of my mouth I let slip: "In case you haven't figured it out, I converted to Judaism." I had not spoken to my mother about my conversion, nor had I told her anything about my prospective bridegroom except that I met him through work. I deflected any questions she had about his religion, telling her it wasn't important. As I expected, she looked aghast at my words; her eyes glazed as if in shock. It might have been more politic to minimize our differences and hide, through an overwhelming display of affection, how much I worried about the possibly of her disrupting my wedding party and turning it into shambles, but I thought that was the least of my problems and allowed myself to visibly show strain.

Not bothering to wipe off the wounded look on her face with a sweet word or gesture, and me not saying another word to change her mood, I escorted her not-so-gaily to my father's table, and then found well-wishers springing up everywhere, changing my mood, making it easy to dispense hugs and kisses, and in that way, imaginary band-aides were applied. The good cheer rubbed off on my mother and she arrived at my father's table smiling and visibly relaxed. My father greeted my mother with a swift pat on the seat recently vacated by Maria as if he had saved it for her. A waitress meanwhile had been by and refreshed the place setting and put out a salad in front of her seat as I had asked knowing how much my mother loved salads, and then the waitress hovered over her and at the proper time followed that up with the dinner plate, bearing the kind of chicken breast my mother particularly favored, i.e. slathered in a cream sauce, served with loads of mashed potatoes with garlic and buttered French green beans.

I thought if we could keep my mother entertained with food, she might be placated and get along with everyone, especially my father, who was busy at that moment talking to his sister, my aunt, who did not get along with my mother. I knew my aunt would be on her best behavior and would, to the best of her ability, smooth things out with my mother. My aunt exceeded my expectations, telling my mother that she had extra tickets to the Museum of Modern Art and suggesting they could all go in a merry bunch. I left them to their planning, thinking I owed my aunt an extra fancy gift for rescuing my father from catastrophe.

Back at the table at the front of the room where Stefan sat, apparently no one noticed my mother's entrance. There were no stray remarks about Maria's doppelganger, not even from Stefan, but then, how could they know whom to look for? My mother is a rounder version of me, but in my experience, few strangers note the resemblance. I found a glass of champagne, and raised it high to toast my new husband, and several people at our table banged their glasses to call for more toasts. And everyone devolved into laughter at some of the stories that were told. Later that evening, I saw my father take a few spins around the dance floor with Ada, the best friend of my new mother-in-law, and my jaw dropped.

Stefan saw my glance and said, "Ada found herself a drinking partner."

I looked back at my father's table and saw my mother busy with the dessert, cheesecake with whipped cream topping, her eyes gloating. Just then, Stefan's ninety-year-old bubbe, his only surviving grandmother, frail and delicate with beautiful thick white hair that fell to her shoulders, stepped up and waved her blue-tinged paper-thin hands that looked like claws more than anything human. Stefan's father shouted for everyone to be quiet.

The ancient matriarch raised a glass of champagne and in her reed-like voice, quavered, "L'chayim!"

Dozens of voices repeated after her, roaring their approval, pushing the dancing and singing crowd to a louder, more abandoned pitch, and in the middle of it all, my father and Ada whirled around the dance floor with their arms around each other, doing a tipsy semblance of a foxtrot. Maria latched onto to Ada's husband, so she had someone to dance with, too. At the end of the evening, when everyone was getting ready to depart, I saw my father talking to Stefan's father, saying that our cultures had some things in common, and giving him a hug.

My father's last words to Heinrich, "I think we'll get along fine."

I realized then, that perhaps for the first time in her life my mother had possibly bent to the reality at hand rather than simply thinking about her own ego—and perhaps she felt some remorse. It's possible that for that reason she was pleasant the entire time to everyone, giving her future in-laws big hugs as if they were best friends and smiling, mouthing platitudes, such as "how nice to meet you," as if she meant it. I'm surprised that my mother never seemed to notice Maria dancing the rhumba with Ada's husband shaking her booty in a deliciously wanton way in front of everyone; somehow the eating of cheesecake minimized her powers of observation.

BOYS NIGHT OUT

Momentarily blinded by the copious sweat running into his eyes, Stefan stumbled as he tried to fake a pass, something at which he was good. Then he was gliding toward the net, and an image of a steep downhill he'd done recently on his bicycle popping up, wind in his hair, singing *pick and roll* to himself, and it sounded as musical as ever. The other men move to give him room, and buffeted by the grind of bone and socket, his best friend Rick attempted to block him, with a smile that said, 'I love you man, but I've gotta do this,' but his effort was ineffectual, and Stefan moved sideways using his arms like battering rams looking like the Hindu god Shiva without taking any missteps, gliding on a blessing, knowing just what to do. He had an instinctual understanding of how to parry and feint.

Playing basketball Friday night at the Jewish Community Center in Old Bridge as a way of honoring Shabbat, instead of going to services, none of them had patience for sitting still that long. They were skilled in the sport; many of them had played in the amateur basketball leagues in Manhattan, and their love for the sport was engrained from the time they met as youth playing hoops in Brooklyn at the schoolyard. Stefan had always been a natural, one of the star players in high school and college basketball, adept at the pivot, jump, and set, but never good at fending off the aggressive players. He consistently scored, but his play was polite at best, if not on the defensive side. He had always been quick, and when the offense was weak, Stefan's confidence grew, and he was able to shine. Just now, bouncing the basketball, Stefan's hands and fingertips trembled with elation, glorying in the natural feel of the basketball, the feeling that he was in his element.

The summer was over, the early breath of hoary winter could be felt in the wind tickling his neck, making him shiver, and he didn't mind leaving the stickiness of summer behind like a bad dream. It had turned into a glorious autumn, all red and gold and the leaves more gorgeous than ever, already several floating down, amber and golden in the sun's low, slanting rays.

The ball seemed to ride off his fingertips near his left shoulder as his knees dipped in one fluid motion. It seemed that the ball was not going toward the backboard, and he'd shot way off. The guys must have thought he was veering way off, too, because they reacted slowly, as if they thought nothing would come of it. But then a wind came up, ushering in a virtually transparent saber of muted light that hit the backboard. A wild boyish spirit rose in the men, wings sprouting at their backs. The ball spun in the darkening air in increasingly tighter spirals in front of a hushed audience before dropping into the circle of the rim and whipping against the metal before heading down. The men stopped and clapped each other's backs, wheezing and winded, lungs feeling like they might burst into tiny bits. Relief flooded Stefan's tired muscles when the others insisted they quit playing. He quit without complaint although he was not happy about ending the evening's fun.

But then Stefan got this idea that they could hit a topless bar after their game. Everyone was down with that. His thoughts caromed in zigzags. Surrounded by his best buddies, he could marshal his scattered feelings. The possibility of seriously flirting with other women not his wife was tantalizing.

Rick's eyelids scrunched down, and he assumed his trademark smile with that little head nod that indicated his good will, his signal that he wanted you to know he meant no offense to anyone, and said, "Looking for the next best thing to having sex with someone other than your wife?"

"The next best thing would be having sex with someone other than my wife," Stefan said. "Anything else is a tease."

"Can't pull the wool over your eyes," Rick said. "Would you be able to manage going to a topless bar in Matawan...just for a tease?"

"Where?"

"It's half an hour east of here, south of Perth Amboy near a former submarine factory—interesting neighborhood."

"Might make the obligatory sex tonight more interesting," Stefan said.

"Definitely," Daniel said. "I could use the inspiration."

The area was away from Stefan's usual haunts and like most of the Jersey Shore, dated from the revolutionary war with eighteenth-century mansions and cute little capes, but Matawan was more of an exception, mostly gritty low-income neighborhoods. Most of the assembled were dressed in t-shirts and hoodies, certainly not the usual garb for a slick Manhattan club, but they would be welcomed however they dressed in Matawan. The seediness appealed to everyone; there were far fewer chances they'd bump into people they knew there.

The guys piled into Rick's car. They kidded Rick that he must be a regular visitor to be so familiar with the streets of Matawan. Rick took it good naturedly, telling them it was his second home. Stefan had yet to see Rick get mad about anything; he was always the first to excuse anyone's behavior, even the most egregious. Stefan imagined that's why Rick and Mattie got along so well. But then he had this thought: if he had a babe like Mattie to go home to, he would gladly put aside his small irritations, his feeble protests over the implacability of things. Then he had the realization that the pressures he was under at work to meet this impossible quota had caused his weight gain, and were likely the cause of his unhappiness. He grabbed his stomach and shook it under his tee and hoody and looked around to see if anyone in the darkness could see his gesture. He had acquired a lot of things, and now he realized that ownership had enslaved him. That knowledge hit him hard. He was responsible for a mortgage that he felt burdened by. And the cars, and the myriad investments that needed constant tending, like a garden, otherwise the weeds would choke the new growth. He used to think that acquisition put him in the position of absolute dominion over inanimate things, but then he learned that is not, in fact, true. Too late, he learned that each of his things had opposing exit strategies. It's if they were aware they would outlive him and have the last laugh.

Stefan rarely ventured out of the Jersey Shore area and didn't know the rest of the state except what he could see through his car's blue-tinted windows on the highway commuting to the train station in Matawan, where he'd catch the train to Manhattan, or cycling the byways of the state while peering through the rose-tinted googles he wore under his cycling helmet, most of it viewed bent over his handlebars, gingerly balancing on the hard, narrow seat of an Italian touring bicycle. He liked to joke to the wife that the blood keeping his balls alive was in serious jeopardy of being truncated. He wasn't entirely kidding. Sometimes when he got off his bike, he found his groin was quite numb. One time, he had been riding through the corn fields to reach Cape May on a century ride in the worst of the summer heat (he didn't want to repeat the experience) and when they reached the midpoint of the ride where they would have an hour to relax, he couldn't walk; his thighs had been rubbed raw, exacerbated by the action on his legs. In their search around Cape May for a beer, they learned that the township still had the blue laws in the books (those have since been amended). They left town without getting any beer. Stefan attached band-aides to his thighs to prevent further chafing. This was after having ridden in and around Princeton, skirting the cranberry bogs around Cranbury and stopping for ice cream along the way, and then riding his bike along the entire section of the Delaware River that ran along New Jersey's border with Pennsylvania.

They passed abandoned factories and warehouses, the kind of forlorn places where people disappear in the thick of the night. An old glass factory abandoned since 1996 looked like a ghostly hulk in the waning light, neglected and forlorn, choked by weeds and covered in peeling paint. Other buildings looked equally run down, a haven for mice and owls. The dews were heavy at this time of year. The fields between buildings glistened as if covered in cloaks of soft color: amethyst, pearl, silver, rose, and smoky blue. And there were piles of leaves rustling in the hollows of the trees, and scattered bunches of them moving like binder paper across the road.

He thought about his children, and his heart melted into an ode to sentimentality. He knew he would always be there for them. Thoughts of his wife intruded, upsetting his sangfroid. Stefan had always shown Shelli consideration, but whatever he did, it was never enough. If he didn't have sex with her daily, she claimed neglect. Why was she so demanding? Women were always hard to read. The girls he dated in college would make similar claims that he dissed them in some way, and they'd stop talking to him. He never knew what drove them to such lengths. Perhaps females did suffer from periodic bouts of hysteria, like the early Greeks would have it. His first real girlfriend would invite him over and he routinely had her clothes off before she could close the door. Afterwards he'd sing to her a few lines of that ditty by Foreigner: "Just you wait and see/How urgent our love can be." After six glorious months they had a fight about nothing really, they started arguing when she kept repeating that she was not a slut. He agreed, but she thought he was mocking her, so she slapped his face, and he walked out. He thought to himself, if this is what feminism has wrought, he'd had enough of it. He preferred the company of guys. They were easier to please. He did not have to be careful what he said nor did; a guy could make fun of a guy friend and no one's feelings were hurt.

This was not their first visit to a strip joint, nor would it be the last. The guys often went to clubs in SoHo and Tribeca, a fun way to blow off steam on weekday nights.

The car jolted to a stop. Stefan looked up and surveyed the dreary parking lot full of battered cars tucked behind a car wash and gas station. They got out and followed Rick to a vault-like door where an affable bouncer in a suit made light conversation and checked their IDs. As they passed through the doorway, the unmistakable electronic notes of Nicki Minaj's "Truffle Butter" washed over them.

He paid a cashier the fifteen-dollar cover fee and followed the others into the main room, a dark, seedy place that had seen better days, where hot women milled about in nothing but thongs, bras, and stilettos so tall their bodies shook like trees in a high wind. The crowd of loud, raucous men emitted a rank smell that mixed uneasily with the perfumed scent of the women and only added to the sense that sex clubs are the new normal in a culture saturated with sexuality, where porn is available at the click of a mouse, and hip-hop videos far raunchier than the racy moves playing on the soft-core cable channels. Sex clubs function as a refuge of sorts, where a man can step outside the anxiety-fraught dating scene or take a break from his marriage or long-term relationship for a night and express his sexuality without being met with a sexual harassment lawsuit and where women parade around nude or nearly so and nobody gets arrested or elicits gasps. Everything is out in the open, sex simply another animal appetite.

Stefan told the guys no way he'd bring his wife to a place like this. Shelli would be jealous of any attention he paid to the girls, and forget about having a conversation with anyone with vagina. Rick agreed. He said wives were way too possessive. If Mattie were there, nothing would be allowed. The problem was not that male sexual fantasies were too complex, but that they were frequently politically incorrect and directly opposed to the female fantasy of being loved above all others. But Stefan knew that if the reverse were true, he would not like seeing Shelli getting involved emotionally with another man, but the reason he gave himself was that women do not have casual sex; they fall in love. A guy can separate the two.

A fit-looking Asian girl with incredible hair, long and unfettered to her waist, came up to their table and looked directly at him, sending shockwaves through his intestines. She asked if he wanted a lap dance.

He looked at her bouncy breasts and croaked "Yes," as if he had a relay of frogs residing in his throat.

She looked only at him, making him feel like he was the only man at their table, leading him to a sectioned-off space, and motioned him to a comfortable chair. With grave formality, she bowed slightly and positioned herself above him, not touching, her thick hair a veil she arranged over them. She was the hottest woman he'd ever seen, with legs that never ended and a body that he could not quite trust was real even though he could see it in front of him, so close, and which she said he could not touch.

She came off as if she really liked him although he could not quite trust he was good-looking enough to attract someone like her without a fat bank account, but he was okay buying into the illusion. He loved being close to a beautiful woman whether something came of it, and enjoyed her erotic dancing. It did not matter that she did not know him. He thought if she were to get to know him, she'd like him.

"I need a drink to loosen up," Stefan said. "What about you?"

She gave the thumbs up gesture. He bought a bottle of champagne because she said she liked it and he told her that it was his first time in a strip club, hoping to score some points.

"Are you married?" she asked.

"I love her dearly, but I need to temporarily escape the shackles from time to time."

"I feel the same way about my boyfriend."

"I wish she had her own friends and a life independent of me, but no. What about you? How did you end up here?"

"Working my way through college. My parents help me when they can."

She moved her hands around her body in a slow, sensual way, as if she were rubbing bubbly soap all over herself. Then she turned all the way around, and in the dim light she became a blur, spinning in a flurry of motion, and started shaking her ass like she was filled with a combustible energy that could not be contained, not unless she was in a steel box.

The more alcohol he drank, the more sexed up he felt. They finished the champagne and started an expensive whiskey that he knew was watered down, but she said it took the edge off and made it easier to do her job, which, when it came down to it, basically consisted of grinding on a stranger's hard dick through the thinnest cloth. Her jiggly tits drove him crazy.

He asked if he could squeeze them. She said, "no touching," when he told her it was a special fantasy of his and that he'd never done it before. He told her he was a virgin. She said the rules still apply, and that meant no touching. He had to be content with being masturbated through cloth. He composed his face to look the portrait of pathetic want, and he felt the kind of impotence that reminded him of a dog's desperate panting and furrowed brow as it waits for table scraps that never come.

She suggested more drinks. He couldn't say no nor did he think he could manage his mounting excitement. He wanted to get down with her right there.

Stefan looked at her pouty lips, her luscious hair sparking a thousand points of light, totally awed by the delicacy of her body, so strong and yet so frail. He told her he had a physical need to touch her, called it a sexual emergency, but she counseled against it, saying there were hidden cameras in the rooms. A couple of drinks later, he could not stop himself: He came in his pants.

Stefan asked her if she could meet on her break, or maybe after work, but she said no. It turned out her boyfriend would kill her if she did. He barely tolerated her working at the club, and if he knew how much she was letting Stefan get away with, well, he'd be super-pissed. That was his one rule, and she was not about to disobey. She was not good at keeping secrets and was deadly afraid if she did anything that he'd object to, the boyfriend would kill them both. If it were him in the role of the boyfriend, he'd do the same, the girl was that hot. He loved the coy way she teased him, but not so much when they told him he had purchased two-hundred-dollars-worth of booze and they would not take a credit card. Luckily, he had the cash. In the parking lot, Stefan told the guys that he tried all his persuasive powers. The guys ribbed him about it. Rick claimed he never screwed anyone other than Mattie, that he had been a model husband; Daniel said the same thing, and Joe, too. Stefan said he never had either, but not for a lack of trying, and bemoaned the situation. The guys suggested a prostitute, but Stefan said he would not pay for it on principle.

"Getting it free is a problem," Rick said. "You'd have to make promises you might not want to keep."

"That's true my man," Stefan said, clapping Rick on the back with a hearty guffaw.

When Stefan got home, he told Shelli about the sex club, and blamed it on Rick, saying he insisted, and he was driving, and the guys made it uncomfortable for Stefan, calling him prissy, so he gave in. She asked him if he enjoyed it; he replied that it boiled down to a big tease. He neglected to tell her about the lap dance and said none of the women were as beautiful or sexy as Shelli, and that he was happy to be leaving those women and coming home to her.

CYCLIST MACHISMO

We cyclists exercised our jaws on pizza and beer at one end of the Seattle-to-Bremerton ferry, the few dozen males and the handful of females, and a few trans, people who liked hard, competitive rides. We'd spent most of the day cycling over a hundred miles, a century we called it, through lush forests filled with rhododendrons, firs, cedars, maples, and giant conifers in the Olympic Mountains.

And while the cheesy treat comforted, we cyclists hung on to Stefan's words for the entire half-hour journey, happy to be entertained.

He repeated the jokes I'd heard ad nauseam. His favorite one: "Of course Jesus was Jewish. He didn't leave home until he was thirty-three, went into his father's business, and his mother thought he was God."

Constant peals of laughter rolled over the group with everyone taking it all in, including me, hovering like a speck of dust floating in the air.

The chuckles died away. Then András piped up, asking Stefan how he survived the ride. Stefan's groan drew shudders from everyone as he spoke of the breathtaking views of Mt. Rainier and the roads taken along the shores of Puget Sound, the heart tasked to take in more oxygen than it can handle for miles on end. No one else said a word, continuing to be happily entertained by this jokester who larded his commentary with stock phrases from the great comedians; he knew them all, having memorized the immortal funny lines for this very purpose, and was able to wow everyone he met with his good memory of famous jokes and one-liners. Ditto for the other cyclists of which Stefan and András were the fastest as well as best friends.

I was the fastest woman in our group, but no women could keep up with the top male cyclists, much to my chagrin—my lung capacity and red blood count were not quite big enough. But the thought that I was faster than most women, cycling at a slightly slower pace than the fastest men in our group, and ranking way above the slow category had no shame attached. And Stefan said my output was impressive, but I didn't know enough jokes to keep him amused, despite my athleticism. He preferred hanging with András, who, unlike me, could remember all the lines from Seinfeld. Maybe there was some manly attraction there, who knew.

"Just for once, I want to make a grand entrance," Stefan said, the green of his eyes deepening into mossy pools. "I never make grand entrances."

There was something about the way Stefan spoke, hitting a theatrical note that suited his role as evangelist for a major software company. He was proud of his ability to remember every joke uttered by the great comedians, as if it conferred on him the same sort of genius. I was amazed at his memory for certain kinds of jokes. Years ago, Stefan studied at the Neighborhood Playhouse in New York and hoped to follow in the footsteps of Robert Duvall and Dustin Hoffman who studied there in the late '50s, but the dream didn't happen, life intervened, and now Stefan performed skits to appreciative audiences wherever he could find them and reminisce about the old Seinfeld jokes.

"You've made some grand exits," András said, completing the joke. András worked as a professional photographer for travel magazines. I'd seen him load his equipment into his car, making his way to assignments around the world, and he dated the beautiful models he met, the kind that make men lose their minds and sometimes their wallets. Yet he never missed a Seinfeld episode, recorded it when traveling or watched it on his iPad.

"Why wasn't Jesus born in Mexico?" Stefan said. "And the answer: They couldn't find three wise men and a virgin."

Someone in the back issued a full on, deep-throated mirth from the gut and that started the chuckles to make the rounds again. This caught like a forest fire, first a lone tree went up and then the whole tribe. I also enjoyed the joke, but I'd heard it so many times before, it was starting to pale. Of course, it was said specifically for András' amusement, and for that reason I joined with the laughter, not wanting to look like a sourpuss.

I don't know how it happened, maybe it was the daily strain of caring for three youngsters and him being away from home so much, but as the months went by, on the marriage front, our relations grew distant, as frosty as a Vermont winter. I started getting friendly with András, flirting with him nonstop. Stefan had become like a grumpy uncle who always has something negative to say. And the kids followed in his footsteps and chose the same route, fighting with each other at every opportunity, making every outing difficult.

Late one night, I had enough. Facing him, my brain function froze, dismay clogging my synapses, and I strangled on the memory of his bottled up, passive-aggressive anger. Steeling my nerves, I sought to define the problem.

"Are you angry at me?" I asked, by way of an opener.

"Why, should I be?" His voice rang clear of obstruction, and without saying another word, he jumped into bed, turning his back on me.

"When we're with other people, you attack me verbally."

"Having three children under the age of twelve has really changed things, more than I anticipated."

"Yeah, it's been an eye opener." I said, feeling utterly bone weary.

How fond the memories of the early days, when our toddlers were engaged in their own pursuits, and Stefan and I would enjoy heartfelt kissing as a prelude for what would come later, after our babies were safely tucked into bed. It was so different now. It seemed that everything I said turned into an argument. I thought it was my fault, told myself I had been asleep at the wheel, and that I had left the vehicle of my marriage running on cruise control. Clearly if I wanted to repair what we had, I needed to get reacquainted with the things I may have shunted aside in my delirium. Not only did I believe I was not looking in the right places, but I also blamed myself for his inflexibility, and for him not wanting to help with the children or the housework. Stefan always left it to me to fix things, as if by silent fiat I had been assigned all matters dealing with spills and broken toys. I tried to keep in mind that his job was terribly demanding, and not take my frustration out on him. And I castigated myself for wanting a more intense experience sexually, thinking that maybe it had been my dissatisfaction that had caused everything to fall apart.

He told me he had another trip coming up. I tried to make up with him and said I would miss him and wished we could go away sometime, just the two of us. A contrite Stefan said he might have been overwhelmed with all his responsibilities, and said he would try to help more, and I melted, thinking I had been too hard on him. But then Stefan went on his business trip, and I was left alone to care for our rambunctious ones. Even András was not around. And when Stefan returned from his trip abroad—London, this time—and showed me more affection than he had in some time, kissing me profusely and asking after this or that little thing, displaying little kindnesses that won my heart many times over, all my tiredness and irritation vanished. I told him traveling was good for our relationship. His good mood stayed with him for weeks. He kissed me more frequently during that time, what I termed our second honeymoon phase. He told me I had a sexier body than any of our women friends, but what puzzled me was that when we went out with our friends, he couldn't stop flirting with these other women. Later at home he said he liked flirting with other women occasionally, and do you mind? I could see the value in it; I enjoyed flirting with other guys as well. In any case, I told him I didn't want a relationship with any other men and expected he felt the same way. He replied in the affirmative. And I meant what I said.

Gradually, though, our relationship began to fray again. Grimly, like a student who needed a better grade, I took our therapist's advice to stop saying things that I knew Stefan would react badly to and say pleasant non sequiturs instead. It took a huge strength of will, and the continual application of an ego-lashing to stop saying the put-downs that came up, creatures of habit, waiting to be released on the tip of my tongue, like a pack of jackals knowing no rule of law or inhibition.

The first time was the hardest; I had to bite my tongue mid-word, but as time went on, it got easier to stop the windup. I had to hear the same old put-down stock phrases he dished out but not react like I had done in the past. To deflect my own instincts, instead of making my usual response, I asked him to explain his statements, whether it be, "Oh, you always do...the following...insert what you want here..." I apologized and said I would do things differently. He protested and said that I'd never change. I did not argue the point. Instead, I followed up with questions, asking him if he wanted this or that, and offering kisses and hugs unbidden. I fetched his coffee and the newspaper, threw out the scraps of paper he left everywhere, and collected the cups and plates he left on my dresser, all this without a word of reproach, and when I heard no word of thanks, when he acted as though this was the way it had always been, I said nothing, enduring every perceived slight in silence. I agreed with the things he said, or if that wasn't possible, I asked him to explain in detail what he didn't like, even his nitpicking over the way I cooked dinner, and resolved to do things the way he wanted. If he said the meat's too well-done, I agreed, and next time, it was rare.

And rather than serve the vegetables he did not like, I made sure he got what he wanted, whether it was mashed potatoes or refried beans, served alongside asparagus or broccoli, whichever he referred. It was infuriating that he took my good humor for granted, but I didn't say a word about that. Instead, I tried to see myself through his eyes, and what I saw wasn't pretty. I appeared colorless, drab, without personality. I tried not to let it affect me, told myself I did not need his validation, but I tried to change anyway, for me, better to be easier to get along with. To Stefan I said that I appreciated everything he did for me and the kids. He wore a tight smile as I said this, as if he couldn't quite believe me.

My stomach seemed permanently knotted with this charade I was forced into. But then I realized this is what marriage was about. A continual biting back when the little daily irritations present themselves, remembering that this other person had his own needs, and that his views would not always flow in the same direction as mine. And then I joined his rides, hoping it would bring us together. And for a time, it did.

On practice rides, we supported each other, patching each other's tires and caring for the wounded. Many times, we had to prop each other up, even to the extent of carrying people with injuries piggyback. Then, it was my chance to shine. But on group rides that at times numbered over twenty cyclists, the rabbits set the pace. These were mostly young males in their teens and twenties, followed closely by men like Stefan and András with legs of steel.

The rest of us worked it as best we could, but we all knew we were on our own; if we got lost, we had the map, there was no waiting for those who did not hack the speed or crashed. The local cycling culture was grounded in machismo, to put it mildly. Stefan liked to joke that I rode his coattails, but often it was me, putting my head down and battling the wind midway through the ride letting others ride in my draft. But I knew better than to boast.

My day of reckoning was nearing, legs getting stronger, lungs, too. I relived the agony and ecstasy of pushing my legs as far as frayed nerves would allow and didn't feel dissed when Stefan reminisced over-long about the day we almost lost a young cyclist on a punishing hill, a one-to-one slope, who talked a mean game, and rode a bike without gears, which was a thing with young male hotshots, and didn't mention anything about my achievement. But of course the hotshot boasted that he could outride anyone over any hill, and gears were for wimps. Just point him any direction.

One of the seasoned cyclists had the bright idea of taking the group across a series of hills that can only be described as extreme, but this gearless wonder, aka hotshot, was able to keep up for the first half before caving. I stayed behind gathering my strength, thinking I was foolhardy to think a female could single mindedly train and gobble up the rabbits like locusts mowing down hayfields. But when the idea of it powered me with renewed energy, I sprinted ahead on the steepest grade imaginable, and a second wind came out of nowhere—heart hammering, lungs straining, throat burning. Charging past a pack of young males, I avoided looking at the dizzying view and powered extra-hard. The hotshot finished in fourth place. It was a happy moment for womankind, but I could see that Stefan would have preferred that I did not break that glass ceiling and instead stayed in my place as the weaker sex and remained in the ranks of women acolytes filled with penis envy.

"Laughing is better than sex," András said, repeating the Jerry Seinfeld line.

That line elicited the head-back, mouth-open-to-expose-the-full-horseshoe-of-teeth kind of laugh out of me, and I rarely laugh like that. Why is it that women are so attracted to men who make them laugh? Paying homage to the greats made both Stefan and András appear more interesting, and it was not just me. Of the two other women in the group that day, both were fawning over Stefan and András. When not commandeering audiences, the two could be found on their bicycles, training for the next endurance ride with massive sprints daily—but their allegiance has always been to Seinfeld, creator of one of the funniest television shows of all time. Both sought to be idolized and not just for their ability to make the good times roll.

"You're the rabbit," Stefan said, referring to what cyclists call the leaders of the peloton.

"You're faster," András said, returning the compliment.

"No," Stefan demurred, "you."

At the end of the hill climb, after we had rested, we clowned around before starting up again. András paid me homage by kissing my proffered hand, and said nothing about my feat against all odds, ignoring the fact that female cyclists have a significant biological disadvantage. Stefan also acknowledged me with a with a high five. And at the end of the ride, the gearless one, aka hotshot, slinked away.

"A few years ago, that gearless cyclist was me," András said.

"It was you who challenged me to become a better cyclist," Stefan said. "I was pretty bad in those days as well."

"Just remember, it's not a lie if you believe it." András arm went around Stefan's shoulder, delighted to have just quoted Seinfeld yet again.

Looking around, I spotted the gearless one. He had come back to the group and was exchanging bemused looks with people that turned into big smiles spreading like butter. It seemed that Stefan's friendship with András was to be growing stronger, the men solid in their feelings of companionship. As time went on and their training rides became more frequent, many times I was not invited along, and that's when I abandoned the idea that I could forge a rift between Stefan and András. Thinking back on it, Stefan may have seen the awareness of that understanding in my eyes. Soon after, he stopped inviting me along altogether on their practice rides, and I rode with other people.

I stayed friendly with the gearless cyclist who kept me abreast of the goings-on in our cycling group and told me that Stefan invited a handful of women who were attractive and much younger to the group's rides, and that the women arrayed themselves around him like flowers angling to attract particularly active bee, and laughed at his jokes nonstop, as I had done in the beginning. It took enormous willpower, but I said nothing about my feelings of being marginalized and left out of the group. I was left questioning how intimate the two men were with the attractive hotties. But I kept these thoughts to myself. I did it for my children, so they could see me treating their father with respect. We all have our reasons for why certain things happened.

BREASTFEEDING BLUES

Both our babies were born breach. Terry showed me her C-section scar. In some ways, this gesture felt healing, as if we were facing our problems together, not so alone, offering a chance for therapeutic discussion about our birth experiences which varied from "not so bad" to "my worst-case scenario" and everything between. Though I had no scar, seeing Terry reveal herself felt courageous if for no other reason than it's not something women typically do—women have been taught not to flaunt this part of ourselves, and it can be scary to expose any vulnerability to the world, no matter how small. Seeing Terry expose herself this way felt intimate, a thing that best friends do together.

I hadn't felt any ill effects from my daughter's birth other than the episiotomy the doctor performed, widening the opening of the vagina to provide more space for the baby to escape the womb. My small incision healed quickly. Terry spoke of lingering pain.

"Too many cesareans are performed because doctors are afraid of being sued," Terry said.

She mentioned a report in the October 2018 issue of *The Lancet* that says the rate of cesarean sections has tripled globally since 1990. In some hospitals, more than seventy percent of births occur by C-section, putting moms and babies at risk. Women who do not need a caesarean section and their infants can be harmed or die from the procedure. It's not to be taken lightly.

We were sitting in her living room in San Francisco's Pacific Heights near Lafayette Park, in a Victorian-inspired home she inherited from her grandfather. It embodied everything beautiful about the forty-niners and the gold rush era. Terry's grandfather made money selling prospectors tools of the trade and raised six children on the proceeds. I loved all that exposed wood, lightly stained.

For some reason I couldn't put my finger on, I felt guilty; I couldn't identify with what Terry had gone through and what she was still going through, and I wanted to offer my sympathy, but I didn't know what to say. I scoured my brain for comforting words.

My daughter, Sarah, only a month old, technically still a newborn, slept peacefully in my arms. Everything would have been perfect, except my belly looked like a balloon, ungainly, with all the air punched out of it. It was disheartening, but I knew my shape would improve. I had a child out of it, a beautiful child with the most angelic face framed by the sweetest cloud of soft brown hair. My labor wasn't painful, though it probably should have been. I chickened out, asked for an epidural when my baby's head started grinding into my spine. They readily gave it. My husband guided my breathing and alerted me when the electronic fetal monitor told me when to push.

But the narcotic turned me into a floppy noodle, and the nurses complained I wasn't pushing hard enough. They had to physically use their hands to push on my stomach, simulating the action of what my own muscles should have been doing but couldn't because my brain had been softened by the drugs. I was ashamed of my sorry performance. As for as being a woman destined by fate to suffer though the birthing process, I was a fraud at least in the eyes of my mother, who said it was the destiny for women to suffer.

I wanted to go back in time and re-experience the birth of my baby. I felt robbed of the rawness of the birthing process. Given the choice again, I would have refused narcotics as Terry did. I vowed to myself that next time I'd do it without drugs.

Terry was the brave one. I had never known her to do drugs that she didn't absolutely have to take. Terry had rheumatoid arthritis and was taking corticosteroids to reduce the inflammation: A double-edged sword that can lead to osteoporosis, cardiovascular disease, and weight gain. She had already experienced weight gain and started taking another drug to suppress the immune system response, but then she had to deal with an increased risk of infection.

"I don't know if I can keep my job," she said. "I may have to go into research. But I love my patients; I can't conceive of doing anything else." Terry was an MD, a family doctor.

Sarah began fussing. The proximity of my heavy milk-filled breasts drove her crazy, and like a sex addict strolling through a high school gymnasium, she reached for them, her expression greedy. At her cry I could feel the pad inserts in my nursing bra getting wet. I sensed what a cow must feel when it's constantly milked, the physical demands, always on call. I took off my bra and brought my dripping nipple to her frantically groping mouth, her hands moving like windmills through the air. She pulled at my nipple with her lips, acting the oversexed lover before settling down to suckle. The vibrations from her suckling thrilled deep inside me—I could feel my contracting uterus radiating to all parts of my body, a feeling that went beyond a mere lover's caress. I recalled telling my husband before I took off to visit Terry that I didn't need him anymore now that I had Sarah. He put on his sad face.

Listening to my little one suckling with her strong, toothless little mouth, her little nose snuffling, and watching her hungry little face lapse into satiated, orgasmic animal bliss, the evolutionary imprint of a primeval, sensual pleasure that dates to the time of the first mammals, tiny sloth-like creatures, filled me with the most intense emotion. She pulled off for a second, looking surprised at the sound of an engine revving up outside, the harsh sound penetrating through the open window, and right away she was searching for me again, mouth ajar, panting.

"Would Sarah suckle another mother's breast?" Terry asked out of the blue, or so it seemed to me.

"I know my child," I told her. "She won't want your breast. Not even her father, whom she has known from the minute she was born, has been able to get her to accept my expressed milk through a plastic nipple. Nor has he been able to convince her to lie against him in the nursing position. He rocks her to sleep every night with her back to him, never facing him. She won't allow it."

"Yeah, but he doesn't have a breast full of milk; I mean she can smell our milk." Terry's baby was still sleeping. Her baby was calm, even stoic, never fussing, even for her mother's breast. "In previous centuries, women used wet nurses. Maybe your child will come to me."

"She's no pushover."

"Come on." Terry the scientist looked excited, her muscles tensing. "I've always wanted to see for myself. If a baby's hungry enough, can she be persuaded? Please let's try with your baby…as an experiment?"

I told Terry again that she had no chance. Sarah was implacable about her feeding, preferring to suckle on me nearly nonstop. I could not leave the room without her strapped to me. I often fell asleep feeding her. Many nights I'd wake up in the middle of the night to discover her still suckling an empty breast, and I'd switch her to the other breast, by that time filled to bursting, and likely what woke me. This is not something doctors recommend. The literature cautions about the risks of the mother turning on her baby and crushing the child. After a time of repeatedly falling asleep as she nursed, I stopped worrying about this; even when I was asleep, I felt her presence. I knew instinctually to stay upright against the pillow and not turn over. When it was physically possible, I took her everywhere; she had a fit if I left the room, content only when attached to me like a little amoeba. Whenever I felt her begin to fuss, I fed her. It didn't matter where we were. If in a public area, I threw a blanket over me. I never saw anyone look at me askance or say anything negative about it. It seemed to me that most people never noticed her under that blanket, suckling away, as oblivious to the blanket as most onlookers.

Casey lay quietly on her mother's lap, her eyes at half mast, her head nodding, seemingly nonplused by all the activity around her. But Terry looked careworn. And for some reason, I recalled reading a description of Mrs. Micawber in Charles Dickens' *David Copperfield*: "a thin and faded lady, not at all young, who was sitting in the parlour…with a baby at her breast." Sometimes I related to that. Copperfield goes on to say: "This baby was one of the twins; and I may remark here that I hardly ever, in all my experience of the family, saw both twins detached from Mrs. Micawber at the same time. One of them was always taking refreshment." That description reminded me of me—Sarah ate enough for two.

As if she knew I was thinking about her, my daughter opened her eyes wide, and, as if she, too, was surprised when I pulled out my novel to read Terry this quote, she grabbed my breast. Gulp, gulp. Relaxing into me, eyes closed.

After I burped Sarah, she vomited most of it on the towels I had positioned around me beforehand. And then she looked up at me, signaling her hungry eyes. I promptly fed her round two until she was satiated. Usually, it took a few feedings before she could keep anything down.

Terry exclaimed over my daughter's vomiting, saying she had never seen a baby projectile vomit like that. I pointed to the bath towels I used to catch the spills; from experience I knew how far away to place the towels, never more than a few yards. Unlike most babies with this disorder, she gained weight and looked strong despite losing at least half of what she took in. The doctors said she would grow out of it. I didn't mind turning into a food factory. Always with a superabundance flowing, I never lacked for milk, perhaps because I never said enough is enough, or let's not overdo it.

I ate as much as I wanted and still the weight fell off me. The forty pounds I had gained at the all-you-can-eat buffets during pregnancy vanished in a trice.

"All babies are connected to their mothers by the pheromones released in the womb," Terry said. "But your baby and mine are bound more closely to us than that. They recognize us by pheromones secreted by the apocrine and sebaceous glands in our nipples and underarms. Babies who don't breastfeed don't have this connection."

"My mother never breastfed me," I said.

"My mother didn't either." Terry gently jiggled her daughter, whose eyes were swiftly closing. "Doctors back then thought formula was better, and then the research showed the superiority of breastmilk, and physicians had to do an about-face. Breast milk is better in all ways: it offers more protection against illness, and the protein and iron levels are beautifully calibrated."

"My mother breastfed her last three," I said, "but they didn't appear to be any more connected to her than the rest of us."

"That must have been weird for our mothers to have all that milk in their breasts begging to come out and not letting their babies at it."

"My dad read the contents of the formula she was feeding my brothers at the time, it was soy-based, and he asked a research doctor, a friend of the family, about it. Doc Halpern advised my dad that soy might not be good. He had been researching this for decades and said that the use of non-fermented soy has been linked to digestive distress, immune system breakdown, thyroid dysfunction, cognitive decline, reproductive disorders, cancer, and heart disease. My mom heard from her doctor to stay away from cow's milk, because there's not enough iron and too much calcium and casein, which makes it even harder to absorb the nonheme iron. On unaltered cow's milk, a baby pees nonstop to get rid of the excess protein and minerals and suffers dehydration. So, she switched to a hydrolyzed formula with very little cow's milk protein in it. And that worked okay, but it wasn't better than human milk. And what did it do to her body to have all that unused milk sitting in her breasts? Could that be what caused her breast cancer?"

"Studies have shown a higher risk for cancer in mothers who don't breastfeed," Terry said, rocking her child, who looked fast asleep.

"Crazy, huh? And she never went for mammograms, not until it was already too late; the cancer had spread to her lungs."

"Doctors and nurses are negligent about their own health. Caregivers often forget we can get sick, too."

"How long will your hubby be gone?"

"Back next Friday. I'm counting the days."

"I'm thirsty," I said. "You don't mind if I get something for us to drink, water or tea?" I stood up and put my sleeping daughter into her Moby wrap, a soft sturdy fabric wrap that secured her tightly. "What would you like?" I kept her strapped on me, knowing the minute I stepped out of the room she would sense it and cry.

"Water's fine."

"I'll be right back," I said and went to the kitchen, found two glasses in the cupboard, and filled them with water from the fridge.

"My dad was the same way, as you know," I said, coming back and putting two glasses of water on the coffee table in reaching distance.

"He was the worst," Terry said. "He never went for checkups."

Terry used to work for my father summers while she was in medical school. That's how we met. I was in sophomore year of high school, and loved learning about human biology, thinking I was on track to go to medical school myself. I read everything I could on the subject, and my father and I would discuss what I had learned. Sometimes Terry joined our discussions. But my higher math skills turned out to be so abysmal, I decided regretfully not to pursue pre-med. Yet I found Terry's advice invaluable; she helped me navigate the treacherous shoals of teenage adolescence and encouraged me to speak up more and take calculated risks.

She was the one who was brave enough to tell my father that he worked too hard and didn't exercise enough; she suggested he walk more. I asked him to take walks with me, but he said he had no time, in this fatalistic manner he adopted when speaking of his health, saying when he could catch a minute, he'd do it. I didn't want to fight him on it, but that response, and others, like the time he said it was "too late" for him, worried me. Terry gently suggested ways for him to relax and get some exercise, too, but neither of us could turn him around to our way of thinking. We knew if he had gone for regular checkups, a doctor might have zapped the cancer he contracted before it spread, and he'd be alive today. Terry was a stickler about checkups. She taught me to develop good habits like getting enough rest and eating healthy.

Talking like this with Terry felt cathartic on one hand and depressing on the other. It was truly one of the saddest things, knowing that if my father had been more vigilant about his own health, he'd still be around. My mother might have been persuaded as well if he'd set the example. Then they would have met my child, my brothers' children, and my sister's daughter. They would have gloried in their grandchildren.

My father waited until he lost weight and experienced the telltale extreme fatigue that afflicts those with cancer to run tests. It was sad to hear his tragic voice with its layers of malaise about everything, including his life. By the time he started treatment, his cancer had already spread to his stomach, and when that happens, there isn't much that can be done; the cancer cells replicate too quickly. His cancer likely evolved from the laryngopharyngeal reflux disease he suffered from, a known precursor, but in the late 1980s there was no treatment, much less a cure.

My father was seventy-five when he died. Not young, but it's conceivable that he might have lasted longer if he had not delayed treatment. With him gone, my mother fell apart and died a few months later.

Thinking about his laryngopharyngeal reflux disease led me to worry about my daughter's immature sphincter causing her to projectile vomit. Medical research shows why it occurs in babies, but not what causes the sphincter to stop performing in adults. The disease in adults is not fully understood. I didn't know if I or any of my brothers or sister had suffered from an immature sphincter, or if there could be a link between the two diseases. My mother and father never talked about health when I was a child, and yet they were both medical professionals, so go figure. The research I've done on my own comes up with dead ends. Doctors I consulted assured me that Sarah's sphincter would mature, probably in her first year, and she would be fine. But a sliver of doubt remained.

I thought back to the day, only six months previous, though it seemed like a lifetime ago, that my father called and said that he had cancer, as though he was talking about a patient that he didn't have a stake in. I rushed home, despite my extreme pregnancy, two weeks away from my due date, flying three-thousand miles to be near him. I couldn't imagine life without my father; I had always assumed he would be alive for me. I thought about all the times he'd had rescued me from some folly, like the time he took me to the emergency room after I banged my head against a car while riding my bicycle with my head down low. And then another time, after a wild horse bucked me off and crushed my teeth to smithereens.

When I thought about those times, and how good he had been to me, how caring he had been, the future turned into a vast shimmering salt flat, as monotonous as an endless stream of white granules going nowhere. Thinking like that put me in a raw, dark place.

But then, I got off the plane and waddled into my childhood home only to see my father looking healthier than I had ever seen him. Gone was the tired affect from overwork and lack of exercise. His live-in nurse, John, crowed about it, saying they were taking lots of walks, and he was eating healthier.

That first morning I was home, we fought over the granola, a food my father had never touched until his diagnosis. I voiced my surprise, knowing how much in the past he spurned it.

"The science has changed since I was in medical school," he said with a sheepish grin. Perhaps he recalled the days he used to make fun of my diet, saying that I ate like a rabbit, telling me I was too skinny. He had been a meat and potatoes man, and he liked his whiskey; he called it a "man's drink". His nutritionist advised him to eat roughage, foods like salads, which in the past he had avoided like the plague. I went out to the grocery store and bought plenty of granola, vegetables, and the making of salads.

About a month after my return to New York, my daughter was born. My father wanted to hold his granddaughter, so I flew with her only a few weeks old, so he could see her; I did not know how long he had to live. She cried when I put her in his arms, and I cozied up with her so he could touch her in the relative safety of my lap, where she enjoyed having him hold her fingers and coo at her. I could tell it tore at his heart, knowing he would never see her grow up. That same day, several of my brothers came in from across the globe and we sat together on the back deck listening to my father reminisce about his own father's end of life, and the friends he wished he had kept in touch with and neglected as his family and practice grew. I suggested he look them up and call them, but he said it was too late.

My father did not want to die in a hospital; he thought them cold and institutional, having worked as a surgeon for most of his life in their operating rooms. He wanted to be at home, surrounded by family. "I'd rather die at home," he said.

I understood what my father meant. The hospitals he had worked in were filled with the sick and dying, sterile factories filled with the smell of antiseptic. I did not find them cozy, either, having gone with him frequently while he was on the job, doing his rounds. But it was weird having him at home full time, weird that we could spend whole days together. Being with my father at a time when he was not rushed or in a hurry to get somewhere made it easier for him to express his emotional side, something he had kept hidden much of my growing up years. I connected with him in a way that was thrilling and heartfelt. We had always shared a love for philosophy, even more so during these days of reading and introspection, both of us reading Karl Popper so we could discuss his scientific approach: How to structure one's observations to test the extent to which a given theory functions as a satisfactory solution to a given problem.

"Popper realizes it's the humans doing the measurements whether it's collapsing wave-function or anything else," my father said. "It's really about the subjective states of the human observers, rather than the physical properties of the particles. It's a mind-blowing observation."

"I love his theory of reflexivity and how George Soros used it to best the markets," I said.

"For Soros, Popper's theory worked well," my father said, "but for some reason, that concept never worked well for me."

"Maybe you didn't have a handle on people's biases and perceptions. That should have been in your calculations."

"Or even what defined the underlying reality," he said.

"I often have trouble spotting those far-from-equilibrium moments. Think it's genetic?"

And there was John, the male nurse, a sweet soul always with a song on his lips cheering us up when any of us felt low. He sang to my daughter: "Baby face, you've got the cutest little baby face."

The day my father died, I held his frail, emaciated hand, and we mused on our memories of good times. I felt helpless, knowing there was nothing I could do to ease his pain. He said that the process of dying reminded him of being thirsty in the desert and searching for water and finding none. As the pain worsened, he was fed through a tube, his pain kept at bay with fentanyl. Later that night he died in his sleep. His death was a blow to my heart. My mother's death followed soon after. For me, the clouds hung heavy, spewing purple and black matter, like brains that had been opened with a scalpel, even when skies were blue. I had never felt so alone. I was an orphan now.

As soon as I was able, I took Sarah with me to visit Terry. I knew of all people, she would understand what I was going through, though I felt tentative when Terry kept pressing me to allow her to put my Sarah to her breast, her eyes glowing with the purity of her intention. Looking at her puffy face, the telltale sign of corticosteroid use, I wavered. Denying her wish made me feel heartless, like someone who takes candy from the dying. I felt my shame like a cold wind blowing through the room, making my skin shiver. Just then Terry closed the windows because of the noise, against the angry clouds forming overhead.

The pleading expression on Terry's face unnerved me, and I felt the walls closing in, the windows sucking out the oxygen. With a wrench of my bleating heart, I disregarded my innate horror of having anyone else's nipple in my daughter's mouth and agreed reluctantly, thinking I had no alternative. Terry would hate me otherwise.

"The minute she starts crying, hand her back," I said. "I don't want you pressing her to you if she struggles."

Terry put Casey down in her bassinet. Casey didn't stir.

Terry sat down again. "Okay," she said, reaching her arms out and flicking her fingers impatiently.

Terry's daughter Casey suckled every few hours, no more. I told Terry she was lucky to have such an easy child, but I was not being sincere. I knew that my daughter was more interesting.

Sarah started wailing when she was put to Terry's breast and flung her arms about, her hands balled up into fists. As Sarah's cries grew more determined, my own breasts tingled and swelled, my nipples rigid, milk leaking, and I begged to have my daughter's tiny baby mouth back.

"Stop," I cried. "You promised." I felt stressed to the point of nausea; a sick feeling rose in my gut as if I needed to throw up.

Terry returned Sarah to me. My baby blinked through the tears that streaked her face and reached out with her tiny fingers. I snuggled her, and a feeling of relief washed over me, gratified that she refused Terry. I sensed that she and I were connected by this invisible force that no one could break. Terry's daughter woke up from the soundness of her sleep—possibly Sarah's crying had disturbed her—and she started crying. Terry took her to her breast.

Terry now specializes in geriatric medicine, the one field where her disease is less of a liability. Her patients understand that she is unable do some things; they know what she's going though.

The research has yet to show conclusively what triggers her disease or how it can be stopped. Scientists have discovered a lot about our bodies and how they work, yet there's so much we don't know, so much to learn. A couple of the most current theories are that bacterial infection or an overproduction of nitric oxide in cells inhibits the natural process of programmed cell death, leading to a host of damaged cells messing up the work of healthy cells. But if relevant theories are slightly askew or missing some element, scientists can easily respond in the Popper vein by changing things around and modifying their angles of attack until they arrive at the truth, but it could take years. I hope science figures out this puzzle before it's too late for Terry.

BIRTHING PREEMIES

Having a C-section unmoored me, sent me reeling. I remembered what my friend Terry had said about it and decided it was worse than she let on. Having staunchly endured the continual contractions, and weakened by the physical necessities of birth, the raw animal blood and ooze, the hurt where the staples nailed my stomach together, ripping my stomach whenever I had to cough or sneeze, I hyperventilated from the excruciating pain, all the while trying to put on a brave face, totally unprepared for the lengthy physical strain of recovering from major surgery. Luckily I had a few days rest in the hospital, the nurses caring for my newborn twins born six weeks early. And when they came home, I did what I had to do, knowing I had to be gentle and loving in a way I had never been called upon to be, not even when my father and then my mother died at home, both from fast-acting cancer.

Even today, years later, I shudder at the memory of the continual excreting and urinating of those early days, the needy helplessness, the double imagery of two little heads hanging from fragile bodies that had to be held gently, and in the words of Anne Roiphe, author of *1185 Park Avenue: A Memoir* "of baby eyes glazed and unfocused, the skull soft and undeveloped," while I had to tend to the splintery sarcophagus-looking fragments of umbilical cords pressed against tiny belly buttons that literally made me wince as carefully I cleaned around but did not disturb. It is not good for babies to have the umbilical cords removed too early, so I allowed the dried bits to fall off naturally. I repeated to myself the mantra each time I picked them up one at a time to take it easy and slow. But the worst was the continual, non-stop crying. They lacked the sucking reflex that sets in during the last month of gestation, so I had to use preemie nipples that limited the flow of milk without needing the mouth's sucking action, and they needed to eat all the time. Probably, that accounted for the continual crying.

That's when my marriage suffered some cracks. I had done and said hurtful things back then, things I'd like to take back. Even today I blanch at the memory. Uppermost in my mind is the time we sat together at 3 am, giving the babies my breast milk that I had pumped earlier that day in bottles outfitted with preemie nipples, and I said to him, "I'd have been happy with just one."

He looked at me as if I was the weakest thing. Hurtful words were exchanged, something from me about him having no empathy, and him calling me a terrible mom. No help for that now. Nothing I could take back, nothing he could forget. His attitude toward me changed after that, a subtle shift, barely decipherable in a look or a gesture, nothing I could pin down, visible, nonetheless. I stopped waking him to help me. I did it alone. I had no other help, other than his mother, who had stayed with us for that first month, but had been more of a hindrance than a help. The worst was feeding time.

Feeding them at the same time took the skills of a juggler and fortitude of a saint. Multiply that by a two dozen feedings a day and it becomes apparent how quickly my life turned into an inexorable march of Kafkaesque incidents revolving around the feeding and cleaning of my new charges that didn't end until they both could hold a cup, a year-and-a-half later. Their father never understood the strain I endured. Stefan had gained forty pounds, too, when I was pregnant, but then I removed all treats from our cupboards until I lost most of it; he still has the vestiges of a tire remaining, like a pimple that won't go away, and I'm telling you this more years later than I care to count, over a decade at least.

And now I have these big, boisterous boys who tear around the house, spilling sticky cereal and marshmallows that get caught in the carpet. It's enough to make a grown woman cry. As Joan Rivers says, "Can we talk?" And yes, they're extraordinarily handsome and a pleasure to gaze upon, thanks for asking. They're everything to me. I ask them in my sweetest voice to cool it with the cereal and to help me clean it up. They do not stop their play until I bend over and by myself start scraping the sticky mess out of the carpet, vowing to myself never to have Lucky Charms in the house again, not until they're much, much older, and wiser.

THE FOURTH CHILD

South of Seattle, views of the majestic Puget Sound shone crystalline blue everywhere I turned. Driving the highway, I struggled to see through the fog. When it lifted, I spied a catamaran pursued by a line of sailboats. Terns, gulls, and pelicans soared overhead. Porpoises broke the surface, trailing the wake as the sailboats drifted toward the other shore.

I had just come from the doctor earlier that day and learned I was pregnant, and I realized I did not know who the daddy was. I preferred my lover be the father. He was brilliant, an extraordinary man, but there was no chance he would want to acknowledge the child. He was happily married, as was I. Curious to know how many babies the world over who falsely believe that their real father is the one raising them, I did some digging, found the *Journal of Epidemiology and Community Health, and* pawed through a host of scientific articles published around the world from 1950 on and concluded that the number could be as high as thirty percent. Makes you think.

Two of my children by my husband, twin boys, age nine, were right then sitting in the back seat where they rocked the car with raucous laughter as they described in gory detail the soccer they played, boasting how they kneed and elbowed their way to the goal several times without getting killed. They started arguing about who was the better player, and my good cheer quickly turned into a wince at the way my lovely sons fought, teeth bared, and claws sharpened, voices raised to foxlike screeches. It took all my persuasive powers to break them up. I had too much on my mind to pay mind to their silly fights.

We headed towards the south part of the sound where the mud crackled and oozed in the wetlands, and the dusty pickleweed had turned into a kaleidoscope of red and green studded with jewels. Birds floated by. Harvest mice climbed and clung to the upper stalks of marsh grasses, the water so muddy that the rising tide looked like a metal sheet rolling over the mud flats, and the creatures that are the life-blood of our ecosystem—the fish and invertebrates—newly emerged from their slumbers, babies in tow, fanning out to enjoy the watery expanse. And I swore to myself that no one would know the truth about this embryonic child, this figment of my imagination.

TERMINAL

My five-year-old boys, identical, down to the exact placement of a tiny mole on their backs, sat watching an animated television show about a sponge called Bob who lived on the bottom of the ocean. Then Seth changed the channel to a wild, shoot-em-up show. Both boys moved to the edge of their seats, listening eagerly.

"All I wanna do is find me a beautiful chick and smoke a big fatty," the actor said in a husky voice.

The boys started chuckling. Did they understand what they were hearing?

"Yeah, smoke that big fatty all the wwaayyyy down..."

I welcomed their attempt to pull me into the story, and laughed with them, happy to see their joyful exuberance. Seth started wrestling with Micah. They had become all legs, looked more coltish by the day, two beautiful youths blooming like flowers, because even male youth can be beautiful. Most people couldn't tell them apart. I often had trouble. It was only when they were expressing themselves verbally that their personalities came through.

Micah tended to be quieter, more introverted, but when you got him talking, he wouldn't shut up. Seth was the leader. Regardless of their differences, whenever one got into anything, the other invariably followed.

I changed the channel to *Where in the World is Carmen Sandiego?* I had to leave to answer the phone, wondering at these boys with their overly vociferous laughter, trying to act as if they understood the world of adults. The call was from my father, who had late-stage cancer. The prognosis was not good.

A few minutes later, Micah appeared out of nowhere, sobbing as if his heart would break, lifting my mood from a black place, and in a rush of emotion, I hugged my son, happy to let go of my sadness. Seth came out into the hallway and joined us. When Seth saw the impact Micah's tears had on me—how effusive my kisses and hugs—he started crying, too, big alligator tears. I opened my arms and hugged both children with equal passion, quelling their cries. The kids meant a lot to me, called up a mix of emotions, never one sentiment isolated from another. The fact that they loved their mother, that's all that I could think about.

They started fighting again. I quizzed Micah and started piecing the puzzle together. It all started when they were sitting in front of the television. They had been playing a game. Seth hit Micah, and Micah hit him back. They pulled each other's hair. Seth chased Micah around the house, knocking over a lamp. I tried to get them to sit down and play a game of cards with me, but they wouldn't sit still, kept hitting each other. I brought them back into my arms and wrapped them up in a group catharsis and asked them to apologize to each other.

When they settled down, I sat with them in the playroom while they played with Legos.

"My nails are too long for this sort of thing," I said to the boys when they asked me to help with some miniaturized pieces. Ruefully, I added, "If I get called upon to do this again, I may have to cut them down."

"No," Seth said. "Keep them long like a vampire."

"So, you like my nails, huh?"

"Sure," Seth said. "They're sick."

Then he jumped up, waving an airplane he built, a grin splitting his face, his merry eyes gleaming. Something sticky had gotten clumped into his hair, giving him a slightly disheveled look, and his shirt had a new rip in it. He looked happy, his cheeks reddened from the athleticism of his play. Micah was putting the finishing touches on his airplane, adding wings with a massive reach. He looked intent, focused, a budding engineer. He showed more interest than his brother in building things. Seth tended to be more the lawyerly type, arguing everything to death.

"Hey, that's a great plane, Micah," I said, pulling at my tangled hair so it wouldn't fall into my eyes.

"Mom," Seth cried. "Look what I made!" He held up a strange, spacey, ship-like contraption with wings sticking out of it at odd places, Star Wars gone amuck.

"It's beautiful, sweetie," I said.

He swiped at his face when I gave him a big kiss on his cheek. "Ewww," he said, but I knew he was just saving face; his grin seemed genuinely happy.

The babysitter walked in, and I got up. I stood in front of my children and the babysitter, hands impatiently squared on my hips. "Be good to Emily, ya' hear?"

They didn't say anything, too busy showing Emily what they had made. I turned to go and the children who sprang from my loins did not even look at me, instead flying their airplanes and driving the trucks they had built out of Legos at speeds that made me tremble. As I closed the door, I realized that my father would never get to see them grow up, and I knew without asking that it was something that tore at his heart.

GRANDPA

Despite Micah's sadness at his grandfather Heinrich's death and having to sit through his funeral—a small consolation that he got the day off from school—his spirits rose at the abundance of rose bushes surrounded by rolling lawn in the cemetery and bordered by forest. To reach this idyllic spot, they had to drive several miles south of Brooklyn to somewhere near Long Island Sound in a quiet, residential old-fashioned neighborhood filled with charming little cottages. It seemed a restful place.

Micah pictured his grandfather the last time he saw him alive: a tall, gaunt man hunched over a deck of cards in the dim light of his kitchen in a wife-beater tee shirt and frayed trousers. On the battered kitchen table, an ashtray sat, filled to overflowing with a pyramid of ashes, and resting on top, always a smoldering inferno of cigarette butts, his newspapers strewn all over the place. A woman came in every day to cook and clean, but she couldn't keep up with his grandfather's messes. Back when Micah's grandmother was alive, the newspapers were always neatly stacked. They lived in a two-story brick walkup in Canarsie, a working-class neighborhood on Brooklyn's south shore. Both his grandparents smoked. Their place stank of cigarettes; the odor clung to the walls, drapery, and furniture as if the very molecules had fused together. His grandparents promised not to smoke in the presence of the children, but it hardly mattered if they smoked or not; the smell was the same. It was as if the windows hadn't been opened for weeks, if not years. And for double good measure, a double helix of curtain and blinds had been drawn against the lurid noonday sun. Micah's grandfather bought the building after WWII on the GI bill and worked in the Brooklyn municipal department in downtown Brooklyn. Micah's father, Stefan, grew up in that house and went to high school in Canarsie and then to Brooklyn College in neighboring Flatbush, never having left that house until after he graduated college.

"No one to talk to," Stefan heard Henrich say. "The days stretch out, no one calls and no one comes by. Besides your visits, we have nothing else to look forward to."

With a weary arm Henrich pushed aside his newspaper, tiredness leaking from his every pore. He was trembling slightly and looked frail, his limbs thin, twig-like, his narrow, bony shoulders bent with the weight of years. He wore a bemused look. In a shadowy corner behind him sat an old black and white television set he bought in the early 1950s on the day Lois and Henrich were married by the justice of the peace. It still worked, but barely. One time Micah asked his father about it, and he said Micah's grandfather never replaced anything until it broke beyond repair.

One time his mother asked questions of his grandfather about the war, saying she wanted to understand it better. His grandfather paused in the middle of his game of solitaire, his face reddening. He started choking; it didn't matter what it was he wanted to say, he couldn't get it out. His choking got so bad, his face turned purple, and he looked as if he was being strangled. His father calmed his grandfather down and turned to his mother and asked what possessed her to bring the subject up. Couldn't she leave well enough alone? Later in the car, his father told Micah and Seth, his brother, that Micah's great-grandfather had been beaten to death in a labor camp by German soldiers when his grandfather was about ten, Micah's age. Micah was tall and slender like his grandfather and father, with the same sweet cherubic face and their moss-green eyes.

His great-grandmother had a nervous breakdown and went to hospital, and his grandfather went to a foster home. He was ill-treated there, used as slave labor. Micah's great-grandmother got him out as soon as she was released, about eight months later, and immediately started immigration proceedings. The Nazis had a way of screwing the paperwork up, and it didn't look good for them. A few weeks before Kristallnacht, a Hungarian diplomat who had the hots for his great-grandmother was able to smooth the way for their escape. But Micah's grandfather never forgave his great-grandmother; it was apparent by the way he talked to her, in a voice of muffled rage.

It was the same for Micah's mother when she asked any questions about that time in Germany.

"Your father didn't like me asking those questions," his mother said, "but I was hoping your grandfather could talk about it—the world should know what happened to him."

"He couldn't talk," Micah said. He felt he understood his grandfather too well.

"That was the least of it," Seth said.

Even as Micah was repelled by his grandfather's frog chin, and his alligator skin offering scant cover for fragile limbs, yet at the same time, Micah felt a kinship with the man. He, too, carried a big weight that prevented him from fully expressing himself. Micah remembered his grandfather declaring many times that the warning on cigarette boxes was a government conspiracy designed to rob them of the simple pleasures of life. No one paid him much mind when he said stuff like that—not that any of it that mattered now. He didn't think Seth grasped this. Micah did this rapid-fire blink but said nothing.

"Better to have left him alone," Seth said.

Micah realized that Seth's understanding went deep. Micah's father claimed his grandfather willed this to happen.

Eddie, his grandfather's cousin, stopped by. Eddie was tall and thin with an angular face and cropped brown hair. He was taller than his grandfather by a few inches; otherwise, they were built much alike. Yet Eddie looked a world apart, very put-together, old-world elegant. His Brooks Brothers suit was perfect. He had a kerchief peeking out of the breast pocket that matched the soft pink of his shirt, making him look every inch European royalty, his hair combed neatly in the Prince Edward school of slicked-back.

His grandfather glanced up when he heard footsteps, pausing in the middle of doling out cards to look inquiringly at his cousin.

"What's up?" his grandfather asked.

This occurred a month before his grandfather died. Shortly after his larynx had to be removed and a voice box put in. It frightened Micah to hear those strange mechanical sounds standing in for his grandfather's voice; it sounded nothing like Peter Frampton's legendary voice synthesizer. He didn't want to think about what it did to his grandfather's soul. An icy shock ran through his veins every time his grandfather spoke through that thing. With his larynx gone, his grandfather refused to see people.

"Everything is going well," Eddie replied.

His grandfather's head shot back down again, his eyes on the cards. Eddie went around the table and kissed everyone on both cheeks in the European manner.

"Eddie stayed in Poland the entire war," his grandmother, Lois, said on the heels of Eddie's warm embrace. She was a physically strong, athletic looking woman, with a handsome oval face and regular features, plainly dressed, and looking like a German Hausfrau with opinions and a wit to match.

Micah had heard this story before.

"I came to New York with nothing but the clothes on my back," Eddie said proudly.

"How did you get out?" Micah asked, remembering that he had asked this same question before, not so long ago.

"During the war, friends of my family hid me and my brother in their barn," he said. "Farm life was boring, but it sure beat the alternative. When we heard the war was over, we left." He chuckled and smoothed his suit jacket.

"Sit down, sit down," his grandmother said, patting the seat on her other side.

Eddie checked for crumbs on the seat before sitting down.

"You want to be dealt a hand, Eddie?" his grandfather inquired from his perch at the head of the table.

"No, I can't stay long," Eddie said.

"They rode motorcycles through Europe," Micah's father said. "Isn't that right, Eddie?"

"In Marseilles, we caught a boat headed for Israel. From Haifa, we took a boat for America. It was the long way to the US, but with the restrictions on immigration, we had no choice."

"He did well for himself here," his grandmother said. "He got in the real estate business and became a multimillionaire."

"I started with a job in construction," Eddie said. "It didn't pay very well and the work was punishing. I managed to get through night school and got my business degree, and then my MBA. There was a need for housing in New Jersey, so my brother and I scrambled to fill it. It wasn't rocket science."

Eddie excused himself and went down the hall to the bathroom.

"You could have done the same thing," his grandmother said to his grandfather. "Why didn't you?"

"How was I to know there was so much money in real estate?"

"Maybe he'll give Stefan a job."

"I like my job," Micah's father said.

"Why? You're not making money."

"We've got what to eat."

"Ma, would you lay off?" His grandfather waved his hand dismissively. "He pays his bills."

"I think dad should go into politics," Micah said. "He'd make a great politician."

"Yeah, right," Micah's father said.

"He'd get assassinated," his grandfather said.

"You're so pessimistic," Micah said.

"So, Eddie," Micah's father said with a smile. "I'm thinking of moving to Poland with all the Hasidim from Israel and America. We need to repopulate Eastern Europe, provide a counterbalance to the Muslim refugees."

"I can't think you'd be welcome there," Eddie said. "The Polish goyim have repackaged the Holocaust as a tourist attraction, complete with kosher-style restaurants, souvenir yellow stars, and a Schindler's List of Treblinka and Auschwitz tours, klezmer music playing in the background. It's Jewish culture without the Jews."

"I'm kidding," Micah's father said. "Why would I want to move to the Third World when I've got everything I want here?" His eyebrows did this dance. "So, I hear you've moved to Miami."

"I needed to get away from the Hasidim."

"You'd make a better Latino."

"Take away the clothing, what's the difference?"

"Torah." Micah's father nodded at Eddie, clapping him on the back. "That's right, my man—Torah."

Eddie said he had to go, motioning to his watch, saying, "Time to pick up the wife. Hair appointment."

"Tell her to come here and visit us for a while," his grandfather said. "She can take a cab."

"We don't see you so often," his grandmother urged.

"She's running late, but thanks," Eddie demurred. "We've an engagement, that's why I'm so dolled-up. You didn't think I wore this jacket for nothing, did you?"

Micah's father clapped Eddie on the back calling him, "my man," and bid him farewell with a hug and kiss on each cheek. Eddie retreated. Micah heard the roar of his car as it sped away.

"Eddie and his wife never do anything with us socially," his mother said. "Why is that Henrich?"

"He's a busy man."

"It's because we're poor."

"No," his grandfather said.

"Yes," his grandmother said.

The memory was tangible yet elusive, as he reached out to hug his grandfather, he felt only air, yet it was hard to believe that his grandfather was dead; he could not wrap his head around the concept of death. He breathed deeply of the sweet scent of rose, and thought, one minute alive and the next dead. One day he had his larynx removed, the next day he was gone. Micah hardly believe he himself could die; he was too full of life, his heart pumping vast quantities of energy through his veins. Looking around the garden they stood in, he watched the friends of his grandfather pass by, a procession of the infirm, bent and shriveled, their movements palsied; it seemed their faces and limbs were decaying in front of his eyes. And soon, they too, would be gone. The velvety reds and flashy yellows of roses by the hundreds surrounded him, their colors refracting and multiplying the light of the sun into a million splinters, making the air feel as if it was brimming over with the warmth and love he felt for his brother and his parents, the happiness he felt belonging to this family, and realized all the roses would die, and their petals would turn black and crumble.

Beyond the roses stretched vast lawns punctuated by headstones of every size, monuments to the decaying bodies buried underneath, a primitive arrangement codifying grief, as if keeping a marker where each of the dead bodies had been placed brings the grieving closer to a person who will never come back, and whose memories are elsewhere. It seemed weird somehow, a grave injustice to the living who love these people. Micah walked up to one of the headstones, noting that it marked the grave of a boy about his age, and the arctic fear of death put its icy hand on his shoulder. He looked around for his father, seeking reassurance that he was protected, and saw his father's tall figure topped by his singular head of reddish-blond hair circulating among the relatives.

"Okay, I shouldn't have asked," Micah's mother said.

"A book we're reading for school says that the Romans put Europe on the path to becoming a world power by forcing one religion on them," Seth said. "Renee, our religious schoolteacher, says that Jews are probably the only people who resisted conversion that have not been totally wiped out. So that's something, huh?"

"If someone said to me, they would torture or kill me if I didn't worship their god," Micah's mother said, "I might not be so brave."

"Is that why Dad called you a Nazi sympathizer?" Seth asked.

"First of all, my family's not Jewish. My great-aunt was the first woman elected to Congress and she voted against going to war against

Hitler. But then she voted against war on the eve of World War I, too. Then there's his thing about my mother being French. Your father hates the French because they caved to Hitler."

"Is that why we hardly ever visit your family?"

Micah saw how aloof his father was with mother's brothers and noticed their numerous faux pas—thinking the Seder was done every Friday night, or that Passover was a stand-in for Easter. Or calling Hannukah a Jewish version of Christmas, as if Christianity predated Judaism. And he knew that his father's family were the same way with his mother. There was nothing they said directly that gave him this feeling; it was just a thought he had when he watched them talk to each other. One time Micah heard his paternal grandmother complain out loud to his aunt and uncle that his mother did not eat enough, and when his mother said something in Hebrew, they would joke with his father, who always made a big point of demonstrating the correct guttural pronunciation, making the deep 'kuh' sound, telling Micah that he had to bring up phlegm to do it right. And his grandmother said often, "Well, she wasn't born to it." And the way they mentioned these things, it gave him the feeling that the marriage between his father and mother was difficult for both sides. He saw his father's eyes glaze whenever his mother's brothers joked about attending Catholic prep school in his presence. And when she said something that showed her ignorance of some piece of Jewish history or custom, he'd say, "Once a goy, always a goy."

"So why did you marry Dad?" Seth asked.

"When we first met and fell in love," Micah's mother said, "we thought none of these differences of lifestyle, opinion, or customs would matter. We thought we'd conquer it all. Easing the pain of Hitler's coming has proved harder than I thought."

Micah felt warmed by the sun, the crystalline air, and the sharpness of the colors. Dewy-faced rose bushes all around lifted his spirits. He thought the garden too beautiful for a funeral home. Creepy to think six feet under, the grounds teemed with thousands of corpses.

FAMILY DINNER

The deck glowed with the same silvery patina as the liquid sky and looked interchangeable, as if an artist's brush had covered the whole canvas with the same colors. Even the hills surrounding the lake looked as though an iridescent gray wash had been applied. The clouds parted to make way for a big, juicy sun that looked like a ripe lemon ready to spill if squeezed even a trifle. And, as if on cue, ready for the spill, Micah's mother carried the roasted potatoes and corn to the table on the deck; the boys followed with the rolls, a salad, and their father brought the chicken that had been roasting on the grill.

"So what gives, Mom, telling us we have to work hard to get into a good college," Seth said.

"You'll have better teachers in a good college, and you'll be surrounded by smarter kids," Micah's mother said. "It's the smart students that make school worthwhile." She passed around plates of food. A silence fell, broken only by the chirping of birds.

"So what does it matter?" Micah's father said. "I went to a college where they accepted everybody with a pulse, and I did fine." He bit into a roll, chewing with unconcealed delight.

"We want to be artists and do things that inspire us," Micah said, "Dad said we can do that anywhere."

From his gleeful look, it was obvious to Micah that his brother was happy to hear that they would not have to work hard to get what they wanted or aspire to be the best.

"You'll have to learn craft before you can make good art," Micah's mother said, her arched brows frowning, a look she assumed when peeved. "For that you'll want to get into the best program for whatever it is you want to do whether it's music, art, storytelling, or designing computer programs. Your sister did that; she's at the best university in Israel for archaeology."

Seth made a wrinkly face that Micah quickly mirrored.

"It's better to learn from people who are good at the craft," his mother said, her voice trembling with the conviction of her belief.

"Give it up Mom," Seth said, with a quick glance at Micah's father.

"So, speaking of school how is it?" Micah's father said breezily, settling his arms on the table. He looked at Seth first, his eyes fierce.

Inside, Micah knew his father's heart was as soft as the butter melting on his roll. And he seemed inordinately proud that his college accepted everyone. Micah's father had told him a few times that his mother was an elite snob, and not to pay attention to what she says. No one said anything. Micah knew he would be expected to say something, but his brain refused to come up with anything repeatable though Micah would have liked to question his father's choice of topics. And why was he posing this question? What was he expected to do, make a list of everything that happened that day? His father asked the impossible.

"Well?" his father said.

"Okay," Seth said. He bit into his roll with a snap of teeth.

Micah choked on his roll, swallowing what little he had left.

"What 'bout you?"

"Okay," Micah said. He felt pity for his father, the most clueless in the world of adults, which was clueless by its very nature, which was saying a lot, to be the most clueless.

Chestnut-backed chickadees sitting on the steel-corded fence stopped singing their bright lilting song and wings sounding the gust of whips stirring the air, and took off, feathers flying. Their plumage matched the rich brown bark of the knurly trees they lived among.

"Sweetie, you need to ask specific questions, like how the presentation went, or how did they score in the spelling bee," Micah's mother said, her voice so soft, it would melt on a corn cob.

"In high school we don't do spelling bees," Micah said.

He was afraid her words would incite his father to feel defensive, to think that he was deliberately prodded. His father liked to challenge everything his mother said. They were unduly competitive with each other. Everything was cloaked in something else.

"They can answer a question about school without me having to jump hoops," Micah's father said.

What was it his father wanted to know? And what was so interesting about this? He was not asking his father how his day at work went. Why relive the horror.

"What classes did you have today?" Micah's mother said.

"Math, American studies," Seth said with a shrug.

The breeze picked up, the stridency of gap winds funneling a bevy of misty cloud formations over Puget Sound. Under a canopy of dense forest, the lake was ringed by the offices of tech giants specializing in the cloud. But the air over the lake and Gryffindor Island appeared as empty of content as always.

"What are you learning in American studies?" Micah's mother asked.

"You really want to know?" Seth said.

Micah looked at his brother and raised his eyebrows, underscoring the joke. How could anybody miss it, it was such a bad joke. Unbelievable that anyone would care to know about the boring and more boring. Did his father really want to know how they liked school— the idea of it was funnier than shit. He knew that answering honestly would not score any points, so he just wore his most enigmatic smile while observing his brother's adept countermoves.

"We took the land away from the Indians and then we exterminated them," Seth said matter-of-factly.

"The Indians didn't know what they were doing when they sold land to the Europeans," his father said. He sounded vexed. "They didn't know the sale meant they couldn't hunt on the land without permission, and they went hunting like they had always done. The Europeans saw it as poaching, and they shot the intruders. That started a war."

"Are you defending the Europeans?" Seth asked. "Seems strange coming from a Jew." His tone was muted, without rancor, but his words cut like a serrated knife.

"With the Indians there was miscommunication and crossed signals," Micah's father said, visibly trying to control his irritation. It was obvious he did not like this withholding of acceptance and adoration, his voice snapping like a wet towel as if to punish Seth for his cheekiness. "What happened to the Jews in World War II was way different. For no good reason, Hitler blamed Jews, who accounted for less than one percent of the population, for Germany's defeat in World War I. And after the war, the amount of reparations demanded by the US and the hyper-inflation that followed sunk the economy, Hitler blamed on Jewish bankers. Hitler used the Jews like the Democrats today use fiscal conservatives—as a collective fall guy. Something like what we're seeing today with most radical of the left wing taking anti-Semitism to a scary level. And I'm speaking as a liberal."

"Oh please," Seth said. "We talk endlessly about that in Hebrew school."

"If you're interested, I have a great book for you to read," his father said, the hope in his voice expanding like the wings on an owl.

Micah hoped they would not have to hear a repeat of the story of his great-grandfather, beaten to death by Germans in a labor camp in the weeks leading up World War II. Micah's grandfather escaped Germany in the nick of time. He was glad of that, but he would rather not hear his father revisit the subject now. Or hear his veiled hatred of Germans, Poles, or Ukrainians, all who served Hitler. One time Micah's father asked Micah's mother if her French grandmother had been a collaborator.

"Hardly, my grandmother was born on St. Croix Island, Maine, and my mother in Quebec." Micah's mother said. "My French ancestors left France in the seventeenth century."

"Ha, knowing your family, they were secret collaborators," Micah's father said.

"Oh, that's why you took the pictures of my mother off the wall and replaced them with your family pictures? I guess pictures of Gentiles don't deserve to be mounted in your home?"

"Papists require extra scrutiny."

Micah looked out at the lake and drank it in, feeling a little woozy, wondering how anyone could talk about the horrible side of life when surrounded by such beauty. And what did it matter? It was all in the past. None of their friends cared much for the religion of their fathers; it was all gibberish to them. Now they were faced with some weird book Micah's father was hawking, probably full of atrocities that they would not care to read about.

"No, Dad," Seth said in slow measured tones. The disgusted look on his face deepened in the downturned lines around his mouth. "I'm not interested in your book. I have enough of my own to read for school."

"Guys, that new friend of yours, Jessica, she's gorgeous. I love her smile," Micah's mother said. She looked from Micah to Seth, all her facial muscles twitching. All she cared about was avoiding confrontation. She was happy to be the whipping boy, replay the guilt of her ancestors.

"Yeah, she's cool," Seth said. His face softened.

"I'm not finished talking," Micah's father said, that snap in his voice again.

"I thought you were," Micah's mother said. "My apologies."

"Come on, Dad," Seth said. "Can we talk about something else? This is boring."

"This is boring?" Micah's father lashed out. "This is your history."

Micah's mother stopped eating to stare at Micah's father.

"I refuse to spend all my time thinking about the ugly things that have happened," Seth said. "Let bygones sort of thing."

A silence followed. Micah reached down and petted Bambi, their pup, stroking her gray and white marbled fur to help him relax. He looked past the glass wall overlooking the Japanese garden, now heavily waterlogged; through the wall of windows shimmering with soft translucence of blue-gray reflections of mountain, forests, and lake, the air smelled pungent and sweet, a combination of damp moss, wet tree trunks, flowers, and pine needles, earthy smells.

"I can't figure out her background," his mother said, sounding like she was from another planet, her voice too agreeable, artificially so. "Where did that lovely cinnamon skin and Oirat Mongol features come from?"

"She's Chinese," Seth said. "Raised by polar bears at the North Pole."

Bambi, their fluffy overgrown puffball that was actually a certified sheepdog puppy scooted near Seth and pushed her snout into his hand.

"Very funny," Micah's father said.

"Guys," Micah's mother said. "Before I forget, we should plan out your summer. I want you to go to a camp or youth group thing. I know summer seems a long way off, but we need to apply now. I found this program in Costa Rica where you'd be teaching kids English in the morning and learning how to surf and sail in the afternoon. What do you think? You'd know Spanish at the end of your three weeks there."

"What?" Seth said. "Let me see the brochure."

"I have the program info here. They run several trips overseas."

"Good," Seth said. "I need to look at this." He grabbed the booklet, and with a practiced eye, leafed through. "Look here! Why didn't you mention this? There's a group tour to Europe, visiting museums and castles, with a side ski trip to the Alps! That's more my style. I won't do the other one."

"Really, you don't want to learn how to sail?" Micah's mother said.

"No." Seth said. "You have been choosing our summer camps forever. It's time we choose."

"He's right," Micah's father said.

Micah looked at his mother, amazed how quickly she capitulated. His father was capricious. Frequently his emotions took over, and most of the time his decisions made no sense. Sometimes she'd argue with him; other times, she let it go. There was no understanding the logic. In this case, it worked in their favor, so he was not unhappy about it. Everyone stopped talking for a few minutes, eating seconds and thirds.

Micah's mother broke the silence by announcing to the table that she and his father were planning a party at the house that coming weekend and inviting friends.

"You're going to crowd the house with drunken adults spilling drinks and throwing up?" Seth asked.

"This isn't like the parties you throw," Micah's mother said. "The people we're inviting aren't going to go crazy."

"Just a bunch of old people trying to have fun," Seth said, "but they've forgotten how." He took a bite of a drumstick. The pup watched Seth eat with close interest, a few drops of saliva dripping from her lower lip, and rearranged herself to lay closer to Seth, who tore off a thick slice of chicken and dropped it on the deck for her to gobble.

"Like you guys know how," Micah's mother said. "At your last party, one of your friends threw up and left the bathroom a mess. His parents had to pick him up."

Seth chewed rapidly. "How'd you know, you weren't there," he said.

"Kiki walked in when I was cleaning up the vomit. She told me."

Kiki was a good friend. She had been there at that party, now famous. Someone brought six-packs of beer and several people got drunk.

"That was just one time." Micah paused between mouthfuls of corn raked from the cob, kernels trapped between teeth.

Bambi scooted over to where Micah sat and bumped his leg. Micah petted the dog, dropped a partially eaten roll at her feet, and watched her eat it in one gulp, his mind elsewhere. Who could forget that kid, he was the type who never drinks and after one beer goes kaput. He had to be carried out of there to his parents' car. Micah's mother had just come home as the dude finished throwing up. She made everyone sit down and listen to her lecture on drinking. Micah could not believe her emotional outpouring, at dagger points about everything. Instantly it seemed, based on quickly gathered information, people go to a hyper-kinetic place, showing the less-than-ideal emotional stability, getting mad about stuff like drinking when all the adults were doing it. Not their fault that this kid had a problem managing his alcohol.

"Why don't you guys stick around?" Micah's mother said. "You might learn a few things. Like you don't need to get drunk to have fun." She took a bite of salad. "I just want the buzz. Then I'm done."

"I've seen your parties," Seth said. "Boring and more boring."

"Take Felicia," Micah's mother said. "When she's looped, she's not barfing in your face. She just gets more hilarious. One time, her daughter Alana was there, and she told her mom she was drinking too much. The daughter taking the mom's role, isn't that a riot?"

"Yeah, I could see Alana doing that," Seth said.

A bluebird landed on the railing, cocking its tiny blue head. And immediately puffed up the dusting of brown on its breast, followed by a dollop of white that extended down its belly. Behind the bird, the trees swayed in the soft breeze, their long limbs rubbing with the sensitivity of praying mantises, their leaves curling.

"Why are you telling him this?" Micah's father said, running his hand though his hair, making it spring up like a spiky hedgerow.

"I thought it was funny," Micah's mother said.

"To you maybe," Micah's father said. "Not to anyone else."

"You have a better story?" Micah's mother asked.

"I wouldn't be making jokes about drinking," Micah's father said. "Drunks aren't funny. Sad, maybe, but never funny."

Micah picked up a piece of bread. With a jolt, as if propelled by the same force that moved Micah's hand, the creature flew away in a twinkling of blue feathers. The excitement over, the dog's head went back down, eyes closing.

"Felicia knows when to stop," Micah's mother said. "I've never seen her drunk."

"She's Jewish and Jews don't drink," Micah's father said.

"What? Like hell," Micah's mother said. "Remember your friend Joe?"

"In any case, you shouldn't be using those words in front of the boys," Micah's father said. "You say the most inappropriate things." His eyes bored into Micah's mother with the force of heat-seeking missiles.

"Right," Micah's mother said. "I'll stop when you stop."

"I don't curse like you do." Micah's father's mouth twisted. He pulled the breadbasket closer to him and rooted for the last roll, which he promptly coated with butter and popped into his mouth.

Micah would rather have seen love or at least acceptance between them, but they were too different.

"Hey, Mom, do you have some jobs you need done?" Seth said, looking from one to the other, a pained look on his face. "Micah and I need to make some money."

As usual, with a few well-chosen words, Seth neatly stepped around the poisoned arrows. Micah could only admire his brother's finesse. His father lost his frown and was already starting to look more his normal self. And his mother stopped looking so picked upon, and gave Seth a wan smile, like someone recovering from a deadly sickness. But a simmering remained in his father's green, tangerine-flecked eyes, Micah knew he was ready to pounce, given an excuse. It made him wish that everyone could just get along.

"I'll pay each of you five dollars for every window you do," Micah's mother said quickly as if she thought that she, too, could deflect his father's venom with a few benign words.

But Micah knew that nothing would erase what she had just said about Jews and drinking. His father did not like his pronouncements disputed, and he did not forget anything anyone said. He had a photographic memory for those kinds of details.

"What about we wash the cars?" Seth said just as quickly. "I could do one and Micah could do the other." Against the deep green foliage that ringed the deck, Seth's eyes looked like mossy pools with occasional flashes of tangerine, as if inhabited by tropical fish.

"I don't want you to do another half-assed job," Micah's father said. "You have to vacuum the carpeting inside and use soap everywhere else."

"We always do," Seth said. His joyous eyes locked on Micah, his lips forming a half circle.

"Last time, you did such a shitty job, I had to do it over," Micah's father said with a trace of bitterness. "And I was out sixty dollars. I'm only paying you this time if you do it right."

"Okay, then Dad's going to have to pay us for wrecking our pot growing farm," Seth said, sounding equally peevish. "Cost us twenty rolls of tinfoil and two of those two hundred dollar grow lights that we bought with money that we saved for months."

Micah looked at his mother to see how she was taking this, but her face did not betray her thinking; she looked inscrutable, like a sociologist gathering information. He could not believe what he had just heard, just when everything seemed to be going back on an even keel, and now this.

"Return the lights and get your money back," Micah's father said. "But I'm not paying for the tinfoil—you've got to be joking."

"The plants that you wrecked were borrowed from a friend," Seth said. "How're we going to pay him back?"

"Did your dad tell you that he and his friend Eddie tried growing pot?" Micah's mother said. "This was way before you were born. But their plants all died, nothing like yours. Yours were freaky big."

"The last thing we need is cops overrunning the place and arresting everyone," Micah's father said. He peered at Seth from under thick reddish-blonde eyebrows squashed together. "How long do you think it'd take before they discover that little operation? The money you spent on those lights wouldn't mean anything then."

"How did you find it?" Seth asked.

Micah sat up straighter, fork poised midair like his brother. His mother said later that their expressions looked the same, but then they were identical twins, why was this such a surprise? It had always been difficult for someone who did not live with them to tell the difference, but even those living in the same house got confused from time to time—his mother, who should know, was the worst offender.

She told them later that the only time she could not tell them apart was when their facial muscles quieted and their hair was the same length; most of the time she knew exactly to whom she was talking. Micah did not mind his mother mixing up their identities. She told Seth it was a slip of the tongue, but Seth did not like it anyway. Micah admired his brother so much that he grew to be inordinately proud of looking like his brother and felt slighted that Seth did not share his sentiment. Seth said several times he wished he was not a twin, saying this reflectively when upset at something Micah did, like maybe he knew that sentiment would upset Micah most of all.

"I was wondering what was causing that huge electric bill—I was thinking hot tub," Micah's father said, "but the hot tub people said impossible, and then I thought maybe someone was leaving all the lights on in the basement, but at that level it'd have to be pyrotechnics—then I discovered your pot growing room in the shed. I couldn't let that go a second longer."

Micah returned to the problem at hand: why would his father wreck those beautiful pot plants, when he himself smoked pot? How is it he gets off yelling at his kids for doing the same? It boggled Micah's mind that his father complained when they toked up.

"No one was going to find it behind that fake wall we constructed," Seth said. He looked at Micah's father as if he were challenging him to a duel, his eyes narrowed into flints.

Micah thought his father should have been happy seeing them adopt the same habits as him, or at least be more accepting. But Micah's father was also not accepting of Micah's grandfather, the Holocaust survivor who smoked like a furnace, mainly because he smoked tobacco, not weed. Micah's father outlawed tobacco in his house, saying he hated the smell, and chastised Micah's grandfather for smoking tobacco, and when challenged by Micah's mother who said he was being hypocritical, claiming that smoking weed was beneficial in the same way Micah's grandfather insisted that smoking tobacco was not harmful. Micah's mother got high occasionally too, nowhere near as much as Micah's father. She used a vaporizer when she did; saying the smoke from incineration aggravated her throat. Micah tried the vaporizer, as did Seth. They agreed with Micah's father that it was like sucking on air. They preferred the kick that smoking toxins gave them. It was one thing the men in the house could all agree on. But Micah's father acted outraged whenever they talked about it, as if that towel he placed under his locked bedroom door could hide the smell. Micah concluded that, like most adults, he had to have his way and pretend he was not doing the very thing that he was castigating them for. Micah squared his shoulders and looked around at the others. He thought they had done an exceptionally good job of it. That wall looked real.

"Our bills were four hundred percent higher than any of our neighbors. It wouldn't have taken the cops long to latch onto that."

"Your dad's right," his mother said. "While it's commendable that you're being entrepreneurial-minded, please steer clear of illegal activities, so we don't all land in jail." She looked serious, all the joking gone.

"Why would you go to jail?" Micah asked. There she goes again, Micah thought, making a problem out of nothing.

"Because we let you do it," his father said. "Why do we have to tell you this?"

Micah looked at his father in shock, mirroring Seth's expression. Oh really? His father always acted certain about every little pronouncement he made, when Micah knew that he was right maybe half the time. Many times, his mother would look up some statement of his father's and show him documented proof that his assertion was wrong. But this time, his mother did not challenge what his father was saying. It was weird to see them agree on anything.

"You should know this stuff," Micah's mother sounded peeved, her out-of-control curls bouncing around her face.

"We were, like, just trying to make money," Seth said. "And now you're taking that away. That's why we're asking to wash the cars." His voice carried the same injured tone as his mother's.

Micah looked at his father with what he hoped was a sweet, conciliatory expression, designed to show his father that he joined with Seth in asking nicely.

"I don't want to have to pay for a lousy job," Micah's father said. He sounded irritated again.

"Nobody's saying you should," Micah's mother said, her voice as gentle as her words.

It was easy to tell that she loved her boys, always ready to forgive them anything. But she should have thought of that before she started in on Micah's father about Felicia. Did she realize that her leaning on him like that was not going to soften him up, just the opposite?

"You tell them exactly what you want them to do."

"They'll just ignore what I say."

"You'll be there to guide them. And don't pay them until they've thoroughly washed it with soap and rinsed it with water," Micah's mother said.

"Mom, after we finish, you and Dad look at it," Seth said.

Micah looked at his brother with admiration. Seth knew how to wax it every which way.

"We'll do a good job," Seth said, his voice ringing with conviction.

Micah wanted to dance for joy. Seth did it again—worked their parents like an artist with clay.

"You're always letting them get away with sloppy work," Micah's father said. His frown appeared again, like a shadow that seemed to lurk right beneath the surface.

"It won't be sloppy, not with you there. It might be instructive if you were to show them what you want done. And pay them if they do a good job."

"I can't believe all the things I get roped into," Micah's father grumbled. "Now I'll have to waste my time supervising boys almost as big as I am."

"And you," Micah's mother said to his father, "need be on hand to show them how to properly wash the cars. I'll help with that, too."

"I'm not going to do it for them," Micah's father grumbled.

"Your dad has a point," Micah's mother said, "You have to do the work if you want to get paid."

His mother assembled the sponges and the car shampoo and filled several pails with water. The dog ran around lapping water from every pail. His mother waited until the dog left the water alone before putting in the car shampoo. "We'll start on the outside. You dad will show you how to soap up the car." Then she stood guard to prevent the dog drinking soapy water, and several times had to drive off the dog and assorted birds.

"It takes elbow grease, none of this 'I'm too weak stuff' I'm always hearing from you two," Micah's father said.

"Let's get some music going," Micah's mother said. "I brought out the boom box. Seth, do you want to put something on?"

"Yeh," Seth said and ran inside. He came out with an armful of CDs, and quickly selected one. "I'm putting on 'Color of My Soul' by Pretty Lights. I think you'll like it, Mom."

"What kind of music is this?" Micah's father said.

"Hip-hop," Micah said.

"Clash Magazine said this song 'swelters with soul,'" Seth said.

"It's pure noise," Micah's father said.

"Give it a chance," Micah's mother said. "Everyone have a sponge. Let's get her done."

"Look at me, Seth," Micah's father said, holding up his meaty paw in which he tightly gripped a sponge as if he was strangling it to death. "Hold your sponge like this and bear down." He started scrubbing the hood of the beamer putting all his weight into his arm, and then asked Seth to take over.

After a few minutes, he cried: "Stop! You've missed all these spots."

"Bird poop is impossible," Micah's mother said.

"We need something stronger," Seth said.

"I agree," Micah's mother said. "We'll get it gooey first with some club soda."

"That's gross."

"Don't you two run off," Micah's mother said. "The poop is only on the hood and windshield. We could do the back of the car until the poop becomes more manageable."

Seth threw his wet drippy sponge into the pail closest to him and passed his hand over his forehead in a tired gesture. And in sympathy, the pup raced around the sopping driveway as if she'd slurped pails of caffeine and not water.

"You're doing an incredible job," Micah's mother said. "Don't stop now. Just a little more to do."

Micah's father went back into the house for several minutes, saying he had to take a piss. Micah figured he was toking up; his father could not last long without a hit from his bong. When his father came back out, he accused his mother of doing all the work.

Micah's mother insisted the boys did the bulk of the work.

"Come on, dad," Seth said. "Next time we'll videotape it."

"You could have stayed here," Micah's mother said. "Then you wouldn't be questioning their work."

"You're always defending them," Micah's father said.

"And you're always criticizing," Micah's mother said.

Micah's mother talked his father into giving them ten dollars extra, saying they deserved it, and pointing out that they went back over parts she asked them to do again. Micah's father looked skeptical, giving each of them penetrating stares as if to divine their inner thoughts. A couple of chattering blue jays landed on the top of the car. The dog barked loud enough to raise a cloud of crows, and the blue jays disappeared with them.

"Bambi," Micah's mother called in an artificially high voice. "Come to Mama."

"You guys did a great job," Micah's father said. "I don't think I could have done it better. Why can't you do it this way every time?"

Micah felt so lightheaded from hearing this unaccustomed praise from his father that he felt himself levitating about three inches off the ground. And then Micah's father pulled out yet another ten dollars and gave them big hugs. Seth belted out a whoop that resounded over the lake.

"Ouch, my ears," Micah's mother said.

Micah's father went into the house through the garage. Micah looked at the money in disbelief. They each received fifty dollars. Micah knew with a certainty right then that his father was going in to smoke his bong and read a history book about World War II. World War II was his obsession, same with Micah's grandfather. And for once, Micah did not mind that his father closeted himself with his books; it kept him from poking around into his sons' affairs overly much.

His father would also have the TV on, likely turned to basketball, the towel under the crevice of the door along the doorjamb, as if that stopped the smell.

Seth made a face to Micah's father's retreating back and nudged Micah, saying, "Let's head out." They went down a trail to the center of the garden where massive ferns and flowering hydrangea bushes fought for space with statuesque evergreens, pines, and spruces.

Gossamer strands of ivy dripped from tree limbs. In the middle of all this untrammeled growth, the laughing stone Buddha took center stage with its head blackened on one side, green moss covering the other. They could not help their delight at simply being alive to surface irrepressibly, wantonly, without a reasonable excuse. Which is not to say that everything had settled down to something that could be labeled normalcy. There was a ruckus from the forest where the pup's ungainly body and feet snapped twigs and small branches, sounding the rustling of fur and coiled muscles as she swept after birds streaking feathers into the wind, showing them how things were done in her world, offering a primer on how the large furry creatures of the world exert power and control.

"Will you take a math test for me," Seth said.

"Fat chance," Micah said.

"What if I promise to take your science exam?" Seth said, smiling coyly.

"Ok," Micah said, "but you'll have to do it."

"Have I ever lied to you?"

"Give me a break."

"Where do you want it?"

PIONEER SQUARE

The next day at school, Micah and Seth were having lunch in the cafeteria when Alex showed up. Around his neck he had his 35 mm with a normal lens on it. There was talk that Alex was bisexual, and maybe he was. Neither Micah nor Seth cared about that; they weren't interested in gay sex, but they were okay with other people doing whatever.

Alex sat down with a tuna sandwich and an apple. "I'm taking pictures of girls doing the shimmy," Alex said. His black eyes looked hard and shiny like opals. "I'm looking for Fuckables," Alex said, flinging his long, flowing hair of Narcissus. "I like to snap them bouncy, bouncy." He took a big bite out of his sandwich.

"I've been snapping pictures of the ravishing Kiki in various stages of undulation," Seth said, "so I can slobber over them whenever I've a yen for some ooh-la-la."

"You never showed me those," Micah said.

"They're mine."

"I can show you some wicked photo shopping techniques," Alex said. "We'll curate the photos and stage a happening."

"So sick."

"Did I tell you I saw the work of this insane graffiti artist in Pioneer Square?" Alex said. "His name's Jesse Edwards. He's staged a show at one of the art houses. Talk about sick."

Out of his backpack he pulled a chapbook of Jesse's art to show around. What surfaced: an abrasive oil painting of a skate park, a still life of a package of Twinkies sitting next to a bong, and a nearly life-sized canvas done in oil of vomiting cheerleaders.

Alex said that Jesse headed a group of people who liked to skate-board and do graffiti art. "You've seen his art around downtown Seattle. Some of it is still out there. Jesse is active politically; he's got a campaign going to make graffiti legit as art."

"Now, that," Seth said, "is hardcore." He suggested they form a caravan to see Jesse's exhibit. Micah texted their friends. Amalie and Shaun replied in the affirmative. Kiki called and begged them to wait until after her cheerleader tryouts at Newport High. She thought they might end around 5 pm. She said she could pick up Jessica on her way.

Alex took them in his mother's gray SUV with deep skid marks along one side. His own car was in the shop. Seth sat with Alex up front. Rick, Amalie, and Kiki got in back with Micah and Jessica, scrunching into the deep upholstery. Something floral and sweet stirred the air. Micah and Jessica fell into a close embrace. The seat in front of them created a wall of separation, and Kiki—on the other side of Micah—divided them from everyone else. In front they were chattering at high volume, mouthing off about every little thing, and teasing each other, too, saying that this one was gay, the other one a necromancer, the voices around Micah all merging into one river of sound bleeding into the CD playing hip hop music. Traffic on the highway was light. Occasionally Alex had to slow down to avoid hydroplaning. A few times, Micah felt like they were floating over the road, other times, it felt like they were skidding across a gravel pit. It was no different than the usual on Pacific Northwest streets during rains that pelted the region all year around. Slowly they exited to Fourth Street and made their way through a downtown filled with jaywalkers; the tableaux changed from the corporate look to the usual assortment of young people dressed in gangsta-style jeans and women in tight mini dresses as they neared Pioneer Square. No one seemed to notice or care about the rain. It became background noise, sometimes audible, sometimes not. Scattered among them, the homeless ambled about like rag dolls, mostly old men stiff with sweat and grime begging for spare change—always a shock to see how dispirited they looked, as if a series of calamities had struck and left them all half paralyzed and brain dead. Alex found parking and they set out, skirting the vegetating carcasses. Seth held Kiki steady. Micah had his arm around Jessica. One of the homeless men, a particularly dirty looking sort, called to the girls.

"Take a shower," Seth said. "She might look at you then."

"Don't talk to him," Kiki said in a low voice. "He might attack us." The way she said that made Micah shiver.

"I'll protect you," Seth said.

They hurried past the man, not relaxing until they walked halfway up Yesler to the intersection with First Avenue. The rain petered into a drizzle while waiting for the light to change. A few feet away, a young couple leaned against an ancient lamp post smooching. All around them, groups of revelers entered and exited ancient brick buildings that gave the quarter its European flavor, many lounging on nearby benches, vaping, conversations ebbing and flowing around them, creating rivers of sound merging with music of all sorts issuing out of these quaint edifices onto the sidewalk: rock, jazz and country. Micah felt the beat of the music course through his veins, making his heart quicken.

Pioneer Square was built at the time of the Gold Rush from hand-made bricks of a quality and color that cannot be found today, clay mixed with straw and grass, the mortar a concoction of gypsum, lime, and sand mixed with a little water to create an adhesive. Brick had been layered to support floor and ceiling beams; gravity held walls in place. In today's buildings, cement and steel are used to keep it all together, but back then there was no cement or steel. The different type of materials used gave the older buildings a more handmade look, less linear. In the 1920s, as the mecca for arts and entertainment in the Pacific Northwest, these buildings housed opera, vaudeville, and stock theaters that drew patrons from all over the country. Now there's a smattering of western-style bars, jazz clubs, art galleries, and furniture and clothing stores, but the square is no longer the center of Seattle's universe, not that Micah cared about that. Seth stomped through puddles, calling to the others to join him and soon everyone was blasting through the water and splashing each other in a coltish frenzy. They celebrated the endless days of rain that for the past few months had been lashing the region to a sniveling drunken stupor, leaving trees heavy and drooping, and turning lacy gardens into seas of mud. Even here, in the urban jungle, the rain combined with a floral extravagance and sea air to create a tantalizing mix, turning Micah into one giant olfactory, his nose filling with fecund, earthy sweetness.

The gallery that held Jesse's art was white and spacious, the walls lined with large colorful paintings of the sort that reminded Micah of the museums he'd seen in Paris. The first piece, an oil painting that depicted a jar of Vaseline sitting on top of a Playboy magazine had Micah staring, and on the magazine's cover, a nude blonde clinging to a huge oversize banana that Jesse called his Mastur-piece, was hanging next to an oil titled Nude with Knife, Revision, depicting a blonde with pendulous breasts holding a knife. All the boys paused at that one. Also on exhibit, a wall with graffiti-style lettering in glowing airbrushed colors spelling the word 'good' with a woman's multi-colored face alongside, her lips puckered for a kiss. The boys lingered on the woman's face, no one speaking, everyone lost in thought. Kiki and Amalie were the only ones talking, conferring in whispers, so Micah could not catch what the exchange was all about, but he did hear one word issuing like a bullet out of Amalie's mouth, "Cunt," which made Micah wonder if she was angry about something. He thought the two girls were mostly friendly with each other. On the street, the word "cunt" was a pejorative. A man with wild, curly hair came over and stood next to Seth. He assumed a contemplative posture, one hand cupping his bent elbow. He was staring at the woman with the perfect breasts.

"What do you think?" the man asked.

"I prefer lube," Seth said. "Feels better than Vaseline."

"Vaseline's iconic," the man said.

"I know what you're saying. My dad still uses Vaseline. He's stuck in a time warp."

"I take it you're Jesse?" Seth asked. "How did you get started...I mean... as an artist."

"I conceptualize on paper and then I use the sides of buildings as my canvases, still do, actually," Jesse said, turning to Seth. "I do my art in my Sodo loft. Why don't you join me sometime, whenever you want?"

"Sure," Seth said.

They all stood in a circle, everyone smiling. It was exciting to be so close to a famous artist, although if they had not known who he was, he would have been just another skinny guy with a lot of hair. Jesse gripped Seth's hand firmly, holding on as if he did not want to let him go. "We could use a few level-headed guys like you, too many hotheads out there."

"I calm people down." Seth said.

Making their way home, Micah saw their father kissing a tall blonde on the sidewalk downtown in front of a bar, his arms wrapped around her as if she were a life preserver and he was drowning. Later Seth told his mother that his father acted as if he and that woman were more than friends, their hands going into intimate places. His mother told Seth he probably misinterpreted, but the look on her face said something else. The next day, Micah and Seth went with Rick to Jesse's loft, but Jesse was never able to give them the individual attention they wanted—he was pulled in too many directions, always at least two or three girls hanging off his arms, with clusters of hangers-on seeking advice. It was a bit disconcerting to see Jesse pulled in a million directions and not paying much mind to them.

Later that evening they learned from their mother that several people they knew, no one close to them, had been found to be high on prescription drugs at an after-school party in the neighborhood earlier that afternoon, medicine they had taken from their parents' bathrooms. The mother of the one of the boys, Debbie Strasberg, called a meeting of the parents. Her son Ian had turned up sick and had to be taken to the hospital to have his stomach pumped. Ian's mother told the dozen or so mothers that showed up that she and Ian's stepfather had decided to send Ian to an out-of-state disciplinary school. Drug treatment experts told her that it was impossible to get kids to stop addictive behavior while living at home. These kids had to be sent to a new place far away and denied contact with old friends so they can be taught new behaviors. After the meeting Ian's mother suggested that Micah's mother consider sending her boys away, too. Ian's mother knew that Seth and Micah had attended some of Ian's parties. Micah's mother and father asked Micah and Seth to sit with them to talk about it. When she mentioned the drug parties, Micah tried to look neutral, but he wanted to smile. He lowered his head. A smile edged the corners of his mouth. Micah's mother asked if they had gone to any of the parties. She said that Ian had named them as among the partygoers, not this time but other times.

Seth admitted that they had attended that first pill party. He said it was a wicked surprise to see Ian pull out a couple of sandwich bags filled with pills, mostly white and pink, a big grin splitting his narrow face, throwing them on the coffee table like they were contraband, his black hair waving high like a beacon. Rick had been at that party and he was the one organizing things. He placed them into categories: opiates, painkillers, stimulants.

"You want to be careful about mixing," Rick said. "Here're the downers." He pointed to the left. "Downers with downers or downers with alcohol can kill you." Then he pointed to the right. "Uppers over there. Doing an upper and then when you're crashing, taking an opiate, can be veeery nice."

Rick pointed out the ones with opiates, Oxycontin and Vicodin among them, and said it was the hydrocodone, a substance like codeine, but stronger, more like morphine, that was present in all these drugs, the opiate deftly manipulating the pleasure receptors so the host could feel just the sublime, not the dross. Vicodin and all the others, except oxycontin, also contain acetaminophen, so there's a danger with those drugs of taking too much aspirin, which can fuck with your brain and liver.

"You'll know if you've done too much aspirin: you'll feel confused, maybe have seizures, or lose consciousness, but if that happens and we can't get you to the emergency room in time, you die."

Practically everyone said they did not want a drug with aspirin in it after that. Rick had Ian go upstairs and find a meat tenderizer to crush the oxy, which he said would make it possible to bypass the slow-release mechanism built into that drug. Since then, Micah heard that drug companies were making it impossible to crush the new ones, but back then it was possible. Ian pointed out that Oxy was stronger than Valium and should only be used by people who've taken opiates before. Micah had ignored Rick's warning, snorted some oxy, just a small amount, enough to float on a sweet euphoric cloud. But he hesitated to do Oxy anymore now that it could not be crushed.

Micah shook his head at the memory. He was sad to hear that Ian was leaving town for some lockdown type of school. His father, luckily, was not willing to do the same to Micah and Seth. He said no to boarding school, too expensive, but his mother refused to let it go. She suggested a private school in Seattle; she'd heard parents say they had a lot of success with small classes and individualized attention. His father put the kibosh on that idea, and suggested meetings with a psychologist who deals in drug abuse. His company's insurance would cover that sort of therapy one hundred percent.

"You're being short sighted," his mother said.

"And you spend money like its water. If we keep going this way, we'll be broke."

■

Later that afternoon Micah and Seth came back from skateboarding to find their parents sitting at the kitchen table, both seemingly lost in thought. Micah was struck by how tired his mother looked, as if gravity had taken over, her eyebrows slanting down on lids that could barely maintain their upright stance, and lips that trembled every so often. The gray of the clouds mirrored the gray of her face. His father did not look much better, slumping over the table as though he lacked the energy to keep his body up, his mouth crumpled like an old newspaper.

His mother said to his father in a weak voice, "This is as good a time as any." She picked up her coffee cup with trembling fingers and sipped its rocky surface, steam coating her face, while he talked. The over-grown pup was lying next to her, looking even more depressed, her facial muscles in a jumble, if that was possible.

"We're getting a divorce," his father said in a flat voice.

"It doesn't change anything for you," his mother said, her voice matching the trembling of her hands. "We both still love you very much."

Micah looked at them both, aghast. He loved his mother's intense caring, her quiet nature. During the past few years, he saw more of his father's weakness, his overly emotional response to crisis and his lack of sound judgment, saying crazy things he'd do to the boys if they refused to obey him, like take away their computers, threats he shrugged off as minor stuff. Back when things had been good between his parents, he had enjoyed his dad's laid-back joking, his story-telling, and the feel-good charisma that he wore like an old shoe. He wished those days could be brought back. When it came to handling prob-lems, his father was a big baby. Even so, Micah wanted to scream at his mother and ask her why she allowed this. His father did not want her to spend money, why did she refuse to listen? When he said he wanted her to get a better job, why did she refuse to comply? Either that or structure an argument for why she needed to do something different that was so convincing his father would go for it, but not this obstruc-tion, this flouting of the man's will: it solved nothing.

"We're selling the house," his father said. "I've never liked this house anyway."

"What do you mean?" Micah said. "This is a horrible time for you to be telling us this," His eyes did this jittery thing. "This is like the worst time." He loved the house; he could not imagine life without it. He did not question his father's right to do this, but he did not like it.

"Your dad was planning to sell the house after you guys graduated high school whether we divorced or not," his mother said. "It has nothing to do with the divorce."

"Why? Where'll we live?" Micah asked. He felt his stomach lurch.

"We'll all be living here until you leave for college," his mother said. "When you go to LA to go to school, your dad wants to put the house up for sale. I love this house, and I know you two love it, too, but there's nothing I can do; I can't afford the mortgage on my own."

His mother reached out to hug the boys, but they sat there without acknowledging her, and shook her off when she came near. She sat back down and started rocking a little, her hands fluttering like she had suddenly acquired epilepsy. She reached down and petted Bambi, who shoved her nose into his mother's hand as if saying that she needed more than petting after hearing the news.

Seth asked if he could leave the room. His father nodded yes. Seth got up; his head bowed. Micah backed away from the table as well. His muscles felt weak, his calcified brain stopped functioning, he could not think of anything to say. A great sadness welled up inside. He gestured to Bambi and turned to leave, taking great pains to avoid looking at the tragic lines of his mother's face. With a heartfelt sigh, Micah followed Seth, the big furry feet of Bambi pulling in behind. Downstairs in the basement, they sat without saying a word. Seth passed around a water pipe. Micah got really stoned, so stoned he could not think straight or talk normal without slurring his words into a fine mash that not even he could understand, which was a relief, because he could not talk even if he wanted to. But he did not like the paranoid feelings that presented themselves. He blew some of the smoke into the dog's mouth. Seth did, too. They thought the dog looked stoned, but it was hard to tell. The dog always looked stoned. Micah got out his notebooks and the box of Day-Glo markers, hoping he could stop the bad feelings that rose up as if to strangle him. He made his name in big letters and painted each letter a different color, and then added ribbons and flowers and little Cuban cigars. He blamed his mother for everything; she screwed everything up.

Micah looked over to see Seth drawing a pen and ink of a girl's face broken into cubes. Where her right eye would be, he drew two devilish faces pressed close together, one of them with big green hair; the other one's hair, a bigger part of the circle, was left blank. The left eye was huge, the iris pink and green flowing through the brown. And under that behemoth eye, the flesh was pink and swollen. The nose had an arrow going through it, and the mouth had a wide reach extending to the ears. The chin looked like a goblin, and on one side of the throat, little cats in bubbles appeared to float alongside a bubble with a pepper grinder with a devil's spiked tail and the word: pepperbomb.

Around the face, Seth drew lots of vertical lines close together to create the girl's hair. In the right-hand corner, above the girl, a stick figure hung from a noose. On one side of the hanging, Seth wrote: 'artificial dismay.' And on the other side: 'discourse of course to Jeny the rply ability of the one true source.' In the middle of the girl's forehead, he drew a face of a boy looking pensive, and next to the face, a couple of stylized graffiti-like letters: F and K and a G, with an arrow pointing to the left corner of the page above the girl, where he wrote: 'got a gate for red news, left loving life four ever.' And on the left side of the page at the bottom, alongside the images of the cats in bubbles, he wrote: 'curiosity killed the cat.' And underneath the throat, in the place of the shoulders, he drew a fat walrus.

They drew for hours, notebooks filled with illustrations of letters and words and pictures of things mostly sad. Micah got thirsty and went up to the kitchen to get something to drink. Bambi followed, padding softly, her body listing like a drunken sailor. Micah gave Bambi a dog bone and let the dog go outside to chew it. He looked around at the peaceful scene, marveling that a hurricane did not suddenly blast them to smithereens. He saw his mother sitting on the deck, a book in her hands, lifting her eyes off the page and staring into space, and then after a time, going back to her book, only to repeat the process a few minutes later. Mid-afternoon, the day had turned sunny, and nearly eighty degrees, which amazed Micah that it could be so beautiful on a day of such sadness. The birds were singing a mournful dirge. The trees leaned toward the deck, whispering softly as if offering their condolences. Even the air around them had quieted. He heard a noise and saw Seth coming up behind him. His face, too, had a funeral-like pallor. Seth followed Micah outside and together they went out to

Micah's mother. The balmy air smelled minty fresh; it did not seem right to harbor so much beauty. Micah's mother looked up. Her eyes were wet.

"Sit with me," Micah's mother said.

"Stay with him so we can keep the house," Micah said. He bit his lower lip.

"I wish it were that easy. There's nothing I can do to make him keep it. Your dad told me he wanted to get rid of the house months before we decided on divorce. Do you understand? He said he never liked the house and can't wait to unload it. I asked him to wait at least until you left for college, which he agreed to do. Even if I stay with him as his wife, he wants to sell it."

"Mom, there's so many memories here," Seth said, his voice sounded a note of animal pain. "It's hard to imagine not being able to come home."

"I know, sweetie, I feel the same way," Micah's mother said. "When we were still thinking to stay together, I pointed out to your father that you guys love this house. It's the only home you've known. I asked him if we could wait until you graduated college. When that didn't work, I appealed to his practical side. I told him that our mortgage was the same as the average rent on a two-bedroom downtown—I know this from a story I did on real estate for a business magazine. He wouldn't save money on rent or even to purchase. And then I brought out my ace card: Real estate analysts predict the value of choice properties on the island in the next ten years will double. He still said no. I lost it—I don't know why I said this and tried to backtrack— said I wouldn't have sex anymore with him if he didn't hold onto the property, and he said well then we're talking divorce. I tried to take it back but he said no, this is what has to happen. Then I suggested to him that we hold off the divorce for a few years so you could have summers and holidays here, and we'd sell when real estate prices move back up, but he didn't care to hear any of it."

"Why?" Micah asked.

"I don't know sweetie. He ignored everything I said, then he joked that he was going to sell it and not tell you guys. He'd move our stuff out and leave you for the next tenants to deal with. I thought that was appalling. It was the worst, ugliest joke I'd ever heard. And then I realized that during all these years he's been closeted in his room smoking weed, he's changed. I don't know who he is anymore. You guys must have seen this, too. He and I don't do things together other than ride bicycles and usually we're talking to other people in the group and aren't with each other at all. And when we do have conversations, it's all this negative stuff. If I tell him my hands are wet, he says they're dry and that I'm hallucinating water."

"Yeah, he's like that with us too," Micah said.

"After six months with a marriage therapist—a man who by the way, sided with me most of the time—your dad said he doesn't want to do what the therapist says. He doesn't want to hash it out. He told me I have a choice. It's either his way or the highway. I chose the highway."

"Oh, Mom, why'd you do that? Maybe he'll come around."

"That's like wishing the earth will stop spinning. I think he's tired of all of us and wants to be alone."

Micah texted Jessica "I need u". She came over on the bus. The boys were sitting on the couch with their notebooks, scribbling madly. The television was turned off and no lights were on; they had lowered the shades, dimming the room, giving it a funereal air.

"Why is it so dark?" she asked.

Seth did not answer. He patted the couch between them, and she sat down. With a groan, Seth put his arms around her. Micah made a motion to move Seth's arms away, but then Seth started sobbing with his face buried in her neck and would not move. Micah understood. Jessica was the only one who could really understand what they were going through. None of the others had been forcibly uprooted.

"Leave us," Jessica said.

Micah went out to the garage, not sure what he was hoping to find, but then he saw the cans of paint stacked in a corner. He emptied out his backpack and replaced his books with a couple of cans of aerosol paints. He put on a thin hoody and went off by himself down the road. A cool breeze blew, making him shiver. It was around 6 pm—early evening, and still light. He was not upset about Seth being with Jessica, but he wished Seth would include him, that they could be a threesome.

He arrived at the school. A couple of boys who looked to be in fourth or fifth grade were shooting hoops in the basketball court that ran along the left side of the building. The sun had slipped most of the way behind the building, leaving only a glittery sliver to hover over the top like a tiara, sending orange shards across the school yard. He went around to the other side, but not far enough to enter the athletic fields. Instead he slipped down the breezeway between the main building and the auditorium. The light was ghostly in there, a darkish subterranean hue, and felt as ice-cold as if he had entered a vault under the earth's surface. There was a section of the wall midway, where the auditorium had this little insert where he could crouch and not be seen by anyone walking by. No one was around, and the air hummed with the quiet, but he wanted to take this precaution. He took out his two aerosol cans and noted that one was blue and the other white. He remembered that these paints had been purchased a few years back to repair chipped paint on bicycles. His father cared about his bicycles more than his own sons. Grimly, with his mouth set in a hard line, he sprayed *my parents are cunts* and then he stood feeling curiously relieved, and went back home, and sat downstairs, playing his guitar. Usually, the act of playing his guitar, just laying his hands on the fret board was enough to pull him out of any kind of funk. But this time his anxiety did not allow for the proper sinking in of the melody, so it could not encode the substrate of his brain, and he mangled the chords. In frustration he put down his guitar, opened his math book, and did his homework, finding a certain amount of comfort in solving puzzles. Yet he felt his depression return with a vengeance. He could not imagine giving up the only home he'd ever known. His head throbbed and his limbs felt heavy; it was all he could do to stop himself from sinking down to the earth.

THE ISLAND

"The kids are doing well?" I asked, hoping to close the awkward silence that fell.

"They don't know how good they have it," Katalin Rappaport, said, elevating her glass of red wine and pursing her lips, preparing to sip. She was a flaming redhead with alabaster skin, blue-green eyes and full, rosy cheeks that looked as moist and soft as a cupcake.

Some of the other adults assembled at this party at the Rappaport house had come from poverty and had vivid memories of challenging times, but based on the comments I heard bandied about, none of their kids apparently had any idea, and they would not want to hear about how hard their parents had it. I wondered if we were doing them a service, living here on this mesmerizing island in the middle of Puget Sound, within easy commuting distance of Seattle, and where massive ferns and flowering hydrangea bushes fought for space with statuesque evergreens, pines, and spruces, truly the most beautiful place I had ever lived.

The only downside was the amount of rain—not every day but close to it in the fall, winter, and spring—but if one kept a raincoat handy, with temperatures mostly mild, generally the living was easy. It was a magnificent fantasy land, a vast proliferation of plant life surging forth like a psychedelic dream, growing to absurd heights and bursting with health and vitality, brimming with needles and cones, plants growing as if fed a diet of steroids. Witness the gossamer strands of ivy dripping from tree limbs; virtually every living thing drenched in vivid green foliage in a way that haunted the soul. Hilly country with amazing views of the water everywhere I looked. It reminded me of Marin County or Beverly Hills; that is, if California were blessed with lots of rain and mist. Easy to fall in love with the place.

I followed Katalin's round, well-padded body to the kitchen to refresh our drinks. Her red minidress threatened to ride all the way up when she moved her legs, exposing chubby thighs crisscrossed with microscopic spider veins and dotted with legions of reddish freckles. Lots of people milled around the assorted liquors arrayed on the wide granite counter under a large window overlooking a verdant expanse. We were greeted by a dense forest of glass towers, magnificent bottles cloaked in logos with the bourbon and whiskey at the back, most of them unopened, while up at the front, the clear alcohols and red wines were quickly being emptied.

"You're not drinking?" Katalin's body vibrated, her eyes widening. And she lifted her upper lip, like a cat. Katalin had been born Catholic, like me, her parents immigrants from a Baltic country (not like me), and religious, in the same way as my Québécois mother had been raised. They all came from stratified communities prone to fanaticism. And in the end, was this apparent guidance from our communities effective? Neither one of us had given up drinking, or sex, for that matter. So what was the point?

"What you having?"

"Red wine. For health." As an ex-nurse married to a cardiologist, Katalin often liked to dispense health advice, but this time she cut it mercifully short.

"My father loved red wine with a passion," I said. "He'd have a glass or two at dinner, sometimes there would be a digestif of sherry or brandy before bed. All while my teetotaler mother called him a drunk, claiming whiskey flowed in his veins. So that's how I was raised, sad, huh? And now I drink like a fish. Nice, huh?"

"To answer your question about the kids, Jeremy just came home from serving in Iraq," Katalin said. "We hoped the army would put him on the fast track to maturity and experience, but he learned nothing in the military, no skills he can use. They had him cleaning latrines and serving meals. These years turned out to be a waste. He tells us he's still not sure what he wants to do with his life."

"The army worked out well for my dad," I said. "He had a bum knee, so he served in World War II in communications, which he enjoyed immensely, but by the same token, he went into the army with a college degree. But Jeremy still doesn't have a college degree, right?"

"No," Katalin said.

"He needs a college degree to get a good job, even in the army," I said. "I heard you didn't let him go to college, that even though he was accepted by one of the state universities, you and Michael forced him to sign up for the army."

"Michael went to medical school on loans," Katalin said, patting her hairdo. The misty wet autumn air that streamed through the open window had turned her hair into a fried ball of red frizz. Completely disregarding anything I said, Katalin continued her diatribe: "Jeremy saw how bad his cousin has had it, so he knows what can happen when you don't apply yourself. Michael wants to teach Jeremy to apply himself. He didn't get the grades for the University of Washington, the only school that Michael would accept. Eastern Washington University wasn't up to Michael's standards, so Michael told Jeremy he had to join the army. We didn't want Jeremy to turn out like Michael's brother, who became a drug addict and lost his job, and was starving when we took him in. Now our nephew is back with his dad, trying to get his dad off drugs. Jeremy saw all that and tells us he thinks it's the worst thing. He tells us he doesn't want to end up like his uncle, and he knows we've got enough money for him to go to whatever school he wants, provided it's a quality school, but all he does is get stoned on pot and play videogames."

"Mine have another couple years yet, but they're stoners like Jeremy," I said. "It's a party atmosphere at their high school."

Gaylene Nowicki, a blonde beauty who, with her height and physical endowments, might be dismissed as a trophy wife, joined us. She had on some dreamy white sweater with boa feathers around the yoke, and tight caramel-colored leather leggings on long slender legs. My eyes travelled straight down to the Christian Louboutin white pumps with their signature red soles, and I must confess my feelings smacked of envy.

"We told Trevor he's got to move out if that's all he does," Gaylene said. She was a Harvard-trained lawyer.

"We said that to Jeremy, too," Katalin said, "but now that he's back from his army gig, he moved into our basement, and has no money, so we made him sign up for business classes at the local community college."

"As long as he follows through, right?" Gaylene said. She was drinking champagne in a large, fluty glass that looked hand-blown.

"I wonder if it's just another delaying tactic," Katalin said, sipping from her red wine.

"I asked Trevor to moderate his drug use so he can make it through college," Gaylene said. "He can hit the party circuit after he's got his degree. But he says he can't wait that long. Even one day is too much." Jeremy and Trevor were in their twenties, several years older than my boys.

"My kids tell me they don't understand what's so cool about joining the rat race," I said. "They say it's too much stress."

"Trevor said he doesn't need to work. I told him he's not getting much from us, so he better be prepared."

I never saw Gaylene socially, outside of a few parties—but I did know that Gaylene's life was crowded with the most exclusive of social events, the kind that only billionaires and celebrities get invited to. Gaylene was another shiksa who had married a Jewish guy, but unlike Katalin and me, Gaylene never converted, and she flaunted her shiksa status like a banner, heading the arts commission of all things, never volunteering at the synagogue, like most of the converts, nor had she done time at one of the religious-themed groups that raised money to feed the poor and provide healthcare to the sick. She took her own path.

"But then Trevor flunked out Western Washington and the school asked him to leave at the end of the first semester, after he got knifed by some anti-Israel assailant on campus, so he applied to one of those colleges that accepts everyone and doesn't issue grades. I told him he should get a job already."

"My boys say they'd rather find some alternative way of making money, like making music or writing movie scripts."

"At least your boys have goals," Katalin shook her head.

"Yeah, but they don't do much to make it happen. Okay, they take music lessons and go to classes, but they could put more effort into it. They could start by handing in their homework on time."

"I hear you, sister," Katalin said. "All we want is for our kids to be functioning and independent at some point. Is that so much to ask?" Katalin paused to sip her wine. "I told Jeremy he can live downstairs in the basement while he's in junior college, but then we expect him to transfer to university and live near campus with all the other students."

"How are his grades?" Gaylene said.

"He gets Ds and repeats the same class again hoping for a better grade but he's too stoned to get it happening," Katalin said, her hands a stew of activity. One hand gripping her glass and the other, pulling her hem down.

"Sounds like he's doing too much pot."

Katalin stopped pulling her hem; her eyes flitted over my face as if she was memorizing every feature, and she spoke slowly, with deliberation. "You know what Jeremy says about your kids?"

"No, what?"

"He says Seth and Micah run the best parties on the island, that's what. He says whenever he's goes to your house, there's a party."

"I don't remember seeing your son at our house—isn't he like five years older than my boys?"

"He likes the younger crowd."

"With so many kids coming and going, I've no idea who most of these kids are."

Katalin joked that her son had it too good and that he'd never leave, not with a full refrigerator and his mom around to do everything. Gaylene was asking if she really did have to do everything. Katalin said she couldn't stand living in a pigsty, but her son wouldn't mind it. I interrupted the conversation to excuse myself; I had a pressing need to find the bathroom, which turned out to be beautifully appointed with tasteful art on the walls—the kind an art collector would have—and plush towels and scented candles.

On my return, in the hallway I bumped into Jon Schwartz, Gaylene's husband, who had made over thirty-million as a lead lawyer fighting asbestos cases, and now served as a state senator, a spare man with a bony face and razor-sharp eyes over which bushy eyebrows grew. He dressed as fashionably as his wife, in an elegant linen tee and gray slacks. Apparently, he also was headed to the bathroom when I intercepted him, but he did not appear to be in a hurry to get there. He stopped to put down his empty wine glass on a nearby table, telling me in a faint voice that he was thinking to bow out of politics. When I asked him why, he looked at me sadly.

"I was telling Stefan about it..." Jon's voice trailed to a whisper.

"What? I haven't seen him all night, where's he holed up?"

"He's telling stories to the crowd collecting around the fireplace..."

"You know, he'd make a great politician. Is that why you want to leave politics?"

"Let me tell you why: I introduced a homeowner's protection bill that would make builders liable for defects in materials and workmanship for two years, and structural defects for ten years—a common sense piece of legislation, with mortgages often spanning thirty years—but the bill was shot down by senators bought off by the builders' lobbying group." His eyes drilled black holes into me as if he would impale me and leave me hanging on the wall.

I shook my head in wonderment, liking his serious intensity and his interest in doing something for the people without a guarantee of a return. Too many powerful people follow the money.

"I heard the building industries got one of the strongest lobbying groups in Washington State," I said. "I'm amazed they're so overt about it." I sipped my drink. "One of our neighbors' kitchen floor started sinking after he and his family lived one year in the house. He took the builder to court because the builder refused to pay for the repairs."

"We had something similar happen to us," Jon said. "We bought this gorgeous house—you've been there—cost us several mil. The first winter, water seeped into our basement, and the next year, same thing. It cost us a fortune to reclaim it." He drummed his fingers lightly on the table.

"You're talking about the house you're living in now, right?"

"The builder never bothered to do an analysis of water flow ... but the law protects him; he's currently not liable."

Gaylene came into the hallway and joined Jon and me, looking glorious, with the pure, unblemished face of someone who cared for her skin with religious intensity. In the indirect light of the hallway, the texture of her skin, so dewy and fresh, looked the product of some clever magician, though I suspected that Gaylene had never required cosmetic assistance, being blessed with good genes. She went up to her husband and gave him a kiss, saying she was headed to the bathroom, and in a few minutes was back and standing by Jon's side.

"I was constantly on the phone about it," Gaylene breathed in that airy, flighty way of speaking she had that sounded as if she was perpetually on the run, returning to a subject we had exhausted.

"But not as bad as that guy who went around the island claiming he was a movie producer and asking people for big loans that he never intended to pay back," I said.

"Who?" Gaylene said.

"Dennis Kilpatrick. Dresses grungy and has long, greasy hair that he wears in a ponytail."

"Never ran into him," Jon said. "Likely doesn't travel in my circles."

"He was found guilty of all counts. Soon to be sentenced, might be as early as next week."

"Who's this again?" Gaylene said.

"His daughter was friends with my daughter," I said.

"All my kids are older than your kids," Gaylene said, "chances are, they never met the Kilpatrick kid."

"He came by the house unannounced," I said, "saying he had an emergency and was making a movie and couldn't get to his funds for a few days, and he desperately needed the funds so he could complete the movie. He had a deadline, he said, and could we lend him twenty thousand? He looked so distressed that Stefan wanted to give him the money right then, but I told Dennis that we didn't have access to that kind of cash. It would take several weeks, I said. Dennis asked for a money order instead, but I told him there was no way we could do that. He said a check wouldn't work because he didn't have a bank account. Alarms were going off in my head, so I told him we would see what we could do. Other people he approached didn't have my qualms. They ran off to their banks and withdrew big sums of cash. One widow gave him all her savings."

"People are so trusting," Gaylene said.

"Saying he didn't have a bank account struck me as too weird," I said. "What movie producer doesn't have a bank account? And the frequency with which he kept pulling out his wallet to show how many credit cards he had ... probably all stolen ... and he kept repeating that in a week, he'd have the money wired from Hollywood as though he was trying to hypnotize me. He stunk of con job."

"This island's a mecca for chiselers," Gaylene said.

"Mucho real estate swindles," Jon said.

"I feel bad for his daughter, her father in jail for fraud," I said.

We looked at one another without letting our eyes slide past, the way people typically do. For the first time in the years that I had known Gaylene—always from a distance, at parties, or sometimes, bumping into each other at school—we were finally talking.

"It's frightful that something like that could happen here," she said. "The island's supposed to be sacred space."

I racked my brain for something else to say. Finally it came to me: "You know there's drug dealers preying on the high school kids, in the same way that Kirkpatrick preyed on their parents," I said. "Kids are so gullible. It's criminal, the dealers getting into the schools."

"I told Trevor I'd pay him for good grades, like it's a job." A note of bitterness crept into Gaylene's voice. She swirled the small amount of champagne left in her glass and sipped delicately. "I don't know if it's going to work. He's been terribly resistant to doing anything connected with school. By the way—I wanted to thank you for taking in our son."

"I didn't know he was living with us." To my ears my voice sounded squeaky, like a badly tuned piano. "Not until he left to go home with you, and I asked Seth where he had gone. I learned that he had been living with us for two weeks. Sleeping on the couch in the basement."

To speak so openly like this with another parent felt cathartic—this thing that had been so long buried now lifted to the light of day where all the oozing abscesses could be examined under a microscope. The fact that we were talking at all lifted my spirits, and I hoped something positive would come from it.

Though our entire conversation, I wanted to spill it all out like a bout of diarrhea, all my pain, the anguish of not knowing what to do, and how bad it felt not being listened to, but I thought this was not the time and said nothing about my personal anguish. Instead, I followed Gaylene and Jon to the teeming living room filled with chatter and the ring of laughter, and reflected on what my life had turned into, with the wholesale discounting of my perceptions, my husband telling me I was imagining things when I told him our boys were using some kind of seriously bad drugs—I didn't know what or where it was coming from. I thought it may have come from Trevor or maybe Shane but then I heard Ian, but my husband discounted everything I said, and was boohooing me in front of everyone. He said they're potheads, period. I told him I could threaten our kids all day and my rage would have no effect. They just did not care.

So he says, "Well how do you think I feel?" Sitting on the tip of my tongue: How was it that I had to spell it out, and lay it bare, painstakingly, with clarity born of experience, and still, even with these repeated warnings, all the males in my house continued to flout me?

What really rankled us was that our boys were so willing to reject even the most basic, fundamental principles, such as that eventually children had to leave to make their own way. It seemed to me that our male children did not want to fend for themselves; they wanted to be children forever. But that could never happen. I could not understand why they did not see that. It was a sort of collective ambivalence. Even my husband overlooked everything I said about it and made it a joke and would not take steps to change it.

We gravitated to the table that held the booze and found ourselves standing in line with people I did not recognize. Most of them seemed engrossed in their own conversations.

"I kept wondering why he showed up for dinner, night after night," I said, as soon as Gaylene settled with a fresh pour of champagne, and me with my cabernet. "What was it, a week before I started noticing? I'm always the last to know."

I was relieved to share this helplessness I felt—the lack of knowledge about the comings and goings of my boys and knowing that they lied about everything with its implications of impending disaster—and wanting to share this with someone in the same situation. Someone well versed in the law. Maybe between the two of us, we might come up with a solution. Gaylene and Jon graduated years ago from one of the top law schools in the country. If anyone could see this quagmire for what it was, it would be Gaylene. I felt delirious, lightheaded even, to think that together we might figure out a plan. I was tired of treading water, knowing it was simply a matter of time before we all would drown.

"What made him return home?"

"He said missed his stuff."

"No, he missed you," I said. "The boys told me he was crying for his mummy." I would have liked to hold the other woman's hand, and feel the blood course through her fingers, to physically connect. But I did not dare reach out; certainly Gaylene would not want that. The woman had a frosty air about her.

"I was so glad when he called. I had visions of him under a bridge somewhere, dead."

"Why did he leave home?"

"I told him if he didn't stop doing drugs on school nights, he could move out. He refused to stop, so I told him to get out. I was just trying to teach him a lesson, not have him killed," Gaylene said.

Someone passed around plates of raw fish and roasted seaweed salad. The fish tasted fresh, the seaweed tangy, and when combined together, rolled across the tongue. I looked around and saw that Stefan was talking with a gorgeous woman unfamiliar to me, which often happened, and then I'd learn that we'd met once upon a time.

"I didn't think he would leave. I thought he'd back down. But instead, he got defiant and said he wouldn't stop taking drugs, even if it hurt his grades. And his grades kept hitting new lows. I couldn't believe it when he said he didn't care. I started to see red, and in one unreasoning moment—I wasn't thinking clearly—I told him to leave. I told him he could earn his own living."

Katalin came up, shaking her hips, causing her vivid candy-colored red hair to fly, turning the strands into a rat's nest. It was easy to imagine that her exact shade was an enhancement, not that I saw that as a bad thing.

"What did he think was going to happen?" Katalin said, with a hair toss.

"He had no plan," Gaylene said, patting her own hair and combing the silk strands with her fingers, making it lie nicely.

"So when he returned home, did he stop with the drugs?" I said.

"He agreed to go to drug rehab. It's a year-long program that will cost us a hundred-thousand dollars. I told him he has to bring his grades up to passing before he can come back home."

"I don't understand why these guys are so resistive to learning skills that'll help them be successful," Katalin said. "And no, it's not an easy road, not for most people."

"I have trouble believing this is my kid. How did I get so lucky?"

"We may be following the same course of action that you're taking," I said. "It seems like a strange, contagious disease has taken hold our kids." I avoided touching my hair, thinking I was better off playing with my opal bead necklace.

"It's the party atmosphere on the island," Katalin said, with another shake of her head.

"Follow the money," I said. "There's too much of it here, people live large, and life is sweet, and many kids cannot imagine why they should work when everything is done for them."

JAIL

Micah Isakson moved restlessly on the thin pad, but nothing could ease the hardness of the metal bunk. Nothing and nowhere was comfortable. His vertebrae felt as if they'd been rubbed raw. His eyes, wide and staring, roved the pitted ceiling of the King County Jail. The cage they put him in was far dirtier and grimier than anything he had ever experienced.

Being on the eighth floor, midway up, entombed in a block of gray steel and shivering from the cold of the place, he felt as far removed from life as if he were buried six feet under. The walls felt as though they were closing in, the room appeared to be shrinking, and he knew that couldn't be happening, could it? He kept telling himself that this was not happening. But he had difficulty breathing, which made him think the air supply had been cut off. How much oxygen could he rely on? He didn't know. From staleness of the air, he didn't think he had long.

He imagined a medieval toilet would smell like this. He ran his hand over the bristles scraping his chin, thinking it nasty not to have proper hygiene. He hadn't washed, brushed his teeth, or shaved in days. He had no contact lens solution, so he couldn't take his contacts out of his eyes even though they were smarting and irritated, nor did he have a container to put them in. This was not for lack of trying. The jailers told him he had filled out the request form wrong and he had to wait two more days to fill out a new one. He looked down at the enormous neon-orange scrub-style shirt and elastic-waist pants they had given him at processing. It made him feel as if he was swimming in someone else's ocean. They had taken his phone, cutting him off from everyone, along with his necklace and bracelets, stuff he couldn't live without. After stripping him of all his possessions, they treated him like they would some rabid dog, pushing him when they wanted him to move, ordering him around in harsh voices, calling him by a number. To the guards, he didn't have a name.

He was only five miles away from home, but he might as well have been in a fishbowl, for all the privacy he had. In his mind's eye, he could see Seth standing at the lake's edge, watching an osprey's quick descent into the roiling, gray water, its wiggling prey leaving a trail of slivery scales fluttering. The image of the bird, headed like a fighter jet straight up, into the dazzling blue ether of his imagination, seemed totally surreal compared with the environment in which he found himself. He missed the forest around their house just as keenly, that vast proliferation of plant life that seemed to surge forth as though it was on a diet of steroids, along with the obligatory water and sun. In particular, he loved the sheltering trees growing with audacity, growing to absurd heights, bursting with health and vitality, brimming with needles and cones. He used to spend many afternoons lying on the grass, gazing up at the dense growth of dark green thrusting skyward, tips disappearing in the gray marbling of the clouds, in parts as mottled and wattled as if the brains of the world had been dissected and left nakedly exposed on God's operating table for public viewing. Trees changed his mood in subtle ways. They were his silent friends, calming and soothing his fears, making things seem less bleak.

The sound of heavy breathing jarred Micah back to his reality. The roommate in the bunk below was an ogre with a broken nose and feverish vulture's eye: a whitish-blue with a film over it that bulged slightly as if he had some medical condition. Whenever it fell on Micah, which it did the minute the beast woke from its slumbers, Micah's blood froze. He had to wait until the ogre had fallen asleep before he could close his own eyes, but even then he kept jerking awake at the man's egregious, harsh-sounding intake of air, cutting through his intestines, making him quiver with fear. Even at that moment, with the ogre asleep, Micah was in a state of tension. His cellmate was in for first-degree murder. It was hard to wrap his head around. During a house burglary, the homeowner had been slow about telling the ogre where his money was, so the ogre put a blowtorch to his face.

The image of the burned, mutilated face of the victim seared Micah's brain. The cellmate said he was thirty, but who knew if he was lying or telling the truth, what with the scars and the tats, and his strange jokes about butt fucking and cock sucking. Micah wondered at this guy who wouldn't stop with his dirt, telling Micah he had a big one for him when Micah got hungry. Micah didn't say a word when he heard those jokes. Their frequency made him feel as if he was hallucinating, the blood rushing to his head, firing up his brain. Mostly he tried not to look scared.

Then there was the big, red-eyed vulture that flew around his head, muttering foul things, unrepeatable things. At night, the voice seemed to get noisier and meaner, the sounds mixing with all the crazed animal screams of the other inmates from inside their steel coffins stacked all around him, a factory of the damned. Above all else, in the outcries of the other inmates, Micah heard echoes of words that Seth had said to him before Micah's arrest: "I wouldn't do it," and "Didn't you hear what Mom said?" Seth had been right about this. What made him think that going along with those guys was a good idea? At the time it had seemed edgy and cool, but now he regretted his involvement. He should have backed away like his brother did.

He put his hands on either side of his head and pressed his throbbing temples. It hurt to reflect so deeply on this. He moaned to think that his brother and friends were living incredibly normal lives, getting up in the morning and having breakfast without him, going to school as usual, and then getting together at night to smoke pot or the Turkish blend of fruit and tobacco in a hookah that they liked.

Meanwhile his stinking carcass rotted in a tiny cell.

Micah uttered a soundless, interior scream to match what he heard through the porches of his ears. The agony never stopped, awake or sleeping. Day or night, the agony was all the same. Each time he reflected back, the pain burst fresh, a new wound layering over the old, creating a crusty tell of accumulated misery.

The other two boys who had been with him that fateful night hadn't been put in jail. They stayed in juvenile detention for a weekend, a mere hand slap. They were seventeen at the time of arrest, and for that reason, they were treated as minors regardless of who did what. At their release, they were told they would have to do some community service, a few months' worth, but that would be it. Micah, on the other hand, only a few months older and considered an adult for criminal purposes, had been shunted off to the county jail.

The judge called it a hate crime, which amazed Micah. Until his arrest, he had considered the whole thing a joke. He had gone along with the other kids on Yom Kippur, to the Yeshiva, and written the graffiti not out of personal conviction but to show his twin brother he wasn't a wimp. This was after a lifetime of Seth throwing down the gauntlet, with the underlying message: Why does everyone have to carry you?

But even more damning, his name had been released in all media outlets with banner headlines "Jewish Teen Charged with Hate Crime." The story even made the *New York Times*. It was plastered everywhere on the Internet never to dissolve. And then, as if he hadn't been bequeathed enough pain, his lawyer advised him to voluntarily remain in jail for a whole month prior to his arraignment.

If you don't show remorse, the judge likely will have no mercy," Michele Cottle, his lawyer, had said at their first meeting in jail, a few days after his arrest. "Having your parents post bail won't cut it. The judge might view you as a spoilt brat thumbing your nose at the law and slam you with the maximum penalty of five years."

Michele was sitting on a tiny, wooden chair at the jailhouse as she was telling him this, her thick blonde hair pulled back in a bun, her face wreathed in an earnest, caring expression. She was a small-boned, thin-lipped woman with high, arched eyebrows that appeared to be painted on, and in her high-necked ivory dress, a rich jacquard fabric that fell loosely over her lean body, draping well below her knees, she looked elegant, an odd sight in that stark environment.

In a phone call, his parents told him to do what the lawyer asked. He had no choice but to obey.

He looked down at the concrete floor. If he hadn't been so scared, he might have thought her sensible white Nike sneakers comical, something like his mom would wear.

He tried to lighten the air. "I like your shoes."

"I wear heels in court, never on the street or in jail."

As she spoke, her soft, even tone made him feel that she was the only person who could save him in a world gone suddenly topsy turvy. He felt a huge amount of relief that she was representing him. He folded his hands, trying to still them, thinking that he was willing to do anything she said, as long as she kept him from having to endure a long prison term.

The lawyer gave no indication what she thought of him. Usually females gushed all over him, but not this one. She had this demure look about her, and Micah thought to soften her with some flirty small talk but the no-nonsense expression she wore on her face stopped him cold. Micah was striking, slender and tall, with finely chiseled features and big, sensual lips in an almost-pretty face, and he had long lashes like a girl's framing these big kaleidoscope eyes that changed magically to match whatever clothing he had on. He couldn't see himself, so he had no idea what color his eyes were with that screaming-loud blood-orange he wore, but that was the least of his concerns.

They sat in the only room where he was allowed to meet her, the size of a walk-in closet, where they could speak without a barrier between them. Anyone else who came to visit had to sit in smaller cubicles on the other side of thick glass and speak to him on a phone.

"I grew up on the Texas Gulf Coast," she said. "My father worked intermittently as a fishing guide—he was what you might call chronically underemployed. I went to law school on a scholarship to save my brother, a drug addict. But he was long gone by the time I graduated." She spoke to him as if he were a child who couldn't sleep on account of having bad dreams, her low, musical voice sounding like the rippling of a stream. She repeated everything twice, sometimes three or four times, and he was glad she did because the clamor in his head sometimes sounded too loud for him to hear her. Other times he heard her words as garble and couldn't understand what she was saying.

Micah's father hired Michele because she had a reputation for getting youthful offenders lighter sentences. Thinking how much power she had over him, he started to shake, which invariably led to memories of how cruelly the jail guards treated him.

"I expect you to plead 'not guilty' when asked."

"Why?" He quaked to think that he was to be arraigned at the end of his month in jail and that newspaper and television journalists would be there.

"I need more time to work on getting favorable terms for you. I'm going to ask that the judge allow you to repay your debt to society outside of prison. I'm thinking of suggesting a residential drug treatment program with an education component. You'll have to agree to stay there for two years while you work for charities that are agreeable to putting felons to work. It'll be like the community service that you had to do in diversion. But getting them to agree to take you on isn't a slam dunk. Many charitable organizations don't want to bother with the paperwork or the worries of dealing with troubled teens. And later, after I've worked out the terms with the prosecuting attorney, you'll be required to face the judge again. This is when you plead guilty. And the reason we do this is so there will be no trial before a jury. I'll use the time between now and then to try and maneuver so you'll be seen by a compassionate judge, someone who's more likely to treat you kindly. What we don't want is to put you in front of one of those draconian types who like to put young people away as lessons for the others."

"But I didn't write the bad stuff."

"It could have been your idea. You could have told your friend to write it."

"We didn't discuss what we were going to say beforehand."

"What proof do you have that you didn't tell your friend to write those words?"

There was nothing he could say to that. His lawyer went on to say that one of his friends, a girl he had dated a few times, had turned Micah and his two accomplices in to claim the thousand-dollar reward. On the basis of this traitor's testimony, they obtained confessions from the other boys along with the word of at least a dozen kids who said they heard about it—one of his accomplices had blabbed about it at school. And now, the lawyer said, he would have to be careful. At his arraignment, he would have to appear contrite. He listened with this feeling of unreality. It seemed so unfair. He hadn't hurt or killed anyone. He didn't steal anything. According to the lawyer, what he did was as bad. He had been with others who wrote graffiti that was considered incendiary, a hate crime, something that would dog him for the rest of his life.

On the lawyer's way out, she shook hands with Micah. Her hand disappeared in his, but her slightness was illusionary. She had a strong grip.

THE HICK AND HIS WIFE

The place they'd chosen for us to meet turned out to be a funky road-side bar a few miles down Highway 9, on a desolate stretch not far from Freehold, an hour and a half south of Manhattan in New Jersey. It was more ramshackle than the pictures on the Internet showed, a barn on the verge of falling apart, cracks and splinters everywhere. It was a hundred years old at least and looked more like an ancient dwelling for farm animals that someone had attempted to refurbish and stopped halfway. It had not been fully brought to life; something was missing. Maybe it needed a coat of paint. Stefan thought it was fine the way it was, a bit tattered, but it failed to bother him like it did me. I told him I liked that it was dark, charming, and romantic, with ivy growing over the walls and a trellis in front, but the smell was something else, musty and damp.

They were waiting inside near the entrance. The male half of our date was fit like an Olympic champion, muscles popping like he was on steroids, which at first intimidated me, and then I noticed how soft and kind his eyes were, and how sweet his smile. He had a big jaw that waggled at every opportunity, and he was quite forward, standing right in Stefan's face when he introduced himself, and clapping him on the back as if they were old friends when they had just met. Stefan went right along with him, not put out at all, laughing and talking as if they had known each other forever.

His name was Clive, and he had a smile so broad it nearly sliced his face in two. He wore a badly cut polyester sports jacket and plaid tie, looking uncomfortable in what was probably his Sunday best.

In greeting, he jammed his face so close to mine I could smell his sour breath, and he pumped my hand, yelling, "Howdy!" into my ear in a voice that sounded like a car without a muffler, loud enough for everyone in a three-block radius to hear. His cheeks operated like bellows, growing into big, rosy apples, and deflating again with a rush of air as he spoke. He looked and sounded like someone who spent his days and nights swilling beer and watching sports, which is what he and Stefan immediately began exchanging comments about—something to do with the LA Lakers. His lack of class grated on my nerves like a bleeping car horn that would not go silent. Some people might laugh about my attention to such behavior; after all, we were simply meeting to see whether we might enjoy a few minutes in the sack together, nothing more. But he was not the kind of people I would gravitate towards outside the swingers' circuit. Whatever spin Stefan might put on it, getting cozy with someone I hardly liked was not going to happen.

"You got an incredible ass," he barked as if he'd paid me the highest compliment and I should keel over right into his lap.

When he saw my consternation, he slapped his hands together like a farmer at a barnyard auction, raising a wind. He seemed to think he was funny, doing that. Yet he spoke with genuine friendliness, as though he was trying to make good, and I should loosen up already. Taking one look at his tough-guy exterior, I thought he was a bit too caught up in himself to be good in bed: the way he held his back, as rigid as a fence post; but then again maybe I was close-minded and not welcoming. I tried to relax.

I told him he had an incredible ass, too, which made him laugh. And then Clive said something complimentary—he said I was so pretty he forgot to look at my tits—and my irritation evaporated. I laughed in a friendly way to show I enjoyed his little joke. I could see Stefan was cottoning to the guy, the way he smiled at the man, so I made a big point of looking appreciative, and making my thank-you sound hospitable, but I was afraid I sounded like a squeaking mouse. Probably he saw me as the introvert I was, someone not used to being addressed in a familiar way by strangers. In any case, it did not seem to matter what I said. Nothing could dampen his spirits.

"I didn't expect you to be this sexy," he said, licking his lips as though he could hardly wait. He spoke loudly again, as if speaking to someone at the other end of the parking lot. "We're going to get along just fine." He pinched my ass. I gasped and instinctively moved a few steps away.

Stefan turned and stared at me, his eyes narrowed, calculating. There was an undecipherable twitch at the corners of his mouth.

I smiled my most winning smile at Stefan. "We lucked out with these guys, huh, Stefan?"

"You sure did," Clive said.

Stefan seemed amused, the muscles around his mouth straining as though he was holding back a chuckle.

The woman looked just like her pictures, very pretty, with a perfectly rendered oval face out of which shone big baby blues framed by the longest, thickest lashes I had ever seen on a human being. She had a tiny blonde head composed of perfectly straight hair, a painted beauty with nipples that poked the thin fabric of her tight little top like tootsie rolls. It was no surprise to see that her hug-my-bottom sailor pants had Stefan gaping. She stood behind Clive, not saying anything, just nodding meekly and smiling until Stefan began asking her about herself, slowly prying her open.

Batting her mile-long lashes, she said her name was Angel.

"Where's the accent from?" he asked.

"I grew up in New Mexico." She suffered from the pin-pen merger, with her *i* and *e* indistinguishable when followed by a consonant—a lighter version of California-speak, which contains even fewer distinct vowels.

"I was in Santa Fe once, for work. It was hot."

"Yeah, it's hot there."

"You're from Santa Fe?"

"I lived in a horrible little town you never heard of," Angel said quietly, her voice sounding like the murmur of a creek. The *or* in *horrible* she pronounced like *ore*, much as a Canadian might, although when Stefan quizzed her about it, she claimed she had never lived close to the northern border.

"How do you like New Jersey?" Stefan had a gentle look on his face. He seemed touched by the girl.

"Much better. The milk in the store isn't sour when you buy it."

The four of us went inside and sat down where the hostess put us, far away from other diners, which suited me just fine. Maybe the hostess had sized Clive up like I had and understood my plight.

Our dates had been right about one thing, this bar offered privacy in spades. We could have been gangsters planning a major heist, and no one would have had a clue. The dark wood of the place leaned into our little group, enveloping us, creating a bubble where we could talk, and making other tables seem far away, like planets from a distant galaxy. The lamp on the table flickered, adding to the sense of seclusion, of being invisible to everyone else. I felt the anticipation of the evening weighing on us. Stefan's questions to Angel echoed in my head, and his conversational agility was a salve to Clive's less-than-subtle greeting. Stefan always had that facility to turn the most awkward situations into something that flowed more easily. He was good at smoothing out the bumps and turning a potential disaster into a slow, sensuous romp.

Clive ordered a beer. Stefan asked what I was planning to order. I told him my usual, a kamikaze—basically vodka with sweetened lime. He vacillated, beer or a mixed drink.

Finally, he decided. "I'm getting the same thing," he told the waiter.

"You let her order for you?" Clive said to Stefan, the twin globes of his cleaved jaw shaking. "A woman does that, and soon she's got you drinking cosmos and eating quiche."

Stefan shot a nervous glance at Clive, but he said nothing. When the drinks arrived, Stefan downed his in one gulp and asked the waitress to bring him a beer, an IPA.

Clive leaned back in his chair, drank deeply of his beer, and looked at Stefan. "What're the small bumps around a woman's nipples for?"

"Her pleasure nodes," Stefan said.

"That's braille for suck here," Clive roared.

"Okay, I've got one for you," Stefan said. "What's six inches long and two inches wide and drives women wild."

"Wait a minute." Clive raised his beer. "I know this."

"You think about it," Stefan said, and patted Clive's arm before turning back to Angel. He asked in a syrupy sweet voice, "What brought you to the East Coast?"

I heard Angel say, "Divorce," which had my attention, but as I could not bear not hearing the punch line of the interrupted joke, I spoke up.

"Stefan," I said. "Finish the joke."

"No, I have it," Clive interjected. "Wait."

"A one-hundred-dollar bill," Stefan said.

"I thought you were going to say your junk," I said.

"That would've been too easy," Clive said.

"Nor would it have been funny," Stefan said, "or true. You know I'm bigger than that."

"What's the difference between your paycheck and your uhmm?" Clive asked.

"You don't have to beg a woman to blow your paycheck," Stefan said.

"Pretty good," Clive said. "You know your jokes."

"That's an old one," Stefan said.

"And so unfunny," I said. "Men like to spend money just as much as women do. They just spend it on different things."

"Don't start," Stefan said.

"I don't like ball-cutting women who drag their wimpy husbands around on a leash." Clive spat out the words like wads of gum and sat back in his chair, clenching his grapefruit-sized fists. "There's them fat ladies with the fake pearls and diamond Rolex watches trying to push their husbands to buy these honkin' luxury vehicles. It's a fuckin' shame when the guy can barely afford his house and boat. The guy's got his eye on a man vehicle, and she's egging him to get her the one that's bogged down with the electric dishwasher and the spa bath. Not that I mind the extra commission."

"Is that what you do for a living?" Stefan asked.

"Do you mean how do I pay the rent? I sell RVs."

"You won't be seeing us looking for RVs, not for a long while," I interjected with a snort, "if ever."

Stefan gave me a withering look. Apparently, he wanted me to make nice. So I did.

"How can you tell which ones are ball-cutters?" I asked in a voice dripping with syrup.

"She'd be the one pulling out the checkbook while he's behind her, meek on his leash, his shoulders squashed in."

"Your wife doesn't handle money?" I asked.

"Of course the fuck not," he said. "Angel here doesn't know how to count. She's always paying too much for things."

I stared at my drink and reflected on how pictures can mislead, and e-mail too, because somehow, we forgot to ask the kinds of questions that might have revealed the man's redneck ways and misogynistic outlook. He might be friendlier than a defanged rattlesnake, but he struck me as the kind of guy who would refuse to go out of his way for a woman. I tapped Stefan on the shoulder, hoping to enlist his help.

"Stefan." The truth of it was I did not want to tangle with a man who carried that kind of baggage.

"Honey, relax," Stefan shot back. "Have another drink." His interest in the woman was visible in the upward crook of his mouth and the metallic flash of his eye.

"Oh, goody," I said, trying to be sarcastic. Failing to get any sympathy from Stefan, I turned back to Clive.

"Oh...um...interesting," I murmured. "So...ball-cutters are buying, huh? How are sales otherwise?"

I offered him another chance to redeem himself, even though the glaring absence of intelligence in his eyes unnerved me. I squeezed my arms to my ribcage, increasing the depth of my cleavage, and leaned forward.

His eyes flickered. What I saw reflected there was a little warmth amid the cold hardness of aluminum and steel, the gray outline of big vehicles, exhaust filling the air. I knew immediately what I was up against. I recognized him as belonging to the tribe of people I grew up with, the John Bircher segment of cowboys and truck drivers of the Old West.

"Terrible … it's bad … I may have to look for another job." He looked at me with those pale eyes and licked his lips. "You're looking mighty sweet today. You know why a woman has tits, don't you?"

Stefan said something to Angel I could not hear; he spoke so low, almost a whisper. It was with great self-control that I forced myself to focus on the knucklehead in front of me. I pulled down the hem of my shirt so more of my cleavage showed.

"So, you like your job, huh?" I questioned Clive in what I hoped did not sound like total tedium, thinking that I could care less about the RV industry.

"The adrenaline rush of making a sale … it's like injecting fifteen cups of coffee—nothing like it." His eyes roamed my chest.

I leaned in closer.

"Why do women have breasts?" I asked.

"So men will talk to them," Clive said.

"You look like you know your way around a woman."

"Women love me."

"You know how to give it to a woman."

"I like to make them squeal."

Just when the talk was getting interesting, Stefan said he had a growling tummy and asked if anyone wanted to order food. With a quick look at Clive, Angel shook her head, saying they had already eaten. That's when Clive decided he wanted a pizza. He ordered one, loudly, with a sweeping gesture of the hand, waxing expansive, master of his small universe. I ordered chicken wings and potato skins, saying I hated pizza. The pinched face of the waitress grew more convoluted with the urgency of my request, or maybe she simply wanted to get away from us. In either case, she bolted for the kitchen. A few of the people seated at nearby tables were watching the hubbub around Clive with amused expressions. I thought Clive would have been more entertaining if I had been seated elsewhere, too.

Clive wolfed down his food, talking all the while, the cheese and grease dripping down his chin. Stefan also was eating with gusto, as if he liked nothing better. They were discussing basketball again, so I delayed saying anything, wishing they had kept to the sexy jokes. I managed to get just enough chicken and potato down to quiet my rumbling stomach. All the while I sweated bullets trying to be social so I would not hear any snide comments from Stefan later. Stefan tended to be critical of my social skills. I asked Angel what sort of work she did and learned that she answered phones. Her eyes glazed as she said this. I asked her what town they lived in. She remained cryptic, saying little. But even with all the conversational dead ends, I could see that Clive was warming up to me, the way he looked over at me and held his beer, telling me that their town was a throwback to an earlier time when people never locked their doors.

Talk of real estate in this context was even duller than hearing about their jobs, but I tried to look interested. I was hoping we could go back to the earlier line of talk, with its undercurrent of sex. To get things back on track, I told him that we had been hoping to meet people as good-looking and with-it as they were. The way I was repeating myself, as if I had nothing in my head, had Stefan raising his eyebrows, likely wondering what was happening to me. I overheard Angel repeating something Stefan had said and laughing at his joke: that a good business opportunity lay in importing prairie dogs to take over New York's garbage cleanup problem. Only Stefan could find a joke in the dirty streets of Manhattan with its garbage cans full to overflowing, litter on the sidewalk smelling like offal. Looking at her shining eyes, I realized that this beautiful woman was probably wondering what Stefan would be like in bed. I wondered did she realize I was wondering the same thing about her husband. I looked at Clive's hands, fantasizing how they would feel on my body. I felt a prickle of heat.

Thinking I would be better served if I could get Clive to talk openly about himself, between bites, I asked questions to induce him to reveal what lay beneath the jokester exterior. At best maybe I could learn something about rednecks, whom I had never encountered before. To that end, I asked him how long he'd been in the lifestyle, and he said five years.

"Yeah," Angel broke in. "He started with his previous wife and liked it so much, he made it a condition of our marriage."

"Veterans?" Stefan said. "You can show us."

"What are you looking for?" I asked him point blank.

"A submissive," he said, looking defiant. "Sorry, but that's how I fuckin' like it. Don't care what you fems think. And she had better like rimming."

"What's a submissive?" I asked. "A slave?" I tried to remember what he had said in his profile but could not recall anything beyond the fact that they worked out like nine times a week.

"You don't know?" He fired back.

"We just started this swinging thing. You're the first couple we've met."

"Shit." He reared back in his chair and growled, "If had known you were this raw before setting up the meeting, I'd never have gone through with it. Newbies are fuckin' no-shows." He plowed his faint eyebrows together and smashed his thin lips into a grinding motion.

"Really? We're here," I said. "We showed up."

"I'm talking about when it comes time to do the deed." His deep voice shot up several octaves. "Let me give you an example. Couple of newbies agreed to come to our house for dinner. We had already met, like now, at a restaurant much like this one, and we all liked how we looked. They promised to be at our house at a certain time, and Angel here slaved over the stove for hours making a special meal. They never came, didn't call, nothing. We tried calling them, but no answer. And this, after my wife scrubbed the house down, set out candles, music, the works—the friggin' works. She bought those candles special. The next day, we get a message saying one of them fell sick. Why didn't they call? Now I just delete e-mails from them. They made me so mad. I thought I was going to burst a blood vessel."

"We'd never do that to people."

"That's good to hear." He said this more quietly, but he did not sound convinced.

"If we say we'll be there, you can count on it."

"We'll see," Clive said. "Come with us right this minute. You'll ride with me in my car. Angel here can go with him."

"Wait a minute," I said. "I'm not prepared to do anything tonight. Stefan and I need to discuss things first."

"See, I'm right. Fuckin' no shows," he said, muttering something about not having faith in newbies.

"I can't be pressured like this," I said, and turning to Stefan I added, "I don't want him to force me into anything. I want to sleep on it."

"Why do you have to make a big deal about everything," Stefan said. "You're spoiling our good time."

Feeling as if they were goading me, their words as sharp as knives, I stood up and looked at Stefan.

"What?" Stefan's frown was mutinous, as obdurate as the blackness outside.

"I'm leaving. Hand me the keys."

Stefan stood up also, shooting me a disappointed look. We paid the bill and walked out to the parking lot, our feet crunching on the gravel. Clive caught up with us next and shook my hand. I kept a stiff upper lip. He snickered at Stefan, who hovered over Angel, his eyes on her tee as it rounded the curve of her breasts, puckering along the ever-erect nipples, the neck cut to reveal a slash of white skin. Stefan looked sadder than I had ever seen him as he leaned down to kiss her wet, shining lips, a painted valentine against the smooth alabaster of her face.

Clive motioned to her to leave. Stefan held her hand even while Clive announced for the sixth time that the evening was over. Stefan looked as if his best friend had died.

She tried to walk away, but Stefan pulled at her.

"Angel," Stefan said in a low, tremulous, drawn-out voice.

At Clive's thundering frown, she yanked her hand away.

Reluctantly Stefan dropped his hand to his side. He looked more dejected than I had ever seen him.

On the drive home, I asked Stefan what he thought *rimming* meant.

"Finger up the ass," he said.

"Really?" I asked, and I looked it up on my phone's browser. "Nope. It means oral-anal contact. Yuck."

"Thanks. I needed to know that."

"Sorry about what happened with Clive and Angel. I don't want anyone forcing me to do anything. I want to take my time deciding."

"They don't matter. The only people that matter are me and you." He paused. "Wasn't it funny, what he said about ball-cutters?"

"A riot," I said. "I wonder why such a sweet girl married that."

"Listen. Not everyone had it as good as you, with a dad who paid for college." Stefan spoke in his best schoolmaster tone, his forehead grooved in shallow trenches like a freshly plowed field.

"Lucky you, there was a free college nearby. What does that have to do with Angel?"

"Her parents not only didn't pay for college, but as soon as they could, they threw her out. She married the first guy who came along. Her husband turned out to be a violent drunk, so she divorced him. With no skills, no job, and a baby to feed, she tossed a dart at the map and moved to Old Bridge, New Jersey, and attended a technical school there. She found a job, but single motherhood proved difficult on minimum wage. But I don't expect you to understand. Hardship is something you wouldn't know about."

"Poor thing. She was sweet."

"I thought so too.

I could not understand why he sounded so hostile when I asked him about the girl, but I realized that he grew up poor and perhaps that accounted for his attitude. I knew it bothered him that he grew up poor. Often in conversation, he'd point out that I had a privileged childhood. There was no getting around that my father was prominent in the community and made millions as a surgeon. It was not something I wanted to dwell on, mainly because my husband was not the type of person who could talk easily about the things that really bothered him: anti-Semitism being one of those things, and poverty another. Nor I could keep up with a conversation about this. I had no experience in discussing painful issues; no one in my family ever talked about things that really mattered; my father was too busy, he was never home, and besides he had a lover whom my mother bitched about constantly. On the rare occasion he was home, she nagged him without letup. They never actually had a normal discussion, so I had little practice conducting one. I hesitated to go where I had little understanding. My way of dealing with difficult subjects was to avoid them. In that way, my father and I were very much alike.

But I did not want to follow completely in my father's footsteps. It brought me no joy. So I resolved to smooth things over, thinking that giving pleasure was the answer. I could not change Stefan's childhood, nor could I pretend mine was not paved with gold. It seemed as though the only good way out was to show Stefan I loved him, regardless of his background or mine. All else was a waste of breath. With that in mind, I decided to try something I thought he would likely respond positively to. I put my hand in his pants.

The RV salesman must have felt the same way because he never got in touch with us again.

FINDING A GOOD MATCH

My husband and I found another couple on a swingers' website that appeared to have it all: they were gorgeous, experienced, and smart. We emailed for a week to suss out more about their personalities before nailing down a time and place to meet. Dave wrote that he and his wife had a swing in their bedroom and a whip made of feathers and assorted other toys—from glass dildos to hot wax. They had been swapping partners since their college days, some twenty years ago, which intrigued us. Partner swapping had been Stefan's idea. He explained it as another tool in our arsenal to keep our libido alive. We had few sex toys other than a dildo I had from college days. We joked that we'd learn from the experts.

"You deserve a good spanking," Dave wrote in an email.

"I demand that you give me that spanking in person," I replied.

"I'd be delighted to," Dave wrote back.

What I especially liked, his proposal for a hot yoga session:"I want to try the naughty dog with you ... plus we could make up all these new poses and holds for fucking and non-fucking ... develop our core fucking muscles ... I'd love to do that."

From Jenny's emails, it appeared she found Stefan amusing, so it seemed out of the blue when she sent the following message:"Swinging rarely gives me pleasure anymore, and I want to forestall another disappointment. I'm opting out."

I suspected it was not about looks. Stefan was super hunky from years of endurance cycling, and his face pleasingly symmetrical, the kind scientists say women tend to like. He was in sales, an expert at getting people to relax. I wondered if maybe she could tell how excited I was at the prospect of meeting her husband, and that's what turned her off.

On our end, it was a go. Jenny was everything Stefan dreamt of— beautifully slender with long legs. I was a toothpick with no curves. But Dave didn't end our correspondence in compliance with his wife's wishes. He switched to another email address and intimated that he might be able to persuade her to capitulate, but we had to plan in secret. That put a smile on my face; it seemed so bad-ass. I agreed to meet Dave by myself to gauge the attraction. If it was not happening between us two, why bring the four of us together?

Most of the men we had met on the swingers' site failed to meet expectations. At times I felt like Jenny, ready to quit swinging and go back to the same old. Stefan had to persuade me to keep at it. Finding a good match between four people is much more complicated than dating solo. It's like building a sports team; everyone must work well together. Stefan was convinced that we would reap rich rewards if we could assemble a group, maybe two or three couples. When we came across Dave and Jenny, we knew one other couple we both enjoyed being with, but they lived two hours away.

The hunt had been exhausting, filled with letdowns. Often it was a personality thing. Sometimes they had misrepresented themselves and were nothing like their pictures—either the pictures were out of date, or they posted another couple's pictures and said it represented their feelings. Sometimes the realization that we had been snookered came after our initial meeting in person at a bar, and then going to a motel or their house, and then when we were smack in bed with the offending couple that's when it hit, and how do you back away from that?

My husband was not interested in a threesome with me and another man, and yet I continued titillating Dave, liking the flirtation, thinking we could convince his wife to give Stefan a chance. Then I began to wonder about Stefan. Was there something I had overlooked that turned her off?

"Was it his pictures or email?" I asked in a text.

"The night she wrote that email we had a disastrous meeting with another couple," Dave wrote back.

I understood Jenny's decision. There's nothing worse in the swinger's world than having sex with someone you consider inferior to your husband. It's not just about looks, or the size of the man's equipment, but about his ability and willingness to do everything possible to please his sexual partner, to ensure that she's facilitated in the best possible way. Few know or care to learn how to please a woman, and many seem to lack a basic understanding of what constitutes foreplay. Dave struck me as different; he had too many pictures posted, and he kept changing them, showing a passion and a sense of play that I was hungry for.

"I can outlast you," Dave emailed. "You'll be begging me to finally come already."

He was the first man to promise this.

"I can do it in every position, and I get a lot of pleasure out of fantasizing about different ways to seduce and delight. I'm willing to try anything you suggest."

I had only met one man in the lifestyle who could give soul-bending orgasm. My husband was jealous of that man—he made that clear by calling me names and starting arguments when Mr. Potent was around, so we had to end our foursome.

Dave promised he would work on convincing his wife. Meanwhile he said we needed to meet, so he told Jenny that he could not handle screwing the same woman for the rest of his life. If she was done with swinging, she would have to allow him to screw someone new at least once a week. Jenny stipulated that the woman had to be sexually unfulfilled and happily married. That was me. My marriage was fine outside of the bedroom.

Jenny wanted to screen requests. Dave noticed that the ones she picked he considered physically unattractive, observing in an email to me that I filled all the requirements except the physical one. But he did not want to lie to her, so he inserted pictures from another woman into an email that I sent him, and forwarded it to Jenny's email, asking permission to put me out of my misery. Jenny said yes.

When he entered the bar, I was struck by his youth. He looked as though he was in college even though he claimed to be forty. I was forty-five. I wondered if he had lied to me about his age, but I was attracted to him and let it go. We sat at the bar and drank Jägermeister, his favorite drink. I felt a tremendous amount of lust, and I could see that he did, too. We knew without either one of us saying that we were going to have sex that night.

His hand on my thigh felt like fire.

His parents were on vacation and their place across the lake in Newport Hills was free, so I would not have to bring him home. Stefan was away on business for the week and my children were all at various friends' houses for sleepovers, still I was thrilled I would not have to bring him into my house. We took off in his dad's ivory Lexus sedan. Ensconced on his parents' patio overlooking the Seattle skyline with the summer air caressing our skin, we kissed and fondled each other, enraptured. We kissed for hours, and the way he plied my breasts sent me into orbit. After that deliciousness, we went from room to room, finishing up in his childhood bedroom.

He did everything slowly, voluptuously, with an exquisite sense of timing, waking me in ways I had never experienced. No man had lasted as long or was as sensitive to the ebb and flow of my animal self. I had more orgasms than I knew I was capable of, and I squirted for the first time in my life, and not just once, but multiple times. I strove to please him in the same way he pleased me, going out of my customary zone of no swallowing.

We met every day that week for an hour after work, so we could be at home at a reasonable time for our families. He told me at the end of that week that it was highly unlikely that Jenny would join us because he and I got along too well. And from what I told him about Stefan, he had a feeling that Jenny would find him wanting. Reflecting on this, I thought it better to keep our trysts secret from my husband. I hoped someday she would change her mind, and then perhaps we would meet. I would have liked to have Stefan share this, and maybe learn from it. But then I realized that likely he would be jealous when he saw me with Dave. I've taught Stefan a few of Dave's moves, so now we can enjoy some of the same. I do not see Dave anymore, but I fondly cherish the feverish delight of bouncing between these two men. I've had more wild sex than I had ever dreamt of. That was when I was in my apex, and it kept my juices flowing.

MICHAEL AND AMY

Gazing at a dazzling glacier-capped ice cream in the sky, Mount Rainier standing tall over Lake Washington and the dense forest surrounding it, I watched my man pull out his laptop and sit with it on our bed: "OMG, check this out!" And after a pause, "Look at these pictures."

A new couple had posted the most beautifully erotic pictures: the woman's sleek, catlike body crawled across the lawn in a G-string and nothing else, while he stood full frontal, ripped abdominals predominating.

"We simply can't pass this up," Stefan said.

The author of the email said his name was Michael. He and his girlfriend, Amy, wanted to invite us for wine and cheese at his house. But we had to decide in the next fifteen minutes, or the moment would be lost to us forever. Otherwise there would be no meeting at all, no angling for a later date.

Michael promised we would not be disappointed, insisting in his e-mail that the pictures were real, taken just that week.

It was obvious to both of us that this was the real deal; they posted too many pictures, obviously amateur shots, enough to convince us that these people were what they said they were. Stefan grabbed me by the shoulders saying, "Check out that ass" and begging me to get dressed, adding "Can't you get a move on?" The guy looked equally impressive. I was in shock at the beauty of these people.

Here and in Europe, where it's more widely accepted, adherents say swinging is a solution to cheating. It's what people do when they love their spouses, want their marriage to continue, and simply desire to have sex with different people without sneaking around.

They might have a point. National surveys suggest that as many as sixty percent of married people cheat. Helen Fischer, an anthropologist who has studied sex and adultery for years, says she has lived in forty-two countries and there is "not a culture in the world that is not adulterous." In other words, we're programmed to do it. But it's not cheating if you do it together.

With that in mind, I decided to go for it and threw on a fitted, cleavage-baring shift, something that showed my assets to the best advantage.

Michael lived just a few minutes' drive away in Newport Hills. His house—a veritable palace—was crowded with bays and crevices lining the banks of windows overlooking an expansive lawn, and in dusk, the glorious swells of Lake Washington were visible below.

At the door Michael met us holding a bottle of Montrachet 1978 in one hand and two empty glasses in the other. He had a big smile and looked very confident and body aware, his face pleasing like a Greek god's, very symmetrical, his nose elegant, and lips full and sensual, made for kissing. He had lovely, dark, curly hair sweeping his shoulders and the most gorgeous body I had ever seen on a man. It turned out he was an architect and had designed the house himself. On the walk through the foyer and wide hallway to the living room to meet his girlfriend, Michael said he worked out several times a week.

Amy was sitting on a couch near the fireplace, where a tiny flame danced cozily over a couple of hefty logs. The room reminded me of a cathedral, all soaring angles and rounded arches, and the ceiling appeared to float overhead, flouting all laws of physics. She stood up to greet us, a tall, willowy blonde with no hips. Amy could have been a runway model with legs that stretched out to infinity and then some. She was the kind of woman I knew Stefan hungered for, the kind that bespoke money and status. The way Michael looked I did not care how much Stefan yearned for Amy. I was happy for him that she looked so scrumptious.

Stefan asked Amy what she did to keep so fit, and she said "sex", which elicited a hearty chuckle from him. Michael suggested we leave them alone, and he led me through an endless array of rooms pointing out this and that architectural detail, each one larger than the last, all of them filled with the dying rays of the sun, with tangerines and pinks and lavenders dusting the cornices. Everything was super clean, nothing out of place. I kept expecting to run into the cleaning lady wielding her mop. The kitchen had been dressed in cherry wood, granite and copper, setting a rich, dark tone that glowed alongside the European stainless steel appliances. He stopped by a mini wine-bar.

"I designed all this," Michael said. He swept his arm out. His dark eyes looked hard and smooth like pebbles.

"Not many kitchens like this," I said.

He opened a wine bottle and expertly aerated it with a vessel created for that purpose before pouring two glasses.

"How long have you been married?" he asked.

"Fifteen years. What about you?"

"She wants to get married, but we've only been going out a couple months."

"How do you feel about that?"

"Much too soon for her to be pushing this hard, but I get it, she's struggling to make ends meet, and she's got a young daughter."

"You're not ready."

"I've been married once already and I'm not so eager to do that again."

We concluded our tour and joined Stefan and Amy. A delectable feast of fruit, crudités, cheese and crackers was spread out on a table in front of a massive stone fireplace that would have overwhelmed a lesser room with its grandeur. Michael, it turned out, was Jewish, and Amy, a Lutheran of German extraction. I told them we also had the similar backgrounds. As a joke, I added that Jewish men hooked up with German women much the same way American men go for Japanese women. Amy looked puzzled, her almond eyes fixed in a squint. In a low, tremulous voice, she said religion had nothing to do with it. Michael looked nonplused and explained that they met in the retail lighting store where Amy worked. These days they spent nearly every weekend together.

At Michael's whispered suggestion, Amy fetched towels and bathrobes, asking if we wanted to soak in the hot tub outside. Amy handed Stefan a towel and a robe, looking at him like she was sizing him up, her face flat, without expression.

I had to acknowledge to myself that Stefan looked pudgy compared to Michael's ripped physique. I hoped that Amy would not care exclusively about things like that. I should have spoken up right then, and personally vouched for Stefan being a good lover and sung his praises, and maybe joked about how he concentrated on riding bicycles for exercise and that's why his abs were in such a sorry state. And pointed out his beautiful, lean legs. But I did not say anything, her expression off-putting, a frown instead of a smile. At no time did she let on what she was thinking. I've never liked people who are not forthcoming with their feelings other than putting out negative vibes; that attitude makes me shrink inside.

The hot tub was a custom-made affair that looked as if it had been carved out of rock. Massive tropical-looking palms and ferns surrounded the deck, holding everything in place under a dusky sky. A profusion of bracken covered the hill behind the tub and lent a wonderful, earthy feeling to the place.

Warm, moist steam issued from the tub, and the air smelled of rainforest. I slid into the water, dunking my head, and then rose up again, sputtering water. I felt I had taken on the guise of a dolphin, with my long brown hair plastered to my skull, my face hot and wet, and cuddled up to Michael, thinking sexy thoughts. The sun briefly fired up like a solar flare before descending behind the trees, leaving streaks of sun glowing on our faces. Amy put her hand over her eyes as if trying to shield them from the sun. Stefan scooted next to Amy. Amy kept sliding over, with Stefan right behind her, until, for all practical purposes, she was sitting in Michael's lap. I was on the other side of Michael, with Amy so close to me I could feel her hot breath.

"The sun's in my eyes," she said to him.

I wanted to tell her the sun was long gone, but I refrained. Instead, I tried to kiss her; she dodged me and zeroed in on Michael. Not wanting to disturb whatever was going on with them, I gave her plenty of space. Stefan stayed where he was positioned, halfway to nowhere. He must have realized that she was not interested in sitting next to him. I joined Stefan, but it felt odd. I was incredibly horny and so turned on by Michael, I could hardly stand it, but I forced myself to remain where I was.

Stefan must have picked up on Amy's snubbing, but he did not say a word to her, directing all his comments to Michael. He started talking about me, saying that I made zilch with my writing, joking that if I did not have his income, I'd be dirt poor. Michael asked me why I stayed with it. I wondered at the direction this conversation was going. I moved away from Stefan. Why did Stefan take his shit out on me with these people who knew nothing about the writing business? Was he trying to defuse any attraction Michael might feel for me? The conversation was anything but erotic.

It appeared from the look on Amy's face that she liked the direction Stefan was taking. She smiled at me as if she were secretly enjoying my discomfiture.

I directed my comments to Michael, and talked about my love for research and storytelling, thinking I could never explain sufficiently why anyone would choose to write under such conditions. I tried to explain my fascination with the process, telling Michael that choosing the right words was more than clever wordplay. As a tongue-tied individual, I found that writing was the best way for me to communicate, nay, the only way, and I hoped to make a better living at it, eventually, but understood that I might not. Writers on average tended to be poorly paid, I said. I pointed out that as a businessman, Stefan did not see the point, but to me it was everything. Michael looked confused, as though he realized that we had strayed away from the purpose of our visit. Wasn't this supposed to be about sex? Almost gleefully, Amy suggested we move the party to Michael's bedroom.

Our host gave me his arm. Grateful for the reprieve, I went along, happy to be walking with Michael and not Stefan, with whom I was irritated, thinking him churlish for bringing up things that he must have known would make me feel defensive and misunderstood, and be the one thing that would put me in the worst frame of mind. Why he would do that puzzled me. Meeting this couple was his idea, not mine.

Amy fell in on the other side of Michael, and Stefan went behind Amy. Our procession wound its way up wide, sweeping stairs and across a vast hallway, through French doors that looked right out of an upscale architectural magazine, into a room that looked grander than anything I had ever seen before. It was on the level of multi-million-dollar spreads like celebrities might own, with monstrously tall windows looking out over flowering gardens. In the middle of this ballroom-sized bedroom stood a king-sized sleigh bed topped with ornate silk covers and skewed slightly aslant as if positioned for a photo shoot.

Michael pulled me to the bed. Amy moved next to us. Stefan was right behind her. I did not look to see what Stefan was doing; I was too pissed off to care. I began kissing Michael, and Amy joined in, each of us taking a side. Michael smooched both of us in turn, his tongue moving from one mouth to the other like a bee gorging on pollen from two ripe flowers. I left Amy kissing Michael and moved down his taut, muscular body to suck on his thick eight inches as though it was salted taffy. Occasionally I had to let it go to take in oxygen, and marveled at how his member retained its shape even when unattended, so I made a game of it, waiting until it began to list to one side before sucking it stiffly straight and hard again.

Stefan reached for Amy and she pushed him away with her hands to the edge of the bed in a move obviously meant to be exclusionary. He sat back, looking crestfallen. I turned my back on Stefan, thinking he deserved it. I had not appreciated his talk in the hot tub. Right then, I felt magnanimous toward Amy, and encouraged her to join me in my teasing play with Michael, figuring that, at best, Stefan might enjoy watching. In any case, Amy had made it clear she did not fancy Stefan.

Amy licked one side of Michael, and I took the other, but sometimes I finagled him all the way into my mouth, leaving Amy sucking air. I always let her have him back after a few minutes, when my aching jaw needed a rest. When it was my turn, I'd jam him down my throat with a perverse pleasure until I nearly gagged. Stefan did not move once to join us; he just sat there with a forlorn expression, as though he was in shock at being thrown aside and forgotten. I did not pay him any mind; he was a big boy and could find his own way. After a time, Michael pushed Amy away and turned me around, positioning his hands on my rump. The minute he slid into me, our good time took a detour. Amy started screaming as if she had been shot.

"Don't pay the bitch any attention," Michael hissed. His rhythm did not falter.

"He doesn't love me," Amy cried.

Uttering a low, keening moan, she jumped off the bed and picked up pottery from various dressers and night tables. He slowed down a bit when the first piece of pottery hit the wall, but after a slight pause to digest the fact that Amy had gone berserk, he kept on pumping.

"Aren't you going to stop and talk to her?" I said.

"She's playing a game," he said between clenched teeth. "If you weren't so hot, she wouldn't care."

I wondered at that but said nothing more. We got back on track. He began pumping faster and with greater deliberation, as if he found his purpose in life from Amy's spewing anger. I thought it strange that he seemed to gain energy from her distressed outcries. But he said again that she was playacting, and that she did this all the time, and to ignore it, eventually she would stop. I knew I was being selfish, but I could hardly help myself, and concentrated on the steady stream of burning hot molecules charging through my body, fraying the tips of my fingers, every molecule in my brain sizzling. We became one plangent current of electricity, as if our bodies had joined into one throbbing unit of fiery human flesh.

Amy continued throwing whatever she could find without let-up, which created the opposite effect to what she was probably looking for. I felt Michael grow hotter, and my own body burned without restraint, like a log that had caught fire and was busily charring everything around it. I felt my energy bursting in a stream of fireworks, one orgasm leading to another, my body moving as if in an epileptic trance, independent of my brain's higher functions. My animal self was in full throttle. Shards of pottery littered the floor, with more hitting the walls, which could easily have ruined the evening, but we kept going on and on and did not stop, not even when, periodically, things sailed by within inches of our heads—books, candles—followed by Amy yelling strings of expletives and threats: "I hate you," and "I'm leaving."

We took on a slithering, writhing serpentine energy that went beyond our two individual selves. It was as if we were bent on gathering together every spark of living matter and fusing them together to create one supersonic, kinetic force. We began winding up along with the entire mass of ions present in our solar system, compressing and bottling our energy until something beautiful and new was created, combustion like no other. I was galvanized and pushed to call on whatever reserves I had, increasing my energy output until I was strained to the max. And even then, I went beyond myself.

Amy continued to scream and throw things. I glanced over at Stefan briefly, hard to do when one is soaring high and heading higher, but a quick glimpse was enough. He was sitting at the back of the bed, spellbound, watching Amy.

"I'm leaving," she yelled.

"Don't let me stop you!" Michael yelled back.

But she did not leave. She stood there looking for more things to throw, her face twisting like a tiger on a kill. Each time Amy manifested her jealousy, I felt a corresponding spike of excitement, although I never got a good look at the objects that went flying by my head along with the hurled threats. It was hard for me to believe that this beautiful girlfriend of Michael's would be jealous of me. I felt a feverish joy, elated that I was finally getting the best of the deal, yelping my pleasure in response to Amy's growls and hisses, which she flung like a shaman hurling her magic, leading our bodies to assume acrobatic contortions, inspired, animalistic, at the height of our sensory and athletic abilities.

Amy was definitely a *Playboy* type of girl—tall, blonde, and slender. There was no question that she had everything over me, with her ski lift nose and wide mouth and big hazel eyes set so perfectly in her lovely oval face. It mystified me why a woman like that would be upset at me, and in fact, be so troubled that she would scream and throw precious objects—beautiful, expensive pottery and artwork not so easily replaced. Each time I heard something smash, my orgasm climbed to dizzying heights. In the middle of screwing, I realized with a certainty that I would meet with Michael on the side without Stefan's knowledge, and that decision fueled me anew, making me climb even higher. At some point Amy walked out of the room, having run out of breakable things to throw. I heard the door slam.

We finished up with savage cries that coincided with my near faint, and together we fell in a jumbled heap of limbs. I lay with my eyes closed for a while, unable to fully take in what had happened. Someone was shaking my shoulder. It was Stefan.

"Let's go home," he said.

I nodded numbly and gathered my things. When we got home, I stopped him in the foyer. I could see Stefan was upset, his green eyes glittered and his mouth was set in a firm line. I decided it was as good a time as any to talk about what took place.

"I didn't like how you talked about me in the hot tub. Couldn't you save it for later? Didn't you know that would only piss me off?"

"You made her uncomfortable. I was trying to get her to relax and show her you're not the paragon of perfection. You probably make less than she does."

"You could have tried to win her over another way."

"I could say that about you, too."

"Look, if you want me to make more money, ok, I'll stop freelancing and look for a fulltime job. Maybe I can find an editorial position at a publication in New York; I was thinking of doing that anyhow. But as far as Amy goes, if you saw that she wasn't interested, why didn't you say something in the beginning before we went out to the hot tub?"

"I thought she'd come around."

I told Stefan that my impression is that most people enter into this lifestyle without any understanding—there are so many misconceptions about it in the media, especially how porn portrays it.

Stefan mumbled something and turned off all the lights. I lit candles and put on Lionel Richie's *Endless Love* with Diana Ross. He fired up a bowl while I took a shower and anointed myself with the most succulent of scents. When we were both too high to walk straight, we snuggled together, gently kissing. I made no demands. He made love to me slowly, sweetly taking deep draughts from my lips, touching me in my most sensitive places, all of which were still highly sensitized, close to being rubbed raw, actually, from being with Michael. It felt really good being touched like that, and I could not help myself—I lunged at him, filled with lust, vitriol, and a huge heaping of guilt. He grabbed my wrists and we wrestled, my breasts slapping against him, inciting us further. He clutched my soft, pillowed breasts, gently squeezing my nipples, and brought me higher, if that was possible.

When we were done, we lay on the bed, exhausted.

"Amazing, simply amazing."

"Yeah, good for you, having two guys."

"The only way to go."

"Everyone should have a handful of lovers, eh?"

The next day, I texted Michael and told him I wanted to meet, just the two of us, adding that I was planning not to tell my husband. I suspected I would not get the real story with Stefan in attendance, and I was curious about his girlfriend—why did she act that way, and why did he react to her as he did. He wrote back that he would not tell his girlfriend, either.

Over coffee, he told me that they had agreed when they started dating that they would have an open relationship. He asked Amy if they could include a girlfriend of hers in their sex play, and she agreed. So the three of them had sex together, with Michael having both ladies, but when Michael suggested Amy's friend join them a second time, Amy said she would rather have a guy join them.

I picked up my coffee and sipped the rich liquid, breathing its earthy aroma, and listened to Michael speak in a low, tremulous voice.

"Amy found a guy on a site for hookups, a dude who had an outstanding body and a gentle, sweet personality. I was okay with it, so we worked Amy over on several occasions. I never got jealous or said a word about this other man fucking my girl. Then I asked Amy if she was okay with adding another woman to the mix, and Amy said it would be fine. The other man, Bryan, suggested we include a woman he was dating, but when I tried to fuck her, Amy yelled just like she did with you, and when I tried to calm her down she went crazy on me. Amy got so bad I had to ask my friend and his girlfriend to leave."

Michael said he was not ready to give up on group sex. He asked Amy to try it with a long-time married couple, saying the woman in question was used to screwing a lot of guys and always went home with her husband; she was not the divorcing kind. But did not matter what he said, again Amy behaved in this crazy way.

"Don't you get it? Amy can't handle you doing it with other women. You might have to accept this about her ... if you want to continue dating her."

"I told her at the start I can't be monogamous." Michael leaned forward, frowning, his steaming coffee cupped in both hands. "Look, I used to be married to a beautiful woman. We have three children. They're with her now. I married at nineteen, and I had no other lover, but I was terribly bored the entire time. I don't want to do that again. Amy agreed to this when she met me. She promised me that she was willing to have different sexual partners. And she has participated in foursomes, but the woman has to be a dog, or she's not happy. You're very attractive with a great body, so she sees you as a threat. I keep telling her it's not fair that whenever I mention swinging, she wants us to get a wonderful looking man for her, and someone disgusting for me. When the woman's nice looking, Amy flames out—she's done this too many times for me to get all worked up about it. That's why I ignored her the night you and Stefan were here. I don't want to encourage that kind of behavior. I want it to end. I want her to realize I'm not leaving her just because I'm screwing another woman."

"She seems incredibly self-assured."

"You're the kind of woman I should be dating. You're smart. Amy's just clings to me like she's drowning and I'm her lifesaver."

"I like being married to Stefan. When he doesn't feel threatened he can be really nice."

"But we can have sex together?"

"Yes, but I don't want to invite Stefan along; he's like Amy. I don't know why he wants to do this; it only makes him jealous."

But the sex did not come close to the explosive excitement I felt with a spitfire Amy in the room. To make things interesting, a good friend of mine, Susan, joined me with Michael, my luscious new boy toy, and Bryan, Michael's friend. It was obvious to everyone that Susan liked this new guy better, which suited me just fine. Bryan had a smooth baby face, a flat rippled stomach, and strong arms. What was there not to like? We swapped partners periodically, and everyone enjoyed the variety, although I preferred Michael, with his dark, curly locks framing strong aquiline features. But it was his gym-rat physique that made me pant like a dog in heat, while Susan continued to hunger for Bryan with his sweet personality and gentle ways.

But then I ended it. I knew I had no future with Michael. He was too young for me, and I do not relish being the one to age first, nor was I interested in prying him away from Amy—she was too volatile to mess with. And truly I loved my main man most of the time, though I felt sorry that he suffered from poor self-esteem, but I didn't know how to change that.

THE SKY STOPPED BREATHING: THE MULTI-GENERATIONAL TRAUMA OF ANTISEMITISM LEAVES SCAR TISSUE

We first heard of fentanyl when Micah, one of our eighteen-year-old boys, was arrested for scrawling graffiti on the walls of a couple of schools on the island where we lived, minutes from Seattle. Only one of the three kids who came along that day spray-painted swastikas on the walls of the yeshiva and wrote "This way to the ovens" while Micah and the other boy did nothing to stop it.

Seth decided not to participate, and he counseled Micah not to do it, either. Micah decided to go along with the scheme anyway. He said later that he wanted to show he could think for himself and not just follow his brother in everything. Seth and Micah looked like the same side of the coin, like Greek gods, tall and athletic, dark blond with hazel-green eyes. Seth wore his hair down past his ears while Micah clipped his hair short so their friends could tell them apart. Micah was seeing a psychologist at the time—both boys were—and never told his therapist about this plan. Micah said it didn't seem important. Micah's psychologist, Matt Gettleman, said they had established a trust, and the last time they met, they spoke about adjusting to a new environment—i.e. going away to school—and dealing with change. Micah seemed happy.

"How did this happen?" Matt asked me, his voice shaking.

I had no answer.

Local and national media splashed the news over the front pages and airwaves. Alexander, the one who conceived this venture and wrote the offending graffiti, also Jewish, had a crisis of conscience and went to his parents to confess. His parents went to the police.

And what was particularly heinous about this prank—because this is what Micah considered it, a sendoff before going to college—was that he had no idea that his friend, the mastermind who conceived and executed it, was going to paint swastikas. The boy who did it might not have thought it through until the moment he picked up the spray can. They never discussed what they would paint beforehand. They had a code to never stop the others from doing whatever they wanted. Micah said, "That's not how we do things."

All of them had tagged walls around the island, and considered themselves to be budding graffiti artists, and usually just drew abstractions, crazy words or images that meant little to anyone outside their circle. They idealized the massive-scale, surrealist murals of the graffiti artist Jeff Jacobson, who used the pen name Weirdo and sprayed the psyche-delic sea life mural at Second and Yesler in Seattle, among others.

The comment about the ovens was the kind of joke Alex liked to say around his friends; apparently, he didn't consider how this would look to people who didn't know this is how he dealt with the reality of antisemitism. And even though Micah didn't *ink* any of the offending words or images (corroborated by professional handwriting analysis) and found it offensive that Alex did this, the lawyer explained that Micah stood by and did nothing to stop Alex, making him equally guilty.

Micah was a year older than the others—the other boys were seventeen and considered minors—and Judge Julie Spector in King County Superior Court, in a nonjury trial, decided to punish Micah and not the others, and make an example of him. Biologically there is little difference between the maturity of youth of seventeen or eighteen; US law makes a distinction where there is none.

That's when we learned that both boys were addicted to the strongest painkiller ever developed in a lab, and they needed to go to rehab. This all was a surprise to us; they had not told us about the drugs they were doing, but then a lot of kids keep their drug use from their parents. As a teenager, I told my father I smoked marijuana occasionally, but I didn't tell him about the time I did mescaline or LSD. I stayed away from meth and heroin. The boys' father smoked marijuana every day—a heavy user, granted, but he did nothing else. I joined him occasionally. We assumed that our children would be equally cautious.

It's hard to imagine fentanyl as the party drug of the year on this particular island — as it was for a few years—in the sort of community where American flags mingle with Seahawks memorabilia hanging from porches of multimillion-dollar homes, boasting one of the state's best school districts and hundreds of acres of parks and open space. Most of their friends came from stable families and didn't lack for the necessities of life. All the parents knew each other, and the kids went into each other's houses as easily as if they were their own. The parents in this group all looked out for each other's kids. And for Seth and Micah, before the drug vultures moved in, it was utopia.

A flash of memory: eleven-year-old Seth and Micah buoyed by limitless energy, holding a contest to see which one could slide the fastest through wet grass after soccer, which they had to act out again in the SUV, pushing each other along long bucket seats in back. Then they upped the ante, dive bombing from the window and sliding upside down. After a time they plopped down, seemingly exhausted. When I finally started the engine, that the two tow-heads were at it again, snapping their seat belts and rocking the car with raucous laughter, taking turns describing in gory detail the soccer they played, with big boasts of how they kneed and elbowed their way to the goal several times without getting killed.

We raised our boys to believe in two things: God and sports. They chose lacrosse after soccer, finding baseball and basketball less appealing, and practiced their lacrosse skills daily. The practice paid off—they turned out to be stand-out players, competing each summer in the regional club leagues. Stefan, their father, loved watching them play; as a teenager he was a formidable basketball player in youth leagues, and shined on the baseball diamond as well. Stefan was always one of the more vocal parents on the sidelines, yelling, "Take the ball and run with it," or, "Make a pass." After games, in the car, he would talk about how to up your game, because it was always about improving the skills. He had these high standards that were difficult to achieve, and often, he seemed disappointed in their performance, pointing out where they could have done better. And they listened to him, but it was hard to see what they thought because they didn't say.

All that changed in junior year of high school. Their father wanted to make them continue with sports, but Seth, the more vocal of the two, said he wasn't going to do it. Micah said he didn't want to do it either. I suggested instead of forcing the boys into something they didn't want to do, why not let them choose their sport. Stefan said he didn't like quitters; I said *what if they no longer like the sport?* Let them choose year by year, so what if they don't stick with any one thing as long as they do that one thing for the year.

Stefan stopped wanting to do things with them. He said if they wanted to talk, he'd take them out to eat, but he was damned if he would go snowboarding with them, not unless they went back to playing sports. He spent an ordinate amount of time in his room smoking his bong, and started hanging out with his men friends, and not inviting me or the boys along.

Seth simply refused to go to lacrosse practice anymore.

I cajoled them into agreeing to play tennis, hoping that would placate their father, but many times they ditched practice. It dawned on me that they didn't want to do a sport at all, and were too afraid to say that, knowing how much their father loved sports. Stefan couldn't imagine them not wanting it as well. They loved sports as pre-teens. But things changed. They started hanging out with an artsy crowd. Their new friends wore their hair unruly, dressed in black, and had tats and piercings in odd places. When they were supposed to be at practice, they went to their friends' houses to smoke weed and drink beer. Their friends worried me, but their older sister had a similar rebellious period and she got through it, and her friends had been similarly attired, and acted clannish, and sometimes off-putting. Sarah came through high school with honors and left for college and stayed on the honor roll. I thought the boys would follow the same path. But then they tried fentanyl.

Addiction happens fast with fentanyl: only a few uses will rearrange the brain's wiring and begin a lifetime of torment for the victim. We hoped teams of the doctors and psychologists that we hired once learning about this horror would shove the no-pain craving into a cave, so until not even a background murmur is left. Fentanyl literally deadens the nerves, so the user feels lightheaded, and a mental clouding occurs, thinking turns fuzzy, and there's a loss of fine motor control. This type of intoxication is highly pleasurable at first, and then no longer works, but by then you're hooked, and you need more and more to have a sense of stasis, to prevent getting violently ill.

We saw what happens when users run out of the Chemical (it's nearly impossible to keep up with the body's growing need). One day Seth got into a rage and accused Micah of doing the last of the Chemical and started hitting him like he wanted to kill him. We had no idea what they were fighting about. It's likely in the psychosis triggered by the Chemical. Seth honestly believed Micah did this to hurt him. Micah had to go to the emergency room to see if his eye had been damaged by the beating he took; it was swollen shut.

=

Neither boy knew anything about the drug when they first smoked its vapor at a friend's party soon after graduating high school in 2010. I learned all of this after Micah started talking about it with us, releasing a torrent of memories in the days after his arrest, when we learned fentanyl had been found in his blood. One of their best friends they had known from third grade said the high was totally awesome and to be careful how much you did because it was easy to overdose. They were told that they wouldn't get addicted from smoking, only if they injected. Everyone gathered around Alessandro who put a thin line of the white powder on a strip of foil that he held in his palm. He flicked a lighter below it with his other hand and soon a vapor smelling like boiled milk rose from the foil. Alessandro told them that the Chemical had magical powers to open their minds to the spiritual. They took turns breathing it in. Micah quickly felt the explosive onset, mostly a head rush. The high is shorter than heroin, one to two hours instead of half a day. The flushing in his face was so intense it was almost painful. He held his hands to his cheeks and rushed to the bathroom and drenched his face in ice water. He felt a shortness of breath as if he had been running; his vision blurred, and his skin tingled as if he were being touched all over. He tried to pee but couldn't. He leaned over the toilet and threw up. All of it felt pleasant. Everyone lay about the couches and floor on pillows. Alessandro took pictures of them in various stages of somnolence with the 35mm camera he always carried with him. Alessandro attended art school summers and took stunning photographs. Later that day, Micah played the keyboards and guitar. Seth played guitar, and Alex played the violin. There was a drummer and vocalist as well.

They dressed in oversized jeans and tees with artistic graphics, and like the Romantics, they championed an alternative culture, criticizing the frenzied pace of learning in the American public school system. Yet they embraced technology wholeheartedly and went to coding camp. Their faces reflected the beatific visions they had experienced and the sense that they were a special breed put on this earth to make life better for everyone.

A few days before Micah went off to college, he joined two friends to do one this last prank. And after their arrest, Micah, the gentle one, one who had been just tagging along, volunteered to go to jail for a month at the advice of his attorney who said this act of contrition would encourage the judge to treat him less harshly. The maximum prison sentence for this type of hate crime was five years. Micah had to withdraw from college the first week of school. We made haste to set up plans to have both boys attend separate residential rehab programs when Micah was released from jail. They weren't going to stop using on their own. We heard the recidivism was high.

His jailors assigned Micah to the violent crimes unit and placed him in a cell with a man who torched a man's face in a home burglary. I was in shock that Micah, never one to start a fight, was sharing a cell with this guy. Micah told me on one of my weekly visits that the cellmate kept making jokes about gay sex. Thankfully, the judge only added another two weeks of jail, along with the maximum sentence for community service. Thereafter he would have four to five years of community service to complete, roughly twenty hours a week of mind-numbing grunt work. He would have to delay college.

I understood the sense they had of being special, of having new insight. And I couldn't criticize them for trying this drug. I couldn't say well, why didn't you look it up first on the internet before trying it? I knew what it was like to be at a party with friends you'd known all your life and be presented with a drug you'd never heard of. Back in the day, I didn't need to know more; my boyfriend's word was good enough for me.

Now that they had been outed, we discussed the drug scene. Seth read Aldous Huxley's *The Doors of Perception*, and said he felt fentanyl would turn out to be as defining an experience for his generation as hallucinations were for mine. I went to university in Berkeley, California, where even now the spirit of the sixties is still very much alive, albeit muted. When I was there, in the seventies, the vibe was still a blatant *Lucy in the Sky with Diamonds*. In a 2006 report in *Wired* magazine, many early computer pioneers were said to have been users of LSD, one of the more popular hallucinogens on ultraliberal college campuses much like mine. Steve Jobs described his own LSD experience as "one of the two or three most important things" he had done in his life. But no one I knew was doing opioids. In fact, the drugs out today are a lot more potent than what I had access too when I was their age, and I had no idea how much things had changed. The night of Micah's arrest, I was in for a shock.

After Seth had been in rehab for several months, and away from the drug, I asked if he could find happiness without it.

"I'm not mad at Micah anymore about what happened," he said, his face earnest. "I love my life now. I have purpose. I love the people I'm meeting, great people. And I'm writing like crazy. I'm working on a screenplay. It's going to happen for me, man."

But the beatific visions that happened in the beginning lost their sparkle. Already he had experienced the psychosis, and the anger, and knew that if he continued, it would eat at his mental capabilities in a monstrous way. It was the dreams that captivated him, he felt cheated without the dreams. I told him that Jorge Luis Borges says that modeling dreams is more difficult than weaving a rope out of sand.

=

Many of their classmates went to rehab. The result: ten deaths from overdose over a handful of years. But you won't hear about it; these families don't talk to the media. Addiction to opioids may have halted in my community after these deaths—that's the scuttlebutt on the street—but nationally it's a crisis without letup. Addiction cuts across every socioeconomic class in America. Although the media likes to talk about it as a big problem in the Midwest, people from rural outposts to major urban areas everywhere in the US are dealing with it, even in the tech centers.

Young, white, suburban Americans between twenty-five- and thirty-four- years-old experience the highest rate of opioid overdose deaths, according to the U.S. Centers for Disease Control and Prevention. No other drug in modern history has killed more people in any one year. UN statistics show that opioid use in the US is the highest of any country in the world, and more than fifty-percent higher than Germany, the second-ranked country of the twenty most populous countries, and two-thousand times higher than India.

Doctors in the US were prescribing opioids for every sort of malady. It seems a natural progression that fentanyl started appearing on our streets in significant quantities in 2013, produced in China. Remember the Opium Wars? Is this payback? Rather than be a tool for enlightenment, fentanyl is a malignant shadow god that has its talons firmly around the throats of our youth. It's rare for anyone, especially one whose brain isn't fully formed, to escape its clutches intact. Currently there's no surefire remedy, other than Naloxone for opioid overdose. Naloxone no longer has to be injected into a muscle— it can be administered as a nasal spray.

In *Infinite Jest,* Hal comes to realize that "we are all dying to give our lives away to something," paralleling what Marathe tells Steeply about choosing one's idols. By giving himself over to addiction, Hal knows he's avoiding some question or realization, and by invoking Hamlet, the narrator suggests that addiction is an attempt to evade suffering, leading to questions about the purpose of life.

The boys went to treatment in Southern California, selected from the *Forbes* list, and very expensive. Nothing was too good for our boys; we just wanted them healthy. A year passed us by, and from all reports, they were thriving. The therapists said that Seth was leading group activities and doing well in his studies. Micah was also doing well, motivated and getting good marks. The following year I wanted both boys to come home for Thanksgiving, though the prospect worried me. On the phone, Seth swore he was out of the drug's clutches, making a lot of friends on the sobriety circuit and actively seeking clarity. The director of the treatment center recommended that Seth come home, after all he reasoned, he would have to re-enter the world sometime. I knew that Micah would do whatever Seth wanted.

The minute they came home we shared hugs, and friends stopped by in an endless procession. Everyone trooped into the kitchen. I watched Seth go through cupboards, saying he wanted to find water bottles. I retrieved a couple for him, saying this brand was the best for hydration, that it had built-in insulation and kept water cold longer. (I was an endurance cyclist and had the latest equipment.)

Seth went to the sink to fill up, and in the process, sprayed water on the floor. He wiped the spill, grinning at my bemused face, his joy breaking out of him in waves of glee. "I don't want someone to slip on this," he said as if he were the happiest person alive to be doing this chore, his eyes round and glowing, his limbs vibrating.

"Just curious, what drug are you on, is it ecstasy?" His happiness seemed a bit more than I would expect if he was straight. It was hard to believe his joy stemmed from sheer happiness at being home, the joy that lit up his eyeballs like a Christmas tree.

"No, not ecstasy." He drank deeply from his water bottle and laughed like a child, with that unadulterated sense of wellbeing, before spraying another layer of water on the slick wood floor, his laughter turning ecstatic, his spirit flowing effervescent like a bubbling stream. He pulled out a clutch of paper towels and bent down again. As he moved, his limbs appeared to shiver like the strings of a violin. "No, I'm just happy. I love you so much, Mom, and I'm glad we're here with you."

"It's not fentanyl I hope?"

He shook his head and Micah said nothing. In their code, the decision whether to admit anything was his brother's. I had my suspicions, but thought after a year of rehab, they should know the drill: how to stay safe, and how to avoid overdose. I put my hopes on their good sense.

After a pause, Seth said in a visible rush of feeling, "I miss our old house. I really cherished that place. It was mystical."

We had to downsize to cover the cost of rehab and Micah's defense, but I didn't remind him of this; he was too high to comprehend anything of weight.

Seth said he couldn't wait to go back to Los Angeles with its young hipsters thronging the streets and clubs. His energy was magnetic; we all hung on his words, especially his friends. After several hours, Seth said he was tired and wanted to take a nap. Micah said he was tired, too. They made plans to go out to a club the following evening.

The next morning Micah found Seth's dead body; his twin had stopped breathing and asphyxiated. The sound of Micah's ear-splitting wail pierced my soul, the sound of desperation and heartache. We held each other for the longest time.

Then the nightmare began anew in a different guise. Micah fell into a deep depression with bouts of sobriety lasting months, and then he would always go back to the Chemical. I could tell now when he was using—his movements were slow, he spoke in a whisper, had trouble getting out of bed, and complained that he couldn't get REM sleep, nor could he converse without a lot of pauses and trailing sentences, his understanding was poor, and he couldn't finish a book. He dropped out of school and lied about it.

Several times he went back to rehab, and each time he got out, he vowed this would be the last time he would use. The stress was unnerving, but I knew I would always be there for him and help him find his way. Then after a period of successfully staying off hard drugs, and seemingly having learned to manage without Seth, he moved to the Bay Area and found a job he loved and friends. Then the friend who had introduced him to fentanyl came to visit and was booted out by his roommate after threatening her and acting psychotic. Later, I learned from his coworkers that a new girl had joined their team. She had just moved to the US from Mexico and announced to others that she was a meth addict. Micah became her friend, and he told the others he was planning to help her overcome her addiction the way he had learned in rehab. I hoped he could handle this, and I wanted to tell him to stay away from her, but I was afraid my admonishments would only spark his interest.

ALONE NOW

Micah grabbed his backpack and extra towels and went into the bath-room as if he was going to take a shower but really, he was going in there to cop a rip. He didn't want his mother to know—she would worry. He turned on the shower and opened the window. Outside, a dark bunting of clouds drew closer, their slick, shiny surface reflecting a metallic sheen, but it was not cold, sixty degrees felt refreshing in the stark dead of winter. Quickly, he felt the explosive onset, mostly a head rush. The flushing in his face was so intense it was almost painful. He held his hands to his cheeks and drenched his face in ice water. He felt a shortness of breath as if he had been running; his vision blurred and his skin tingled. He arched his back like a cat in heat feeling his nerve endings deliciously fire up all along the ridges of his spine. The sudden flash of Jessica's face in his subconscious, her mouth opening, telling him it was so cold in Alaska people could not kiss on the lips for fear their skin could be temporarily glued by their combined frozen saliva, and remembering how she looked the day she tried to sever the umbilical cord that connected him to his brother and he said he would have none of it. He dismissed her as if she was a bee buzzing too close for his comfort, shooing her away.

He tried to pee but failed to get anything out. Then he leaned over the toilet and threw up. All of it felt pleasant. He put one of the candies he had in his backpack in his mouth and threw the wrapper on the floor. He could not be bothered holding onto trash when using, his muscles could not bear the load. The mess felt homey. His mother was such a germaphobe, she'd follow him around and clean up after him with this sad sack look on her face. Again Micah washed his happy, hot, sensitive face and spit big wads into the sink and slinked back to his room, a wet noodle, and fell on his bed, where he lay in a coma for an hour or so, suspended between life and death, hovering between life forms with one foot in each, his voice to his own ears sounding as if it had exited his body on the wings of a bird, soft and ethereal, a whisper. This is when he could best imagine his brother alive again, talking to him in the mutter they perfected for camp and school to deflect authoritarian adults, ready to slap them with detention or take away their phones. Having to telecommute with his brother using the Chemical as their medium felt strained, not like it used to be, and he heard Seth say he could not always make the leap. He faced the hush with something akin to acceptance and did not gag at air thick with its plague-like semblance of impending death. Late afternoon noises intruded: The harbor wind slaking against angled cement on the nearby roadway, the slush and sheen of highway traffic, horns blaring, the ominous gravel crunching with the impact of someone heavy-footed walking by outside.

His mother came into his room. "You feel better numbed," she said in a low, soft voice meant to be soothing, and went to the window, opening it wide. But what she said next only made him feel more anxious. "I think it's time to talk about you going back to rehab."

He shook his eyes open and took in a lungful of fresh air smelling of fresh-cut grass and pine trees, and viewed the curtain of trees that rimmed the yard. They hung silent, motionless, as if waiting for him to say something. And he did have questions, plenty of them. "What about my depression issues?"

"The doctors will help you learn to cope."

"I won't be able to hear the therapists over the voices in my head," he said.

He told her that the voices in his head had been growing louder, angrier, harder to deal with. They were driving him crazy. He could hear nothing else. He stared at her, wondering how to explain in terms she would understand what happened to his sense of well-being when the Substance was removed. He could not articulate exactly what would happen, had already happened, only that he did not want to go through it again. He could tell her this much: When his withdrawal was full-blown, it felt as if a blistering-hot liquid had been slaked over every inch of his skin and covered with rows and rows of red ants fornicating endlessly, creating a raw, oozy feeling not unlike what he imagined being flayed alive would feel like. And the shivery pain in his bones felt as if his inside core was the center of an arctic squall. Then there was the other pain, the pain of loss, always resident, never far from his consciousness. He did not have the courage to end his own life; death was too final, yet life in its present incantation did not appear to be a viable solution either. It was his brother's death that had led him to this horror, needing drugs beyond all hope of redemption. He dreaded each day and needed to be high all the time to cope, but even then it was hard to carry on. His feelings of loss-trauma flooded his soul, shaking his very essence, creating the sort of despondency that festers like an open wound, making it hard to feel motivated, impossible to do anything—at least on the Chemical he could revisit his memories.

His mother told him that they had remedies for his kind of sadness, and personalized therapy for the rage and powerlessness issues. The doctors would give him something to block the aching desire for his substance of choice and mask the physical discomforts accompanying withdrawal. "But you know this much already," she said, "it'll be the second time for you in rehab."

"I'm hurting too bad," he said from somewhere deep within his catatonic shell, blinking blurry-eyed. "I can't leave home just yet. I need to grieve here, not in some strange place with people who don't know Seth."

Through the window, clouds the color of brackish water knotted up, blocking the sun. The room suddenly went dark. He still had an overriding need to be loved, despite his soul being blown to smithereens by his brother's death, only to be nurtured like a baby sapling by his mother. He looked at her with the knife points of his eyes. Her sorrow-crusted face loomed above him, her tears visible through the netting of his lashes. She did not make any moves to leave his room. She wanted more suffering, then?

Her tremulous voice droned on. "Like you, I long for your brother's presence every moment of every day. On one hand, I feel that you and I should grieve together. But I still believe you need to go; the question is when."

"If you send me away now, I'll run away," he said in his hollow, corpse-ridden voice, heavy with the sadness of his brother's passing. "You'd never be able to find me."

"If they catch you, they might send you to jail. Do you really want to risk that?"

"If you allow me to stay and grieve with you," he said craftily, wearing his best poker face, "I'll stop taking the Chemical. A few more days is all I ask."

"Sweetie, you make this so hard."

"You have to let me stay," he continued, his voice rising. "Otherwise, there's going to be another death to disturb your consciousness."

In the aftermath of the violence in his voice, her voice sank to a whisper. "The death of the one person we both treasured lost to us forever." She capitulated faster than he anticipated and left the room.

He fell back into a place of skating sleep, more like dozing, but still lovely. Seth's face came up from behind his eyelids, asking if he was up for jamming, and Micah told him he was always ready. He heard the creaking of the chair near his bed. He opened his eyes expecting to see his brother, but it was his mother again.

"What do you think happens when someone dies," she said. "Whether Seth's still around in some form, or has his spirit dispersed, having been absorbed into other life forms?"

"I like to believe his spirit is still out there, but I don't know." He could feel the intensity of his grief splintering the clutched, twitchy muscles around his eyes and mouth.

"I could never know what you're going through. Never had a twin who looked just like me whom I loved more than myself, someone I lived with in lockstep from the moment of conception, I who have been addicted to nothing other than sugar."

"Sugar?" he said, raising his hands to his flushed face as he said this. "Seriously?"

He told his mother this is what fentanyl does to a person, raising their body temperature to an intolerable heat. He got up and went to the mirror. His face looked thin, childish, eyes as large and luminous as headlamps on a car. He promised to get on the plane for rehab when she told him to, his voice barely audible. He did not know how many days had passed, or how many he had left. It did not matter. He was in freefall, not thinking, just feeling pleasant sensations. He was with Seth and happy again.

"I want you to start tapering down day by day by small amounts. You won't be high, but at least you won't be in pain, so that, in a few days when you get on that plane, you won't be suffering."

"Yes."

"It's not good if you stay this way. You can't hold a job or go to school. You want to go to back to school, don't you?"

"Of course, Mom."

She left him and went to work in her office downstairs. A few hours later, he sat up in bed, playing music on his guitar, a lullaby. He felt better, even if he was only partially lifted out of the plant-like proto-plasmic state that kept him insulated from any kind of pain, there was just enough Chemical in his veins to keep him from howling.

His mother came back into the room.

"I can't deal with the anxiety," he sobbed.

"I have a lot of anxiety, too."

"But mine is monstrous, and it never leaves me alone."

"You have a choice. You could continue to be sedated, and your brain functionality will slow down to a crawl. You won't mind, because the feel-good syrup will be clogging your synapses, and a lot of time might pass, could be decades, but one day you'll wake up and realize that you've wasted talent and ability that you can't get back. Your brain will have rusted and calcified. It'll no longer be able to wrap itself around a new complexity or puzzle or think deep thoughts. Emotionally you'll be wrecked, unable to connect with people except as a beggar seeking alms. All your feelings will be a gray muddle."

"I don't want to be like that. I don't want to be like those old, dirty guys I see sometimes on the street. They look so sad."

"You could face your fears and learn to live with them. It'd be hard at first, but that's really your only choice."

"I'm not happy about it either. But my stomach is starting to tighten already. I need a line right now, or it's going to be horrible. The pain's insufferable."

"I wish you'd take the Suboxone the doctor gave you."

"My bones feel cold when I'm on Suboxone. And it makes me feel slow and stupid. I'd switch to heroin—the high isn't as good, though, but it's cheaper."

"You look emaciated," she said.

"Oh nice. So you came all the way up here to insult me?"

"The loss of muscle from the opioid is extreme," she said. "Can you get a hard-on?"

"Why you asking this?" He did not need to tell her fentanyl was more satisfying than sex.

"Sweetheart," she said softly, speaking to him like a child. "The toilet in your bathroom is clogged with your spit-up tobacco again." Her tone was light.

"I don't feel well." His snarl deepened.

"You can't do drugs and chew tobacco. Your stomach can't handle it."

"Chewing tobacco keeps me from doing more of the drug. My need is overwhelming otherwise. Too many memories everywhere I look."

"A friend who was in a car accident has to take fentanyl to stanch pain from a damaged spinal cord. He's trying to ease off it and told me that he's been using this product called agmatine sulfate so he can lower his dose of fentanyl. It's a supplement that weightlifters use to increase stamina. He adds it to fruit drinks, allowing him to cut down on the amount he uses. He said he's a lot healthier, his brain is more active, and he can do more. It might work for you."

"I'll try it."

"Oh, good, I'm so glad to hear that. I bought some through Amazon. I'll make you a drink with it." She left the room.

Prying open a tin of chewing tobacco, he turned to the wall before sticking a hunk of the stinky, gooey plant in his mouth. He promptly started chewing. The tobacco was thick in his chipmunk cheek. It felt relaxing to chew the giant cud of tobacco leaf, its fibers strong like hemp. Chewing blankly like cow facing blank wall, he looked over at the poster of Wiz Khalifa smoking a fatty. Somehow his mother's face got in the poster. He closed his eyes, and lay back on his pillow, chewing. But there was no pretending that his mother was not there. She loomed larger than life, her presence burning shadows into his closed eyelids.

"How much tobacco do you chew?"

"I'm tapering down."

"Drink this blueberry shake I've made for you now. It'll taste good."

He drank the spiked fruit shake she blended. Then he went into the bathroom, closed and locked the door, feeling a sense of relief. His anticipation for what was sitting on top of the counter caused his hand to tremble. He readied his foil and brought the lighter underneath. He could see in the mirror that his expression was greedy, his mouth opening like a fish out of water getting ready to suck in the juices, acting the lover with his chemical sweetheart. He made faces for the mirror as he pulled in the vapor, releasing a faint cloying odor like sweetened condensed milk that had been put to boil. The ritual was delicate and precious to him. It felt spiritual.

"What did you think of the agmatine," she said later in the day.

"It's okay but it made me have this huge poop. Like elephant poop. And I did the same amount of fentanyl, anyways."

"I don't trust this agmatine to work for you like it did for my friend. He really wanted to reduce his dose but I'm not sure you do."

"I have too much anxiety."

"It's the craziest thing, seeing you like this."

The agmatine did nothing but make his stagnating blood race. He disliked the tingling in his fingers and turned away from his mother's hawk eyes that were always assessing, and looked out the open window where the landscape glittered like sequined art, bits of color flashing everywhere from the rain. The heavy scent of decaying leaves filled the air and the chirping birds sounded a melancholy note. He went back upstairs and walked softly down the hall to the bedroom she shared with her boyfriend. He went through her closets, looking for money or something valuable to sell. She snuck up on him, scaring him with her witch's eyes.

What are you doing?"

"Looking for a lighter."

"You know I don't smoke."

He shrugged. What else could he say? Of course he knew she did not smoke. His mother brought several valises down from storage and asked him to pack his things. Later that day, two men from the drug treatment center came to the house, there to accompany Micah to the treatment center. He was putty in their hands.

From inside the car, he looked out, his stomach unsettled, his emotions on a yo-yo. He opened his mouth to say something but then a big heaving muscle spasm shook him to the core, and he could no longer say a complete word. Instead, a couple of stutters came out. The heavy rainclouds had dispersed, creating a tiny blue patch that continued to widen, allowing the sun's magnificence to spread out unfettered. He averted his eyes at the bursting sunlight, chilled to the bone and tired beyond all endurance.

He made a last-ditch effort: "One of Joyce's characters in *Ulysses* says that giant poppies growing in Chinese cemeteries produce the best opium," he said. "Reading that didn't trigger anything." He spoke as if his mouth were filled with pebbles. It was hard to get the words out.

"I'm glad to hear that sweetie. It gives me hope."

He could not believe she was doing this to him, her only surviving son.

Many times Micah did not appear to understand what people said to him, the numbing in his brain was too great. He heard what was said to him in a fog and spoke in a mumble that was hard to understand. His mother said to him that she found it unnerving and stressful to watch a beautiful, highly intelligent young man function in a coma-like state, unable to grasp fully what he needed to do to maximize his life. He tried to explain that girls could not compete with the Chemical high, even Jessica, the girl he loved before his brother died, and there was the added complication that any girl would not understand what Seth meant to him. And he had a spotty record with school attendance, and no skills other than musical, and he felt too laid back to marshal anything together, even putting together a resume highlighting his achievements in music. Each time he came back from rehab, he swore he was done using. Micah's mother said she had trouble with the notion that she was standing by and watching his decline, and suggested he do something different, change things up. He had already tried methadone and Suboxone and didn't like the effects. He said the methadone was fatiguing and made him nauseous, and the Suboxone made his blood run cold. She told him about a promising new therapy she heard about, where patients micro-dose on psilocybin, the psychoactive component of magic mushrooms, taking a tenth of a regular dose three days a week, making sure there were several days between with no use. Scientists say that psilocybin enhances neuroplasticity in animals and helps combat depression. Micah found there were dozens of posts by people who said they had successfully climbed out of heavy meth use, and others saying that they had exited a daily habit of alcohol and marijuana without undue hardship. Others said they were simply walking away from a life of a depressive, lonely soul and finding satisfaction in listening to their pain bodies, and finding the motivation to work on their careers, with no mental issues to derail the way. He knew it would take discipline; he had to avoid sliding, even when things turned difficult or ugly, but he thought it might work for him, and resolved to ask his therapist about it. Surprisingly, his therapist agreed to prescribe it for him, and he started on a dosing regimen.

Soon after, he had a dream that he decided to go with Kiki and a few friends for a weekend of skiing in Whistler to celebrate Shaun's entry into the coast guard. Shaun also swore off drugs.

He had been to Whistler plenty of times with his family and his dream took the same trajectory. This time instead of his parents in the car, he was driving his friends. They drove north through tall canyons of sheared-slate cliffs, some of it a type of black slate not found anywhere else in the world. The cliffs looked straight out of a fairytale, hewn out of rock by giant pickaxes, much of it topped by white angel dust. The slate appeared to glow by infinitesimal degrees, a nearly imperceptible thing, and he might not have been aware of it except for his eagle eye that watched for these sorts of changes, the subtle kind that he heard might happen, as the magic mushroom fostered visual and mental acuity. He was awash in ideas for songs that he wanted to write. He pulled a notebook out of his backpack and started writing lyrics to a new song brewing in his head, a crooner's lullaby about his lady love, which he promised he would play for them when they reached their destination. At the entrance to the town of Squamish, nestled at the foot of these massive slate formations, they passed several fast-food restaurants, a supermarket, a Lucky Loonies Dollar Store and a motor inn. Kiki asked if they wanted to stop at Starbucks in the strip mall designed in faux Swiss chalet that stood underneath the highest of the hills the locals call the Stawamus Chief.

Everyone piled out of the car, and everything looked frosted-over as if they stepped into a freezer. Micah loved the look of the frozen land, the icy sheen over everything, including metal that looked more slivery than the Metallica documentary *Some Kind of Monster*; even the sound elicited a glowing presence, something that he could almost taste, i.e. rank bitterness. Back in the car with their drinks, Micah felt warmth spread to the marrow of his bones, the air no longer coming out of his nose and mouth in an icy stream. Micah nursed a chai tea with his scone knowing that caffeine might not mix well with the 'shroom, as small a dose as he was on, however given the fragility of his mental state he wanted nothing to upset his equilibrium. It would not do to fall back so easily into his bad habits of taking whatever, and not knowing how things interact in his body. He shivered even in the warmth of the car, not having any familiarity with this degree of cold. In Seattle, it rarely fell below 35 degrees Fahrenheit. Here the temperature gauge that hung outside in the air nearby said it was -3.8 °C (25.1) °F. The extreme cold made everything look flinty to Micah and he imagined if he reached out of the car, he could chip pieces of slate from the mountain with a putty knife. Snow began to fall in soft, airy clumps swirling around them. The individual snowflakes moving in a synchronized arc counterclockwise at different speeds in dizzying arrays, presented a choreographed ballet dance with literally thousands of dancers immersed in their own little bubbles as if remotely controlled from on high. Micah gazed out at a vast forest that stretched over the mountains of trees looking magnificent in their fluffy white hats, their limbs completely blanketed in snow.

The trees staggered under their massive loads, too burdened to do anything but sway. The effect was mesmerizing. They were driving what used to be called the highway of death, but now, after the 2010 Winter Olympics, many of the kinks had been blasted out so the road had far fewer curves, having been widened from a twisty two lanes into a spacious four lanes in many areas. The time and attention needed for navigation had been significantly reduced, cutting travel time by as much as a third. That day the roadway was packed with vehicles. They were five cars down from a snow plow pushing a large accumulation of the white stuff, leaving in its wake a light dusting on the roadway. The snowplow drove slowly behind its expanding load. On either side, the tree limbs seemed too small and fragile to carry such thick layers, some of them appearing to stagger underneath. Every so often, some of the snow resting on even the steadiest of limbs would fall in a cascade of cottony fluff, adding to the fleecy white blanket below, covering all the earth in the same stark blinding version of whiteness.

The forest was as quiet as a temple. A hush had descended everywhere, even on the road; not even the sound of their tires broke the silence.

Micah felt this beauty to be cold and metallic, the scene of a heartless love. Micah thought he had never seen anything so beautiful in its stark rawness, and for some reason he could not fathom, seeing that profusion of untamed nature, he felt the pain of Seth's passing like sharp knives assaulting him anew. *I'm alone*, he thought. *Truly alone now, Seth's gone.*

The snow continued to fall, regardless of whether people lived or died. He could die here, right now and the snow would continue to fall without a pause. He was struck by the finality of it. People would continue to make their trek up the mountain. His friends would care, like they did for Seth, but nothing would change. Seth had been right: it didn't matter what they said or did. As he thought this, he felt Jessica's hand tighten around his and he squeezed back. She leaned into him, warming him, as if she understood what he was thinking. But the feeling she engendered was not the same as it had been previously. Since his brother's untimely death, all his feelings were coated in layers of sadness and despair. And yet her presence helped him recover from the brink where he had been, though he was not sure he could love her as completely now, not the way she wanted to be loved, not the way he was feeling. Even so, it was comforting to have her with him. He needed her more than ever now.

Kiki was driving. Behind the wheel, she looked small and delicate, her golden brown hair a luxurious marvel the way it flowed down her back like a river's song. Shaun, sitting next to her, took up the passenger side with the solidity of a craggy mountain. He suggested for the second time that he could take the wheel if she got tired of driving, parsing his offer delicately: "Only when you get tired, of course."

"Yes, yes, of course, that's so kind of you, but I won't get tired, and I know how this car drives, I'll be fine," Kiki said. "Plus, I'm loaded up on caffeine."

"You don't have to worry about me wrecking your car," Shaun said. "I've taken lessons at a driving school on my dad's stick shift." Then without preamble, he told Kiki that he had stopped doing hard drugs. "Cold turkey the minute I was accepted into the Coast Guard school," he said. "It had to end."

"Me, too, I stopped," Micah said. "I couldn't study high."

"I'm so glad for you both," Kiki said. "You guys are awesome."

Behind them, Micah and Jessica held hands, their legs touching. She was looking out the window, away from Micah, so he could freely exhibit his feelings on his face without worry that his sadness would upset her. He marveled that she was so intuitive, and he had to hide his true feelings sometimes, so as not to look like a depressive. He felt the fresh splatter of pain that was his life without Seth, though his sadness was mixed with the intense love he had for his brother and colored his every move, every expression that flitted across his face. The last day of Seth's life replayed in his head in a nonstop loop. His mouth crumpled at the memory of the excitement in Seth's husky voice, telling Micah about the screenplay he was working on. But then Jessica turned to him and said something in his ear, making a swishing sound with her lips, jerking him out of his bittersweet daydream, followed by the baritone of Shaun. The conversation lighting up the front seat set him on fire.

"I'm back in school," Shaun said. "Getting good grades."

"It's so cool you got that soccer scholarship to U-DUB," Kiki said. "Glad we're going to the same school."

"So you're not in the Coast Guard anymore?" Micah asked. "When did that happen?"

"Nah. That scholarship changed everything."

"I'm glad I'm not using," Micah said. "I wouldn't be able to snowboard if I was high."

Kiki waved her hand at the view in front of them. "Look at those waterfalls and the glaciers," she said. "Drink it in."

"Breathtaking," Micah said. And he meant it. On one side, every few feet, another waterfall that had been flash-frozen at a gallop, reminding him of Greek sculpture.

"Too bad you can't look down," Shaun said. "Or you would see the swimming seals."

Shaun had binoculars trained on the rearing, surging, purple-tinged waters of Howe Sound, a triangular-shaped basin lined by dense forest on sheer cliffs scored by tributaries hidden by massive tree limbs. Micah didn't need binoculars to see the large, forested island plunked in the middle of the basin, which looked to be as large as San Francisco Bay but likely wasn't. Without the binoculars, however, the seals popping out of the water were just black dots. Howe Sound looked huge, taking the shape of a lake halfway down the Juan de Fuca Strait, a ninety-five-mile-long canal that is the Salish Sea's outlet to the Pacific Ocean, and looks like a big gumdrop surrounded by strands of licorice with the biggest licorice being the strait. Micah hoped that Shaun would pass the binoculars, but he didn't ask. Asking felt like too much trouble. After a time, Shaun passed them around, and Micah got a chance to see the seals up close. As he looked through the binoculars, in his mind's eye, he could see people walking by and inadvertently kicking his heart beaten to a pulp, subsiding into a dull pain that he imagined he would have for his whole life, a living testimony to what it means to lose a beloved twin, his body double, his heart severed and left to bleed on the concrete. And why did he have to bear the pain internally, and paste on a brave smile? Though the last thing he wanted to do, parade his sorrow in front of his friends, he knew they would do what they could to make him feel loved, and he did feel loved, but what he wanted, his brother back alive, they could not give. So he kept his feelings to himself.

"Yeah, well," Kiki said. "On the way back, you're driving. I'll see the seals then."

They reached Whistler Village. It took them about an hour from the time they left Squamish, not bad for a snowy drive. The rustic beauty of the place stirred pleasant memories. Micah roused himself to look around.

"I love this place," Micah said. "It reminds me of the Alps."

"I really wanted to go to the Alps with you," Kiki said. "Remember? I couldn't get my mother to let me."

Her words brought tears to Micah's eyes. It was wonderful the way his friends rallied around him in his time of need. When Seth was alive, all they seemed to care about was Seth, and now he knew that they cared a lot for him, too. They went out of their way to make him feel loved. And if he could bring back Seth alive, he would not care about any of the other stuff. He felt intense waves of love for his friends pulsating through his veins, knowing that they cared for him. And Kiki wanted to do this trip as a salve for him, to make things right for him, and her thinking (rightly) was that doing something he loved to do would help.

"I'd have taken you in my suitcase, but I didn't have one big enough." He tried to assume a jocular tone, but part of him was watching the side of him that talked and acted normally, and Micah the observer was amazed, as well as somewhat appalled, feeling lightheaded at the weirdness of seeing the public persona half of Micah play this game of normalcy, and see that the other people in the car actually believed that it was him talking.

The real Micah, essential self in the interior behind his rib cage was crying huge buckets of tears and feeling as if an actual leg had been severed, as well as a hand and arm, and that internally he was bleeding to death, by infinitesimal degrees. Would he ever learn how to walk again on one leg? He wanted his leg back, the real thing, not a prosthetic. And the same with his hand and arm. How could he go on like this in his crippled condition?

"Well, now you don't need to hide me in a suitcase." He forced himself to say this, feeling that he needed to act the part, and play dual roles, act the joker, even though he did not feel it. He did not need people so much when he was on the Chemical, but sober, he did.

TOP OF THE HILL

It was late afternoon. Micah told his weeping mother he was going to take the dog for a walk. He didn't feel like it, but he had to get away from her. She grated on his nerves like a rusty saw. He took the dog to a park near the Lake Washington waterfront, about a mile downhill from where they lived.

Standing at the edge of the Luther Burbank Park, slices of lake could be seen through the netting cast by the tall, full-limbed, densely furred trees that ringed the water. He watched Bambi scamper after a poodle, the two dogs barking excitedly, Bambi looking like a big balloon compared to the stylish and slender poodle. The dogs seemed to get along well for a while, despite their differences in temperament. Bambi was all big personality, lively, playful, even foolish, leading the other dog, a finicky thing, in circles.

Before they broke up, Bambi and the poodle stood at the water's edge as if soldered to the ground. Then a loud crack in the air sounded like a bullet. Bambi jumped around like she was going out of her mind from the shock, encouraging the other dog to bark forcefully at a tree that people in the neighborhood said was home to a nest of a nearly extinct breed of eagles. Nothing stirred, but still Bambi braced her legs as if she was preparing to jump up the side of the tree and had the other dog bouncing like an automated windup toy. They continued to bark, insistent, their voices shattering Micah's delicate equilibrium. Just then, two large bald eagles with white feathered heads, chocolate-colored bodies, and massive wingspans flew from their perch at the top of the tree and headed skyward, becoming smaller and smaller until they became specks in the wide blue bowl of a sky. Only then did the dogs wind down, their voices losing volume, splintering into a series of little half-barks.

Bambi turned on the poodle and launched a feint attack, not intending to hurt, but boisterous enough to cause the dainty poodle to shrink back. Bambi teased mercilessly, relentless in her playful biting.

Micah decided the poodle needed a breather. He called to Bambi, who ran circles around Micah and then doubled back to the poodle, barking madly. Micah moved slowly toward Bambi, speaking in soft tones, calling her by name, telling her to calm down and come to him. When he came close enough, he grabbed Bambi's collar. The poodle's owner came over and they exchanged pleasantries. The poodle owner was super cute, and Micah was glad for the diversion, but then thoughts of Seth came crowding back like a haunting by a feverish ghost. Seth was unable to leave Micah for more than a minute. Micah could not give this girl the attention she required, so he grabbed Bambi and walked away from the poodle's owner without saying good-bye, heading toward the other end of the park, toward a big grassy knoll where he hoped he could sink down and die. He was bored of being alone. He wanted his brother back in the flesh, and not a ghost, feverish or not. He hated the outdoors. He could not be anywhere without his brother for long before he felt nervous and out of sorts. Feeling uncomfortable, he headed back to his mother's place. He could not think of it as home, not without his brother there.

She was sitting at the kitchen table working with a pencil on a manuscript. When he came in, she put it away.

"Funny thing, I used to feel that Bambi preferred Seth," Micah said. "But I don't see Bambi missing Seth at all."

"Dogs only deal with literal realities—if the pack leader, the person who feeds her—that would be me—"

"Sometimes Seth did that," Micah broke in. "Me, too."

"Very occasionally," his mother said, "not enough to establish him or you as chief caretaker. But say I disappeared, or all of us were gone—

me, you, and Seth—it would upset her. If one of us disappears, it's not as traumatic; she has the others."

"She was upset when we found his body."

"And now she's eating and playing, just like she's always done."

"Yeah. Weird."

"It's the way of the wild."

"It's callous as all get-out."

"It wouldn't be smart evolutionarily speaking for her to waste time on something she couldn't do anything about and didn't physically cause her to suffer."

"I wish Seth had listened to me. None of us could ever tell him anything. He believed he was like Odysseus, and that the gods were watching out for him."

"I can't help having these regrets, too. I wish that we had known. We might have been able to do something to save him."

Micah looked at her speechlessly, his eyes glazing over, thinking about Seth. The image of his brother's closed eyelids and that sweet, angelic expression rose up. He couldn't help but blame Seth, asking out-loud why Seth hadn't been more careful, why he hadn't paid closer attention to the possibility that he could take too much, understanding how easy it is to overdose. He knew Seth was aware the worst could happen. He was with Seth when they heard about several others, people they knew and had partied with, who had died this way. Because of the drug's way of clearing out every shred of misgiving, it was only logical that Seth would believe he was in control and knew what he was doing even when he was not. Micah told his mother that Seth boasted that he could estimate with unerring accuracy his own tolerance level. Seth got angry at Micah for questioning him. Seth committed this act of hubris, and Micah couldn't forgive Seth for thinking he was so special, nothing bad could happen to him.

"Even if I had come to you and said that he was overdosing, do you think you could have talked him out of it? Likely not. He would have had a tantrum like he always does, and you wouldn't have been able to fight it. He never listened to me, and he certainly wouldn't listen to you."

His mother joined Micah and his father on the speakerphone to discuss the funeral arrangements.

"Now you'll have one less mouth to feed," his father said. "And the cost of drug treatment just dropped by half. So that's the good side of it."

"You never cared for him much, did you?" Micah's mother said and hung up.

Holed up in his bedroom, Micah got busy trying to track down Jessica, but no one answering Jessica's description had been admitted to any of the area hospitals. He tried Jessica's cell, but it came up disconnected, just like Seth had said. Micah didn't have any clue whom to call. Seth had said he had tried calling around, and Micah had talked to Kiki at her visit the day Seth died, but maybe something turned up since. It was also possible things had slipped her mind. Kiki was at the University of Washington. He texted and Kiki texted back. Her outpouring of concern and sadness made him feel loved and connected, but her response about Jessica through the digital landscape seemed muted, not suggestive of her usual high-pitched vibrato.

No idea appeared across his screen. No joy or hope flowed from those words.

He texted Kari, their goth friend with overdyed black hair, nose ring, and extensive leg and arm tats; maybe she knew something. Her outpouring of grief over the loss of his brother made him realize how much he and his brother were loved. He could tell her sorrow was genuine. It's hard to say why he thought there was any question about Kari's love for them both, but he realized from the spontaneity of her expression that she was deeply affected.

There was a terse reveal: Kari's brother had died of a heroin overdose. It was something she had never talked about. Micah asked her why she had never mentioned it. She wrote that it made her cry, and who wants a crybaby around. But then, almost as an afterthought, Kari said that she had run into Jessica at a party over the weekend, words that flashed across the blue screen of Micah's phone with a stridency that stopped everything in the world; every gesture, every sound was stilled. The low drone from cars that usually could be heard from the highway had halted in their tracks. Even the birds had stopped singing. It was like the earth had suffered a complete meltdown. He took a deep shuddering breath and, as he took in oxygen, his ears popped, and the sounds resumed again as if nothing had happened. Then he realized he had held his breath with such force, and so completely, that his ears had plugged up, leading him to imagine that everything had stopped.

Kari texted. "Oh, my god, Micah, I'm coming over right now."

Kiki must have been thinking the same thing. Within minutes, both Kiki and Kari were at the door.

Amid tears and hugs, what Kari told him about Jessica had him gasping for air: "It was like I was seeing a ghost, but a very red-blooded one. Jessica came striding into this party like she was this rock star, arm-in-arm with these two husky, muscle-bound dudes and wearing the tightest miniskirt with the highest heels I've ever seen on her, platforms at least five, maybe six inches. The guys looked like pimps, wearing these L.L. Cool J. style white hoodies, a big red stripe across the front, and red lounge pants that looked like they were made out of silk. They had skin black as night, I swear to god, with these huge gangsta tats, accessorized by scads of bling, wearing more gold than my grandmother at Christmas."

Kari had Jessica's new address. Micah grabbed his coat, telling her that he would send information about the funeral, and headed out. The day felt cold with the breeze picking up. He shivered and turned on the heat in the car so high it created thick, furry warmth and smelled like air twice used, making him feel sleepy. To shake off his drowsiness, he opened a window, letting in a funnel of ice-cold air, and drove with the hot and cold mixture swirling around him like a hurricane.

The address he had been given was in Seattle, south of the Mariners Stadium in the heart of Columbia City on a nondescript block with humble-looking houses, most of them peeling paint, their doors sagging, the yards hardscrabble. He drove past the house with the right address and parked several houses down near a little coffee shop at the intersection with Martin Luther King Boulevard. Micah went inside, bought a passionfruit drink, and took it outside to a little table on the sidewalk where he planned to wait, and think, not sure what he should do. Bilious clouds gathered overhead.

He was about to head over to her house when he saw her walking down the street. He knew it was her without a doubt. Her skin had that caramel sheen and that peculiar way she wobbled on her heels, her hips swaying like a ship on high seas. It made his heart skip. When she drew alongside, he accosted her.

"Oh my god, Micah!"

They embraced, tears gushing out of her eyes like a geyser. She smelled sweet and flowery, and her skin felt soft, a sensual odyssey for the fingers. He liked the long-sleeve tee she was wearing under her parka that said: Orgasm Donor above a red cross.

Micah kept his arms tight around her. They stood like that, just holding each other for the longest time.

"Sit with me," he said, motioning to the table where his drink sat, looking forlorn.

"I'm so glad you're out of jail." She looked up at him, her full cheeks flushing from the effort of twisting her head back. The sun glinting off her tears made him want to kiss them away. "I got so scared when I heard that you'd been arrested without bail. I thought you were done for. I freaked out..."

"It was fucked."

"I dropped a tray loaded with food all over the restaurant floor, and then in a totally unrelated move, I dropped coffee on someone's lap."

"Hah."

"I dropped the second cup of coffee, and the manager fired me."

"Know somewhere we can get beer."

"I've got my fake ID on me, what about you? You'll need one."

"Let me check." Micah pulled out his wallet from his jean pocket and peered inside. He lifted a small, laminated driver's license out of his wallet. "Okay, yeah." It did not have his name on it, the license was a copy of a legitimate one belonging to a twenty-one-year-old-friend who had graciously allowed Micah to borrow his identity, but the picture that Micah had spliced in was his own, and then he had the card laminated to look authentic, and to hide the fact that there had been work done on it.

"If I'm old enough to be incarcerated in an adult jail," he said, "I'm old enough to be served beer in a bar."

"I've never served time, but I've adult responsibilities. I've been working and paying my own bills."

They passed a candle shop and a ceramics studio. Further down the street, past the intersection with Rainier Avenue, they stopped at a sports bar with big cheerful windows. Inside the place looked clean-scrubbed, smelling of earthy red brick, mixing uneasily with the astringent odor from an astroturf carpet designed to look like a football field. TVs at every corner beamed snapshots of Richard Sherman of the Seahawks bruising receivers in front of Earl Thomas, the deep safety, in the manner of Theseus who vanquished the Minotaur, or so it looked to Micah, who never could get over the brutality of the sport. It was a late-afternoon crowd, most people looking like they were just getting off work in low-wage jobs that required a uniform or were otherwise physically demanding. There was a mix of ethnicities, mostly white with a few blacks, and a handful of Asians, which did not surprise Micah; he suspected Columbia City was the most integrated of Seattle neighborhoods, gentrified enough to attract whites with all the new, cool-looking retail springing up, yet cheap enough to hold the working crowd.

Jessica led him to two cozy seats nestled in a corner, away from the hubbub around the bar. They sat facing each other over the glossy surface of the table where Micah found a blurry reflection of his face shining back at him, making him feel like he was looking into lake water. They ordered beers. Through a sublime mist, Micah gazed at Jessica, not quite believing that she was sitting in front of him, thinking that she looked like a mirage, the way her image kept changing. He had dreamt this very thing so many times in jail that her presence seemed another of his imaginings.

Jessica nipped at her beer, the foam clinging to her lips. Micah took a deep draught of his.

"You know about Seth?"

"I haven't been in touch with anyone, not even Seth, particularly Seth."

"He OD'd."

"Micah." She pulled her chair as close as she could arrange and put her arms around him. "I couldn't get through to him. He was doing so much of the drug he turned mean. But it was only when he hit me that I left him."

"I can't believe he OD'd." He said this in a monotone, his voice husky, eyes staring straight ahead, unblinking.

He listened to himself say the word 'OD'd' with this sense of unreality. With all the things that had happened to him, death was the most real event, yet how could it be real: to cease, never to wake up, the blood to pool, and the body to decay. The only living creatures that have been able to escape that fate are asexual, like bacteria and some protists, or some unicellular creatures that have sex, like certain types of algae. Hydras and a certain type of jellyfish, *Turritopsis dohrnii,* are technically immortal, although they could meet their end by accident, disease, or being eaten. For most of the living, birth by its very nature carries with it a certainty of morbidity, the yin and yang of life, especially for multicellular creatures that internalize the division of labor between the somatic (body) cells and the germ (reproductive) cells, for them, death is an essential part of life, with its ghoulish implications of pain and suffering, its macabre displays. He shuddered.

She squeezed him and he hugged her back. They began swaying, holding each other. "I'm so sorry," she said, her mouth to his ear, her voice barely above a whisper, tickling his skin. "I'm near death myself."

"Don't say that."

"This is hard to take."

"Oy." He sobbed quietly, hardly making a sound, but the tears were clearly visible. He did not try to hide them. "I've never known pain like this."

"I can't believe what happened with Seth. I have this sense of unreality about it, like it's a nightmare that I'm hopefully going to wake up from."

"I've been asking myself if I had stood up to him, could I have stopped it?"

"I'm sorry I wasn't there; maybe I could have prevented it."

"Why didn't you let my mom know where you had gone?"

"I lost my job and got kicked out of my apartment. You wouldn't understand what that's like."

"What do you mean? I was in fucking jail." He drank a mouthful of his beer.

"Okay, but now you're out. You'll be back in school before you know it." She took small sips of her beer, licking the foam off her lips watchfully, like a spooked kitten.

"What you did, running off without a word to anyone, that was horrible. I missed you terribly."

"I was afraid. The cops might have been looking for me, too. For all I knew, my parents issued a missing person's report. I have no money. My sister, luckily, was there to help me. She and I moved here to Columbia City to be near her job. We couldn't afford that place on the island anymore."

"I wish I could have been there to help you," Micah said. He felt a sharp pang as he said this. All the pain of the past month hit him, and he choked back tears.

"I was afraid to contact you, or anyone else. Like I said, I didn't know if the cops were after me. It wouldn't have done you any good if I got arrested, or worse, sent back to my parents under lock and key."

"I hate separations," Micah said.

"Are you home then, for a while?"

"For another week or so." Micah had another swallow of his beer. "Then I'm going to California for residential drug treatment. I'm going to miss you."

Around them, the noise level from the dozen or so conversations grew louder. More people had packed into the little bar, filling all the tables around them. The place was rocking with laughter. Jessica started to say something. Micah leaned forward, seeking to pick her soft voice out from the din.

"You've survived the worst of it," Jessica said. "You'll come through this okay. I can't believe this about Seth. It's so crazy."

"I can't have visitors for the first three months of drug treatment."

He looked at her tear-stained face and wondered if she knew how much pain he was in. It seemed to him that she did not want him, and was sitting with him because she felt sorry for him, otherwise why not leave word where he could find her? It seemed from her expression she thought the prospect of residential drug treatment the most boring subject, a big nothing, merely cause for time to slow to a crawl, as if his troubles were analogous to a discussion of the way cement is made or how tires are manufactured. She said something that sounded as if she wanted to be with him, but either he did not hear it, or it went in, and his brain could not register any of the words. His mind went completely blank in the way he had seen his father do when his mother talked. After a time, his brain snapped back as if he had been jostled and brain parts rearranged to function more clearly, just in time to hear her wonder out-loud whether rentals in Los Angeles were expensive.

"In jail, I couldn't stop thinking about the night we were camping, and we were looking up at the stars. You said you loved me."

"I remember." Jessica tightened her hold on him.

A pleasant-looking man in his late twenties or maybe early thirties with a rugged, weather-beaten face came bounding up with an athlete's easy grace. His worn, frayed jeans and tee shirt looked as if they might have been torn apart by wolves, the teeth marks still visible. Micah half-expected to see blood trickling down his side. Deeply etched lines edged past his narrow blue eyes. He called to her in a hoarse whisky-soaked voice, "You Jessica?"

Jessica looked up, startled.

"Jessica?"

"Arnie." Jessica said, and jumping up, hugged the man. Turning to Micah, she explained, "Micah, this be Arnborg, the man who speared a whale and single handedly put all the local boys to shame." She sat down again, gesturing Arnie to a nearby seat. "What brings you to Seattle?"

"A fishing job," Arnie said. He grabbed the chair, scouted over, and added, "Don't mind if I do." He sat down. "You're the last person I expected to bump into on Martin Luther King Boulevard, of all places."

Micah stared at their interloper in disbelief, hoping he'd go away. Micah made his expression look as sorry and hangdog as possible, his eyes watery and his lips pointed down in half-moons, his chin and forehead crumpled, but Jessica's eyes were elsewhere. By her expression, he could see she was totally into talking up Arnie.

"Your sister here, too?"

"I'm living with Ila down the street."

"What's with Ila?"

"I don't know, Arnie, Ila never said anything to me."

Micah wanted the man to go away, but he also knew that forcing the issue would not sit well with Jessica, so he tried to call up a more forbearing attitude. Jessica and her friend were reminiscing about people they knew in Alaska. Micah was bored; his attention wandered. He fell into a daydream that Seth had barged in on them, not Arnborg, asking how it was they had run off without telling him where they were going. Were they trying to ditch him? That question upset Micah so much, he came back to reality with a start, only to hear the voice of the seaman rudely intervene.

"Been out at sea for months, and I'm weary to the bone, girl."

"Arnie, you're the only one in all of Seattle who knows what my life up north was like."

"When I left Anchorage, I did Ila a favor."

"Why do you say that?"

"Your daddy was getting ready to kill me. He didn't like seeing her with a sourdough works fishing boats."

Jessica had this look on her face, like she was secretly amused. But then she glanced over at Micah. "Look, Arnie, I got to get back to Micah," she said, "his brother just died and we're having a heavy conversation, so here's my sister's number if you want to talk to her?"

Micah felt tears well up and his chin trembled. He was glad Jessica got busy making their goodbyes to Arnie and did not appear to expect anything from him. They finished their beers, and she invited Micah to visit her at the house where she was living with her sister. Micah accepted eagerly.

The house was indistinguishable from the rest of the small and humble pastel-tinted cottages that lined the street, even the siding looked downtrodden. Inside, they entered a dark room with the shades drawn.

"I can't believe this is happening," Micah said, running his hands along her shoulders and arms. "I'm not looking forward to leaving you."

"It's impossible. You'll be in drug treatment for years."

"You could run away with me. We could leave now for Mexico—no one would find us there." He looked at her expectantly, but what came out of her mouth next sent a shiver down his spine.

"And then we'd have to hide forever. You'd never see your mom again."

"It'd be worth it, to have you." His response was automatic and skirted his conflicted view of the matter. Overriding all else was his desire to hold on to this girl.

"If they catch us, they'll ream your ass."

"Truth is I don't have the heart for running away, not unless you wanted it, too."

"You're not the most cautious person," Jessica said, kissing him. "Poor baby, I want to cuddle you. Come with me to my room," she pleaded, her eyes boring holes into Micah's, making it hard for him to blink. He just wanted to stare into her eyes and put his arms around her forever.

"No one's around," Micah said, looking down into her eyes soft and moist like black gummy bears.

"They could walk in and surprise us," Jessica said softly. "I wouldn't want them to see us bare-assed." She took the comfort of her arms away and took him by the hand.

Jessica led Micah down the shadowy hall over a reclaimed wood floor to a room hardly big enough to get around the cot and small chest of drawers that had been shoehorned there by some enterprising soul. Above the chest, a small window covered by a heavy blind made the place seem darker and smaller than it really was. Jessica led Micah to the bed and kissed him. They stood holding each other and kissing in the semi-darkness.

"I'm hurting right now."

"Me, too."

She opened the blind. Without speaking they peered out the window at bleak gray skies that had come out of nowhere, the blackbirds and finches silent for once. A pallid light filled the room. Inside him was a bottomless yawing, crazy mouth of need that took over his brain, analogous to a desperate clawing for survival that looked in his mind to have a physical presence like an ancient mythical god, its enormous mouth and vacant eyes shielding an emptiness that threatened to overwhelm him. He hugged her. Her warmth made his despair less. Jessica looked at him unblinkingly. Her eyelashes were so long they looked like starbursts. She lit a doobie. He could no longer see her eyes because smoke was seeping from her ears and collecting in pools around her skin. The smoke came from within her pores, fell to the ground and pushed from there upwards to the ceiling. When he could no longer breathe without taking in bits of char, he got up and ran out the door and up the hill heading toward Seward Park, his lungs pounding in his chest. He stood at the top of the hill and looked out over the lake and Mount Rainer and saw that all of it was submerged in fog or smoke, he could not tell which, and through it all he shouted for help to the empty vista below.

ZERO EVIDENCE

Stretch demanded to see the casino floor as soon as we dropped off our things in the hotel room. His breath quickened as he said this, and he brushed his glossy brown hair back from his forehead in that characteristic way he affected when excited, exposing thick eyebrows that looked like overgrown hedgerows. Having never tamed his inner gambler, he behaved like a young dog, ready to soil himself and roll in the glossy rectangles of the cards.

He says playing cards soothes the beast in him, makes him tractable, but I think it has the opposite effect. Seeing Stretch like this brought to mind the words of Dostoevsky in *The Gambler*, "Even as I approach the gambling hall, as soon as I hear, two rooms away, the jingle of money poured out on the table, I almost go into convulsions." For Dostoevsky, it was never something he could get a grip on. He had to crank out *The Gambler* and rush the ending of *Crime and Punishment* to pay off gambling debts.

I've seen Stretch in action and know from experience that usually he cannot have just one bite; he must eat the whole thing, and like Dostoevsky, he's had to borrow money to stay in the game. So you can imagine my horror when it turned out we were headed down the elevator to find the poker tables; this was not part of the original plan. I might have objected, but then I thought, give him some slack. He's been good for the past year. Maybe he's gained more control. Before online poker was outlawed in Washington State, he used to play online poker daily, losing more than he was winning, frantically finishing apps he'd been coding to have the money to pay debtors. Wins served to kept him hooked, saying things like, "I'm due to win," and "shouldn't be long now," and "I've got the math all figured out."

He loves the Venetian in Vegas and plays the nosebleed deepstack poker series but only because it's two hours away from Seattle where we live, adding that he wants to be like Tom Dwan, master of the bluff. In the next breath he admits that he cannot hide what he's feeling which is like a death warrant in poker. He is terrible at reading people's 'tells,' the hints that players try to hide their hidden thoughts: indications of mood in the eyes and mouth, the lack or profusion of hand gestures, the changes in the pulse visible in the throat. He says he often forgets to check these indicators. Sometimes they're blinking neon signs.

He's tried downplaying the merit of his cards by looking bored, although he's never sure if his face reflects what he wants to project. A lot of times other players at his table, to his puzzlement, immediately fold when he gets a winning hand. When that happens, sometimes his vision clouds and he does not know what comes out of his mouth. The few times he had to be escorted out by security, he could not say why. He's felled by an all-in, and only sometimes has the ability to climb out of a short stack.

Somehow Stretch was able to stop himself before the roof caved in.

During the worst of it, he neglected family. Many times, his daughter begged him to watch her perform on her debate team. The few times he did show up, he was on the phone talking about playing, disrupting the audience. Other times he'd promise to go, and then at the last-minute, book poker tournaments instead. The losses kept mounting, and once he had to take a loan against the mortgage on his house.

But the turnaround came when Stretch realized how much he had hurt his daughter. He experienced the profound despair that this sort of addiction engenders, and he started thinking suicide. He purchased a gun and had plans in place.

The National Council on Problem Gambling estimates that one in five gambling addicts attempts suicide—the highest rate among addicts of any kind. There are plenty of anecdotes: the police officer who shot himself in the head at a Detroit casino, the accountant who jumped to his death from a London skyscraper, the student who killed himself in Las Vegas after losing all his financial-aid money to gambling. In Europe for centuries, publications were full of breathless reports of people ending their lives at Monte Carlo Casino, at the tables, in the garden, in the hotel rooms. According to Cassell's Magazine, no other gaming tables in the world can be said to be responsible for as many suicides. One table alone was said to have claimed one-hundred-and-thirteen lives in a ten-year span between 1890 and 1900, though Historian Mark Braude, author of *Making Monte Carlo: A History of Speculation and Spectacle*, says there's no evidence that suicides along the Côte d'Azur are any higher than any of the other famous casinos.

I do not know how I prevented him from pulling the trigger; I like to think it was me sticking by him and pointing him in a direction. The clincher might have been enrolling him in golf lessons. Everyone needs a consuming passion.

"I realize now that nothing will totally satisfy my craving for big windfalls or attention," he said, "especially not gambling." Now he's modeling himself on Rory McIlroy, one of the best drivers of the golf ball, and practices his swing daily.

Golf made it possible for him to religiously hold to his spending limits, so his shortcomings do not deter him. He tells me this, and his breath quickens while driving by a casino near the Canadian border, brushing his big hair waving like a peacock's tail back from his forehead.

He first developed the love of cards watching his mother and grandmother play at their home, and seeing their excitement, began hosting impromptu games with his friends. As a young boy, he played stickball with his siblings against a casino wall in a San Francisco suburban parking lot while waiting for his grandmother and mother to emerge; they still don't allow young children to hang around the slots. His mother played in the hopes they would get a windfall, although they lost more than they won. Stretch lived for the wild tales they shared on their return, their wins and losses part of the fantastical journey.

Then in deep winter, we decided to fly to Tahoe from Seattle to meet my son living in the Bay Area to take advantage of the record snowfall at Tahoe resorts, over four times the average. We got a chance to ski a few days before the resorts closed in the aftermath of eighty-mile-an-hour winds tearing over the pass, nixing our skiing plans for the foreseeable future. The winds were expected to die down for a few hours, and then resume again with greater intensity. Early that morning, my son took the bus for the Reno airport, an hour drive east in treacherous conditions so he could make it back in time to show up for work in San Jose. A few hours later, we took the same bus to catch a flight to Seattle. The snow started up harder, and winds ripping through the naked, exposed hills. The whiteout was surreal, like a dream.

At the airport, we heard that the winds had gotten worse, cancelling all air travel. Stretch talked me into one of the many casino hotels in downtown Reno, saying the food would be better there. For the past few years Stretch has not gambled, mainly because I found it dull watching him play, we knew we might not recover from ozone-sized hole in his savings, and I hated what it did for his disposition.

The bus took us past some of the city's more cautionary tales: boarded-up motels, pawn shops, and failed theme casinos that reminded me of old Vegas, presenting herself like a whore, legs spread, bad teeth visible in the toothy leer and surrounded by vast stretches of empty parking lot covered in snow, fronting strings of rundown honkytonk bars and lonely motels that looked right out of the Deep South. There wasn't much traffic, only the most desperate of gamblers in their rentals with the windows blacked out, the wheels making the chinka chinka sound of money rolling, coming for the impossibly low buy ins. Someone sitting next to us on the bus said, "Don't think they're pushovers in Reno," and cautioned that Stretch would lose everything when they're dealing out of shoes at the Silver Legacy or Peppermill on busy weekends. Stretch thanked the man for the tip.

We entered the thriving middle where the larger casinos are located—appearing right out of a Disney theme park that wishes it were Vegas but falling far short, looking more like a group of suburban Indian casinos attached to each other with plenty of tiers, like any of the newer malls, each tier set back from the one below. There was a look of excitement on Stretch's face. He told me he wanted to play the two-dollar tables at the Sands or maybe the Eldorado. Immediately I was hit by a shortness of breath filled with foreboding. Out on the street, the winds tore at us, making each step a battle. We stepped inside, thankful that the buildings were connected, and strolled through the Silver Legacy, Circus Circus, and Harrah's, all seeming the same with the array of dizzy colors and lights, and then we hit the Club Cal Nev, where there had been no attempt to modernize, everything dark and claustrophobic, low ceilings throughout, and the dealers sporting bikinis or leathers. But Stretch did not like the dark, saying he could not see anything, and wanted us to break out.

In the plush lobby of the Silver Legacy, he acknowledged he has this problem, saying "yes, yes," but then brushed it aside with a wave of his hand as if he was removing invisible cobwebs from the air. Imagine my horror when he wanted to find the poker tables; this was not part of the original plan. But then I thought, *give him some slack. Maybe he's gained more control.* He knows the reason he sustained these long periods of losses isn't a matter of intelligence, or understanding, but due to his pernicious inability to hide what he feels at exactly the moment he needs to bury his emotions. His acting ability is nil—he's what people call an open book, displaying too much intellectual ferment to be a good poker player. His anticipation is palpable; the not knowing delights him.

"Maybe blackjack is a better game for you," I said, trying for diplomacy. "No psychology needed."

We toured the cavernous casino floor of the Eldorado. Disorientating, psychedelic carpets lay underfoot, with a sensibility born of voodoo and the occult. The architecture gently curved in, moving us towards machines that radiated hypnotic rainbows of blinking lights. My mind melted. I gazed at the dayglow beauty on the screen directly in front of me and I was miles away, dreaming of sugary beaches to the sounds of heels muffled in the carpeting that pass me by, reminding me of the sucking sounds of whirlpools. I could not tear my eyes away, even when sounds of winning could be heard—the *bling bling bling* of sirens and the clang of jackpot bells announcing that someone hit a jackpot.

He never misses a credit card or his mortgage payments, which I'm thankful for, proving he can control his impulses as long as he stays out of the casinos. His trouble occurs when he lets himself do even a little bit, and then it's the bipolar igniting. I know this about him: he's impulsive, triggered by obscure forces leading to frantic emotional upheaval. But now that we're in the casino, can he master his gambler's itch?

In *Infinite Jest,* Hal comes to realize that "we are all dying to give our lives away to something," paralleling what Marathe tells Steeply about choosing one's idols. By giving himself over to addiction, Hal knows he's avoiding some question or realization, and by invoking Hamlet, the narrator suggests that addiction is an attempt to evade suffering, leading to questions about the purpose of life: "… the questions why and to what grow real beaks and claws". The bird-like imagery alludes to the image of the shadow that Kate Gompert uses to describe her depression. Which begs the question: Is addiction the best defense against depression and insanity? Against failure?

Stretch makes a lot of money as a software developer, having graduated from a prestigious university and now working for a high-flying company, and it was not as if he was financially bankrupt, not even close, but like a Monet, from a distance everything looked beautiful and vibrant, but when you got up close, the real picture was a cloudy mess. I was especially attuned to this tendency as I had just come out of a period when my ex-husband's neglect of me made me think my love of art and fashion would fill the lonely spaces, the more expensive the better, which led to him asking for a divorce, shocking me into questioning everything about myself.

Post-divorce, I avoided shopping as it had become something toxic, and instead, I worked at developing myself apart from my wardrobe. I ran marathons and took up endurance cycling, and gradually liberated myself from the self-doubt and pity that colored my life.

Cycle to seven years later and Stretch and I found that we understood each other's addictive personalities and how to help each other stand firm against our worst instincts. From that basis, we worked to form a relationship. But it took the assistance of a therapist to let the other have the breathing room to develop our separate selves and let loose the dependencies that did not serve us. At one time a semi-professional surfer, and now as a body builder and golfer, Stretch continues to utilize the singular focus and ability to forget losses and play through pain. It's the same focus whatever he does, applying the work ethic he learned as a youth. Stretch has not played poker in a long time and knows when to walk away. What the pros say: The work ethic can turn malignant. It's hard to distinguish between person who has a hobby they love and an unhealthy problem. The hobbyist who maintains outside interests and takes part in activities outside of their game usually does not have a problem. But even as he says he can handle it, I feel a painful twinge when right off he wants to visit the poker room.

When I asked Stretch, he said he's convinced there's a fine line between what constitutes obsession and addiction. He's more interested in another question, perhaps related, the one thing that both repels and excites him: the inherently unfair and amoral position of preying on the weak. The thought of this basic unfairness makes him bridle. But he quickly added that he enjoys bluffing, enjoys pretending he has something he does not have; wishes he was better at it, and realizes he may never be good enough. He wants to do it for the enjoyment, he says.

"I have these seemingly contradictory beliefs," he said.

Personally, I dislike casinos, but I hold my counsel, realizing that dabbling occasionally in personal vices—as debased and sordid as they might appear to be to someone who does not share them—will not harm him, though I hoped that I could come up with a reason he should not play. But it would be a fight I could not win, and I might alienate my man in the process. And what's the harm if he adheres to his limits.

"I have to keep telling myself that I'm not entitled to win the money just because I was dealt Aces," he said.

We found the corner of the vast casino floor where a few lonesome poker tables stood looking forlorn. As my head filled with notes of caution, remembering how easily we can talk ourselves into bad spaces, noting the care that went into the construction of this room with its velvet walls, soft carpeting, tables made of exotic woods. The management put a lot of effort into making the place attractive. Someone with a problem gets so caught up playing that they miss their daughter's field hockey game—at least they're trapped in a beautiful environment. But without anyone there, it felt like a red-light district with no patrons. Stretch said he had been on the fence about playing poker anyway, that he'd rather try blackjack, having studied the charts, claiming that's what he was doing on the bus ride into Reno. Now he knows when to stand, ask for a hit and when to double down or split. He reminded me that his engineering background provided the perfect training.

"Did I tell you that some of the top money managers on Wall Street started out playing blackjack?" Stretch said.

"Well if you can make it profitable," I said.

"Who knows, I might actually have an edge if I play correctly."

I asked him why he liked playing casinos.

"I love the atmosphere," he said.

"I can see your point," I said, eying a waitress in a push up bra showing too much cleavage, her narrow hips doing a little dance, her feet shaking in skyscraper stilettos. She was chanting an unending refrain: drinks, drinks, drinks, what can I do you for?

"Cards are as addictive as playing slots but with cards," he said, "you have some control over what you're doing. And unlike bingo or horseracing, it's the perfect mix of gambling and skill: the better you are, the more skill there is and the less gambling."

I hoped in the thick of battle he would remember his words and clamp down on his emotions. They seemed to run away to run away from him overmuch. We went into the Eldorado. I breathed in the filtered air, relishing the sounds of a beat-driven music, a rhapsody making my blood thump, merging nicely with the tantalizing ripple of cards being shuffled, and the slip-slip-slip as they were dealt over the sounds of laughing card players and the occasional drunken yell. Sopranos! Altos! Tenors! Bass! Baritones! The chorus never seemed to slow down long enough to inhale.

The click-click-click-click-click of chips dancing across green felt seemed to dance in synchrony with the flickering lights in a smoky, synchronized show. I understood why casinos appealed to him. My spirits bordered on ecstasy.

"Every time I walk into these places, I feel a rush like I just snorted cocaine," he said, mirroring my thoughts.

Stretch found a table, and we slid into the remaining two chairs. Stretch whispered that a table full of people is good for a player; it allows him time to think. I remembered something else Stretch told me early on: Proficiency in math is important, but even more so, to make a great player, one also needs to project a certain image: other players should think he doesn't know what he's doing, and the act must be convincing. I noticed that the other players were dressed in tee shirts and jeans, and looked like truck drivers, many sporting pot bellies. Stretch was lean and muscular, and looked like an executive in his golf clothes.

I wished he blended in more, and I thought that I was being too paranoid; maybe how he dressed didn't matter as much as I thought. Perhaps this is why people love the game so much. It's only in part a desire to get rich; it's also bound in the struggle to find the core of one's essential self, to reach deep inside and to act on one's beliefs. To appear to make a stand, the truth less important, or maybe it's that illusions are as important as the reality, maybe even more so.

Card games encourage the erecting of temporary walls and the mounting of a defense and like real life, reward lies and deceit. Stretch knows to hold his cards face down like secrets that aren't revealed until he's forced to divulge them. But really when it comes down to it, he's not comfortable in the lie.

A ball skipped along the roulette wheel in hypnotic tympani.

A round-faced Asian woman in a glittery costume with a high neck dealt the cards. She had a fancy way of moving her hands. I could not focus on the cards; I found myself drawn to her magician's hands and could not help noticing the meticulous grooming of her gaudy paste-ons in overlay of electric colors, and the way they flipped and scrolled through the air mesmerized me.

Stretch drew a ten on the ten he had already—making a twenty, beating both the dealer's hands. This happened several times, with different amounts, plenty of them doubles. Then he drew two fives in quick succession. Each time said he wanted to double down. And every time he drew cards, he checked the blackjack chart that he had left open on his phone before making his move. The dealer frowned at him but did not say anything. Stretch put his phone on his lap under the rim of table and kept on playing.

The dealer glanced at the pit boss standing next to her. The suit looked visibly disturbed. He stared hard at Stretch, as if his glance was designed to light Stretch on fire. Stretch had at least seven hundred dollars' worth of chips stacked in front of him, four times what he initially put in. With trembling hands, the dealer started dealing the cards faster, making it hard for Stretch to play along, but he kept winning.

There was a change of dealers. And the new dealer, a man, his attitude as serious and dedicated as any junior executive on the make, was not one for small talk. His eyes bored holes into Stretch as he pulled out a new deck of cards and his mouth formed a thin red line like the police line that says do not cross.

Gambling can be found in almost every aspect of social life, from personal relationships to international politics, and has been a factor in our lives since the dawn of time. In some ancient societies, gambling was part of religious or communal exercises, and the outcome was thought to signify the blessing of the gods—underscoring that the most important aspect of life has always been about luck. But people have always known there's a darker side to gambling. The *Rig Veda*, a collection of Hindu religious hymns more than three thousand years old, contains a section known as the "Gambler's Hymn," which laments: "Without any fault of hers I have driven my devoted wife away because of a die exceeding by one [an unsuccessful bet]. My mother-in-law hates me; my wife pushes me away. In his defeat the gambler finds none to pity him. No one has use for a gambler, like an aged horse put up for sale."

Blaming a bad result on an offended spirit or a good result on divine favor is far more comforting than accepting the cold indifference of chance. And rather than admit there's very little we can do about something that's outside our control, we invoke the power of magic and the occult to manage our terror.

The dealer kept hitting face cards, which did not seem natural, and Stretch kept losing, in a stunning reversal.

"I should have left the table the minute I saw that happening," Stretch said. "But I couldn't believe a dealer would be that brazen."

"Me, too, I couldn't believe it either, not until it all your chips were gone, and then it sunk in."

Every game is an attempt to disrupt the odds, but it's difficult to prevail when the casino can basically jimmy the game in their favor, and do it blatantly, like a banana republic, trampling on individual players' constitutional rights—that is, if you were on public property, treating people like that would be illegal. I wondered what would happen if enough people complained or even boycotted the casinos until they amended their rules. What would have happened if everyone simply said no?

By invoking his intuition at the gaming tables, for a time he gets out of having to obey all the myriad rules that govern our lives. But if governments across Asia, Europe and the Americas tried to tamp out gambling, would society as we know it cease to function? That's the question I asked Stretch.

He shrugged and said he didn't care. He just wanted his money back.

"Fat chance of that," I said.

"You're right," he said. "The chance of that is exactly less than zero. That's pretty fat."

I found it exceedingly curious, my muscles froze, and I couldn't say anything. I could only soak in the sounds and lights as if paralyzed, though I remembered to click the video feature of my phone and surreptitiously recorded. Someone told me that they had played two-deck games in Vegas and no aces came out and that this someone asked the pit boss if he could check the cut-away cards. All eight of them were behind the cut card. I wanted to say something to Stretch but I struggled to speak, and no words issued forth, not a sound.

A man sitting a few chairs away whom we had spoken to a few times looking meaningfully at Stretch, said, "It seems like a good time to step away from this table." He had not lost much, not like Stretch.

Stretch could not move. It was as if he saw the guillotine aimed high in the air above his exposed neck, and still could not move. I imagined his body throttled in death throes, covered in a sticky substance stronger than glue. The man stood up and clamped his cowboy hat down on his head, hitched his jeans past his hips, and came up behind Stretch, jingling his coins in his front pocket. He paused for a few minutes but did not say anything. Then, slowly shaking his head, still not speaking, departed.

The cocktail waitress came by again asked pointedly if he wanted anything, forcing Stretch to look away from the dealer to address the waitress. This happened whenever the dealer was handing out cards. It seemed too much of a coincidence, but I did not think about it at the time, but it registered with me all the same and gave me an unsettled feeling.

Stretch pulled out of his reverie. All his chips were gone. He was down a thousand. He got up, on shaky legs, his eyes glazed and mouth crumbled. Right off, he stumbled against the chair he had been sitting on, looking as if he had been punched in the gut. The smirk on the dealer's face deepened; his mouth puckered as though he was trying to stifle a grin.

We left the table and went into the lounge.

"How do you think they get the cash to build these palaces with," I said and suggested we go to the management to register a complaint.

"Yeah but we have zero evidence," he said. "They'll laugh at me."

"Look, here's a video on YouTube of a dealer doing in slow motion exactly what happened to me." Stretch said, his voice shaking with anger. "But he doesn't say if he was able to get justice served. And here's a story about a lawyer who represents gamblers, Bob Nersesian. He won seventy cases similar to mine and returned millions of dollars to gamblers. Nersesian was interviewed in the *New York Post* in 2016 about it. In the cases Nersesian won, the management clearly overstepped and violated peoples' rights."

In one case, a card counter playing blackjack at Hard Rock Hotel & Casino in Vegas—the same place that Ben Affleck was kicked out of a few years ago for card counting—won nearly six-thousand dollars his first two days in Vegas, and was actually losing on his third day, when a Hard Rock employee stopped him. "Cash in your chips," the casino suit said. "You're done."

He was handcuffed and bullied into a back room. An hour or so later, Thom Kho was released and given his possessions back, including an envelope containing nearly thirty-thousand dollars, but the casino wouldn't let him cash out chips worth three-thousand, six-hundred and twenty-five dollars. Kho sued the casino and won.

"If they offer a game to the community—and it's their odds, equipment and rules—how can they exclude smart people from participating?" Stretch said.

"This is how," I said.

THERAPY FOR DOGS

Micah concentrated on working for the charities to fulfill his obligations to the court, spanning years in a feverish slog. He spent at least two years doing this brutal and soul-sucking work, sorting clothes for Goodwill; cleaning trash on the highways, parks and other public spaces in Southern California. The litter kept growing with the tent cities and homeless camping on the byways, especially around the coast. He passed the time telling his fellow laborers jokes and riddles. They told him he shoulda been a comedian.

Then there was his supervisor, a dude with a low IQ, stretching his patience to the max. Someone he couldn't talk to, telling him to do this or that in a gruff voice, telling him to move faster, stop clowning around. Micah had to dumbly obey. Even so, he felt gratitude that he wasn't in prison. That would be far worse.

He had spells of sobriety lasting months, even years, but then he would meet someone out of the blue at a party or whatnot who offered him weed or an opioid, and he fell back into his old ways. In a last-ditch effort to kick the on-again, off-again habit he'd fallen into, Micah decided to move to Las Vegas and join a boot camp for aspiring paratroopers that a friend from rehab told him about near Nellis Air Force Base, to challenge himself and lift him out of his funk. His father agreed to pay for the three-month program. He told his mother that he loved the comradery—everyone was warm and friendly, and they assured him they had his back. Borrowing a car from his roommate was never a problem; anytime he needed anything, someone had it: extra socks, toothpaste, soap, a pitcher of beer to pass around.

He loved the discipline of getting up at dawn for four-mile jogs along the Las Vegas strip, and afterwards going to a local park to perform a grueling military-style workout, followed by paratroop exercises like jumping off cliffs or rappelling down, and spiraling out of planes mid-air, and then, exhausted, taking a dip in the lake at the day's end surrounded by good friends, bonds created under physical duress, the tightest kind. He said this camp was better than rehab, which consisted of mostly talk therapy and motivational lectures, and activities like soccer, and the golf lessons the therapists talked him into. He loved it all, every hour accounted for, never having to rely on his own ability to get up and make something of his day, which he admitted was difficult for him. On his own, he'd get on his phone, reading posts from friends and viewing entertaining snippets from news services, forgetting the time, and whiling the day away, and then get up bored, not sure what to do, dreaming of the good old days with when his brother was alive and good friends perpetually stopping by, their greetings filled with good cheer, some of them expressing their love, and their eagerness to share a fattie around. These feelings were not deterred by reason, they were the anti-reason. Thinking about those days gave him joy and filled him with warmth, his heart beating strong, not for purely physical reasons, but because these memories made him truly happy.

"I realized my need to have every minute accounted for," he said in a phone call to his mother, "When I'm busy I don't miss the Chemical."

They went on three-day fasts once a month—Micah loved the endorphin rush of fasting while exercising. Micah came home for a weekend visit and talked his mother into grocery shopping for essential keto ingredients and told his mother to buy almond, cashew and pea protein milk, his tone messianic, his voice taking on a passionate tilt. He offered to prepare meals: cheese and mushroom omelets with spinach salads. His mother was struck by the beauty of her son's personality shining brightly like the sun's glow in his fervor for the extreme clannish lifestyle of the training camp; something about him said he had arrived at a joyful peace.

Micah and his mother shared a comfortable, companionable togetherness, now finally, that he was constantly sober, they could converse normally, without the irritability that Micah demonstrated when constantly under the throes of heavy narcotics which made normal conversation impossible, his senses not marred by traces of fentanyl. Micah said he was considering the military; the man who ran the training camp urged him to join, said he was a perfect fit, but the thought of being far from home, trapped in a foreign country, unable to see his childhood friends, gave him the willies.

His mother told him it was his choice, that she would always be there for him, and, as much as she could, help him find his way.

He decided against the military and stayed around Vegas looking for work, liking the glitz and the wild entertainment crowd, performers and actors crowding the streets of Henderson. He especially liked visiting the Lion Habitat Ranch and hiking the trails around Lake Mead. But throughout his time in Nevada, he found he disliked the desert air, tough to suck in. There wasn't enough oxygen, period. Breathing desert heat was nothing like the coolness of the air buzzing with oxygen from the plants of the Pacific Northwest. But he let that go. For a time he was seduced by the huge number of job postings, though he couldn't apply to many of them because of his felony conviction, but easy to line up promotional gigs for nightclubs. But working on commission made it tough to live on, though he met guys who were killing it and living in comfort. He found the high sales expected of him to be contrary to his nature; he'd rather make friends and shmooze and not care about meeting quota. He found hustling to be stressful, but he tried it while staying off most of the recreational drugs except for ketamine to relieve his anxiety. He didn't like either the drug or the lifestyle. Even so, he hung around his high- achieving friends so he had a social life and went through the motions for about a year and a half before he got fired. In a phone call to his mother he acknowledged this about himself and told her in no uncertain terms that he was through with Vegas. He decided instead to move to a sober-living house in the East Bay near San Francisco. Town called Hayward. His mother told him she had never been but it was near the San Mateo Bridge with easy access to communities like Palo Alto and Los Gatos. The people who ran the sober-living house promised him a job and guidance to help him transition to life outside rehab. There were daily drug tests, and a houseful of similarly challenged individuals. He worked as a landscaper for close to two years, while working at least three days a week for Bay Area charities, as he wasn't done satisfying the court's requirements, requirements that seemed to be constantly shifting. He was always amiss in something they required, which he found dispiriting. Three times a year he flew back to Seattle to meet with the judge in person to discuss his progress. He thought the judge was being overly strict, but he tried to please her all the same. All of that time he successfully staying off hard drugs, and seemingly having learned to manage without Seth around, although he said that he didn't like some of the people he lived with and resented the lack of privacy.

He thought about going back to school. His mother found scholarships he could apply to, but he couldn't muster the energy to fill out the forms. He complained of lacking motivation and having chronically low energy. And he was sick of the landscaper business, sick of the constant feeling that he had transported himself to a prison-like chain gang with the commensurate low pay and punishing hours. It seemed fortuitous that just when he couldn't stand waking in the pre-dawn hours anymore, he found a job as a therapist for dogs, having discovered a nascent gift as dog whisperer, calming and soothing strays and family pets alike. And he started making friends, lots of friends, sometimes he forgot himself and had periods of happiness. He started a class on mediation and met a musician there. The musician friend and he started work composing music for an album. He spent many hours on Mount Tamalpais composing music that was beautiful and appealed to his friends. Micah kept at it and thought it would not be long before the pair could produce an album. About that time he met a woman at his meditation class who impressed him with her beauty and intelligence, a software engineer who devoted all her free hours to animal rights advocacy. Stephanie Ioannou made life exciting; even the small moments were infused with meaning. They went for walks around Berkeley though the winter and spring months and developed a friendship. Her presence made him feel an irrational sense of happiness, almost deliriousness; he thought they understood each other and had similar views of the world. For one thing, they both loved animals, and could speak about the beauty of the purity of heart and playful spirit of animals.

He looked forward to their dates together; she told him it was the same for her. They talked about his work and her dreams of freeing animals from slaughter. Micah did not like the idea of animals being slaughtered either, though he still liked to eat meat. He rationalized this seeming contradiction by saying that he mostly ate beef and chicken, and his mother, who grew up on a cattle ranch, told him that cows and chickens are low intelligence and would not be around except that we like to eat them, which he acknowledged was crass, and no excuse. He told her he agreed that the world would be a better place if, please God, we stopped the barbarism, but did not feel troubled about this implied contradiction. And he felt they were communicating openly and fearlessly, laughing together, touching hearts and minds. A few of those times, he forgot his brother and then invariably, he'd remember with a sharp pain to his chest. He learned that Stephanie was living in an artist commune in Berkeley and wanted to find a condo in Oakland to share with a few likeminded people. She asked if he would be interested. The only catch—he would never be allowed to cook meat in her condo.

"I want to warn you that I take it seriously. Only the cooking of plants will be allowed my place," she said.

"Sure," He said readily, now used to compromise, thinking to himself that he would eat meat elsewhere.

They sealed their commitment to animal rights with a hug and kiss. A few weeks later, he moved in. They went hiking and camping, and one night became lovers. Then Alex (the one who introduced Micah and his brother to fentanyl) came to visit and was booted out by his roommate after threatening her, acting psychotic, and threatening violence if she did not comply with his wishes. Stephanie's brother, who lived a few blocks away, came over to help convince Alex to leave peacefully. Stephanie said Alex was not welcome in her house ever again. Micah drove Alex to the airport so he could return home.

To smooth things over and help erase the unpleasantness that Alex caused, Steph bought a piano for the house, which she said Micah was free to use anytime he wanted. He started composing music again in her home, practicing his craft several hours a day. He composed a song that he said came to him in a dream. His musician friend liked it so much he wanted to include it on the album: he called it "Micah's Dream".

Steph said she was ridiculed by male colleagues at her job for her volunteerism as animal rights activist. She did not talk about it much, knowing that many of the guys at her company did not seem to get it, though many of her afternoons and weekends were devoted to this work. She organized marches and wrote to her representatives in Congress, urging them to ban the eating of meat and decrying the carnivorous lifestyle of many Americans. Stephanie could not talk Micah into joining her on marches to protest the transport of pigs to slaughterhouses near Sacramento, where she would stand outside state legislative meetings while in session and lead the chants with her bullhorn. She would sometimes get arrested but always was released within hours. Micah could not get the time off, which was just as well, because the one time she mentioned it at work, a couple of the male engineers offered a few choice derogatory remarks that made her fuming mad, and Micah worried that he would end up saying something that would get him in trouble with her. She could be touchy.

Micah's mother called every few days and texted often to check up on him, feeling a sense of dread, knowing Alex was not content to leave Micah be, he wanted a dependent Micah. His mother hoped Steph would be able to keep Micah on a good path. But it was difficult for Micah who did not feel as committed as Steph to the protest movement. Often she went alone. One day Steph went to a 'flash speak-out' in the meat aisle of Ralphs Supermarket to support a Direct Action Everywhere protest. With other protesters, she crowded the store chanting and holding signs, blocking people from accessing the packaged meat, texting Micah several photos of the twisted and angry faces of protesters juxtaposed with the faces of frightened shoppers, disturbing his equilibrium. He felt anxious, and did what the rehab counselors had suggested, to sublimate, finding something else to address his upset. He thought of his craving for chicken. Stephanie was not expected until late. At the corner grocery he picked up boneless chicken breasts on sale. He planned to air out the place before she came home.

As he was sitting down to eat, Steph came into the room, "What are you eating?" she said, and then screaming, "No, no, no."

It was as if she was being beaten with a switch. He had been living with her for a few months as lovers, though he had become increasingly turned off by her fixation with public protesting; even so, he was stunned, and apologized, saying he had been dying for a piece of chicken for days. But she was not to be swayed. She turned into a raving lunatic and tossed his plate with the chicken still on it against the wall.

He called a few rooming houses and moved out of Stephanie's a few days later, his life totally upended. He left all the furniture he had purchased behind; he thought it was too much of a hassle to get past the hydra-headed Medusa to claim his stuff. He went from opulence to living in a dilapidated house a few towns away. The landladies, a couple of middle-aged Filipino sisters who charged an exorbitant fee, seeing that he had no other place to go took advantage, and he knew that, but felt powerless to do anything. He paid the rent including first and last, thinking he'd find a better place at his leisure. At least he had his own furnished room, though the common living space accessible to him was cluttered with thrift store finds, a porch swing, a piano, a bed in a corner occasionally occupied by the landladies' visiting family, clothing heaped on the floor. But he did not realize what living with people with different cultural norms and no curiosity about the world would do to his soul. He promised himself that he'd go out with his friends as much as possible to be away from this place, and tried to convince himself he was better off. Still, the thought that he would never see his brother again intruded, his loneliness descending on him like a lead blanket. The minute he opened his eyes in his new home, he faced a herculean struggle to get out of bed. His circumstances seemed to have become bleaker.

He could not articulate this pain to his mother; he told her everything was fine, that he was coping; he did not want her to worry. He talked only about the good things, like his job, and how much he loved the people he was meeting through his therapy for dogs. He did not tell her that he felt at a loss, the friends he had thought would be with him forever were busy with other things or people; they were not around anymore, not really, even if they did text or call every now and then. There was no one to run with every morning before work; no friends lived around him except for Nick, an old friend from the old days, a former habitué at their house on Gryffindor's Island, but Nick was too busy with his new job as pastry chef in a busy four-star kitchen in Berkeley to hang out like they used to.

Shortly after getting kicked out of Stephanie's, totally stoned on pot, Micah called his former therapist Matt Gittleman to reconnect, even though Matt seemed defensive, asking Micah why he never said anything about the graffiti. Though he asked politely and calmly, still a note of hurt sounded in the keening-like despair curling the edges of his voice—practically accusing Micah of ruining Matt's marriage.

"I couldn't think of anything else," Matt said. "I kept replaying our sessions like a windup toy. I couldn't get past your calmness telling me you were looking forward to school in Southern Cali. I couldn't believe that you would hide that from me. I thought we had a good relationship … better than most … I believed we had a deep understanding forged over the three years we'd known each other. I'm usually good at reading people, knowing when they're hiding something, but I found my past, training, and experience meant nothing."

"What about me?" Micah said, "You didn't come to see me in jail. The one time I needed you the most."

"Don't you understand what it is I'm saying to you? You never said a word about your plans to ink the yeshiva walls? You led me to think everything was fine. How could you act so calm when you were planning this ... this ... horror ..." Matt's disembodied voice had a certain aspect of vaudeville, but it was not comic; hearing Matt's voice was too distressing for that. More like tragicomic.

Micah listened as if in a trance, thinking disjointed thoughts, questioning why a man like Matt would put himself into this nebulous state, finding a foothold in this absurdity of existence, calling himself a psychologist and professing to love his fellow man specifically Micah, meanwhile did not Matt at one time say "knowledge is power?" pressing him to talk, wanting to know everything, never satisfied, always wanting to pick him apart with sharp beak and claws drawing blood in a quest for more so-called knowledge that leads to what ... if not power ... was it all about control over another human being, even if the stated goal is to help? None of us has the slightest reason to be here, everyone living in a tangled heap, muscle and bone, irritated at each other and the world, and trying to act as though we are not hidden embarrassments full of cascading anxiety, juggling dismal thoughts that terrify in the middle of the night.

Sometimes Micah woke up screaming, thinking spiders were crawling over his body and nursing an overriding obsession to delay the crumbling of his world. He was also getting tired of holding his finger to the dike.

"It didn't seem important," Micah explained. "I had no idea that anyone in my group was thinking to draw swastikas. So okay, I was there, that's all, and I didn't tell Alex what to write ... I'd never do that; you know that's not how we do things ... and they decided to ruin my life because of that? It's called being in the wrong place at the wrong time. And people like you accusing me of not saying anything when I did nothing wrong."

Micah remembered the dreams they had, mostly they were Seth's dreams, but Micah valued them as if they were his own, and incorporated them into his essence, and in some ways they were his own as part of their shared DNA, the white fire that burned in the heart of Seth that Micah absorbed like an amoeba, that Micah believed made the pair of them unique in the history of brothers, the spirit of Seth that imparted more worth, more value, than the others not sanctified by this unity of purpose. With these others, what you see is what you get. Not that they were better than other people, by any means—but at birth, they were luckier than most. Ribbons of grace passed through and around them—for whatever reasons this was recognized by his brother, who thought it conferred a measure of immortality and invincibility, which led to his hubris, and certainly in some ways undeserved, unearned, or monetized.

"Now my wife filed for divorce because I can't get past this thing," Matt said. "It's haunting my dreams." He sounded bitter. "I thought you were in a good place."

"I was at the time," Micah said. "Not anymore, not since my brother passed. I'm dead now, too."

Micah thought if he couldn't talk to his therapist without feeling his world was falling apart, perhaps acquiring a pet would prove therapeutic. So he spread the word around. A friend at work said she found a puppy for him, the perfect companion: a screwball like him. Micah was heartened and called his mother to tell her about his plan to adopt a pet. He sounded excited and happy, and was talking about going back to school, saying he was planning to fill out the scholarship forms, he still had them around, and he was more than ready now to get on with his life.

Not long after that conversation, his mother learned from one of his coworkers on Fakebook that a new girl had joined their team, having just moved to the U.S. from Mexico. In a phone call to his mother, Micah joked that the new girl, Kayla, had announced to everyone in the room that day that she was a meth addict. He told his mother he wanted to help her learn ways to abstain. He said he was planning to help her overcome her addiction the way he had learned in rehab. When Micah's mother learned that Micah befriended this girl, the dread the mother harbored in her heart increased to a roaring inferno and thinking she was going crazy, started exhibiting signs of helicopter mother not able to let her twenty-something son live his life, she started calling him nonstop all that day and many of the next, she reached for the phone to text or call, wanting to say that he needed to avoid this girl like the plague. But she stilled her voice thinking that he has to make his own mistakes, all this she told herself while texting some joke just to keep the lines of communication open.

A few weeks later, Micah called his mother to say he was in a park on a trail, smelling the sharp sweet smell of blooming flowers, and he stopped jogging to talk about the girl. He told her he loved the way Kayla wore black as an emblem of pride, or despair, he wasn't sure which. Some of the time he felt it was the color of the callous, or the rebellious, depending on the time of the day he was thinking about it, and how he was feeling in the moment, the color was attractive in any case. "And black is the only color she wears," Micah said into the phone. "She manages to make black look like all the colors of the rainbow are represented. Never have I felt that the use of this color is exclusionary, everyone a rebel."

One day she wore a black cotton dress that looked gray—the color was so washed out it was almost purple, what they call vintage black, worn with deep black nail polish. Another day the same week, the black was an overly saturated black layered on black and iridescent nails that were blacker than black. The opposite of the whiteness of her perfectly rose-tinged pale-white face that looked as if it had never seen the sun, but not dead white, it was a living, breathing, healthy white; a vivid white framed by the blue-black of her thick ropy hair, and her lips, the impossible red of vermillion that in olden times was made from the mineral cinnabar, toxic to the nervous system, so probably not from that source; likely her lips were coated with a dye made from crushed cochineal females, a sessile parasite that lives on prickly pear cacti, feeding on plant moisture and nutrients—this he learned from an art teacher. Knowing that the females of that species use the red as a biological marker made her use of this dye even more potent.

With rising passion in his voice, he told his mother that while red is commonly found in the physical world, women seek to remind men of their red, aroused labia by displaying or wearing the color red, especially in their use of red lipstick, but the idea of black being a color adhering to a standard is absurd, is there such a color in nature? He went on ruminating, saying to her that the blackbird male is black, but not a true black, there's a blue sheen on his head grading to greenish iridescence on his body. And the black bear actually comes in a lot of colors, from black to blond. Black animal fur and natural (not dyed) human hair is actually neutral black that occurs naturally in charcoal, soot, graphite, some types of coal, certain types of marble, granite and basalt, and probably many other minerals. There's black agate and onyx, translucent quartz that is not pure, strands of other colors weave in. Pure black does not exist in nature.

Creating an ambiguous color that also mimics a bruise, and melts into a darkness that looks like something that came out of the earth, not something you could see without x-ray eyes—sight being just another one of man's inventions. He realized this knowledge surpassed everything he had previously understood about life, surpassing his sense of smell, touch, hearing, taste. The present moment is all there is, he realized. Memories are fluid, shape shifters, and existence has no memory. His brother's life extinguished at a time where everywhere else life was blossoming. If his brother could not be brought back from the dead, he wanted to be dead, too, and yet his very flesh throbbed with possibilities, his body open to it. But why so many duplicates...why would God require that he carry on with life when his brother fell? His brother who did not believe he could die. So much life is engaged in a relentless struggle to exist, living things seem to know that a great number of their duplicates will stumble and fall to their deaths. It's a vicious plan; a lifetime spent avoiding the voracious claws and mouth devouring all available food. He recalled that in *Magic Mountain*, Thomas Mann's character Lodovico Settembrini thinks "...of course [Naphta] would defend the primitive religious level on which death was a terror wrapped in horrors most mysterious..." and then Naphta, as if to underscore Stetembrini's thoughts, says, "without which, of course, there would be no such thing as architecture, painting, sculpture, music, or poetry." He would put a positive spin on death.

How much was Micah's attraction tied to Kayla's obsession with the color that represents black? He puzzled over this compulsion he felt viewing the black that she wore like an emblem. But he did not say the obvious: Black as a symbol of death equals the negation of life. It was as if he was telling the world he had placed one foot on the boat to Hades. "What you will win from me here will be death and black destruction (kêr); and broken under my spear you will give me glory and give your soul (psychê) to Aides of the famed horses (klytopolos)." Homer in the Iliad said this. And in Thomas Mann's words, "death as form ...death as something austere...bloody, the Inquisition, starched ruffs, Loyola, the Esorial."

His mother stopped herself from saying, "No!" knowing that would only serve to make the girl appear more attractive. His mother had to display the patience of Job in the withholding of her anguish and fears. And in turn, Micah downplayed her addiction, saying it was in the past, she was fine now, only does it occasionally, and otherwise how could she hold a job?

Micah's mother felt her fears for her son would overwhelm her. She wanted to tell him to come home and she would protect him from people like that but she said something else, something to the effect of going slow and being careful. She learned the girl's full name: Kayla Sanchez. Micah's mother looked for Kayla on Fakebook. The account was open to public view. What she saw in the girl's profile and posts made her gasp. The girl reminded Micah's mother of Amalie, Micah's first love, down to the athletic body and large breasts, the intense gaze, the sexy clothing. But Amalie paled in comparison. Kayla's makeup was hard, slutty: Her lips a fire-engine red and with exaggerated swooshes of eyeliner thickly applied and curled where the eye ends in an arabesque, the eye shadow purple ala Amy Winehouse. In fact, Kayla resembled a more voluptuous Amy Winehouse, down to all the tattoos and scars, her hair the same intense shade of blue black falling down her back in waves. Except this girl did not look anorexic, she was curvy, more like model Ashley Graham, the first plus-sized Vogue cover girl with enormous breasts and attitude that could only be called snarky, the way she pursed her lips as if she were daring someone to pump her full of semen. Looking at Kayla's profile and the remarks on her posts gave Micah's mother the chills. She wanted to warn her son to stay away but knew that would only draw him further into the girl's orbit.

Later that day, Micah's mother saw from her phone that her son had tried to call her several times, but she been away from her phone, having left it behind in the car while shopping. Now that she had her phone she tried calling him back but got no answer. It must be something important, she reasoned, and felt a wave of anxiety. He had called six times. She left a message that she had been away from her phone and now had it back and to please call, but never heard his voice again. She immediately called some of his friends, those living in the Bay Area, to ask if they had heard from him, and hit dead ends. At a loss, Micah's mother texted a couple of his Vegas friends, one of whom said she had received several texts from Micah the previous night. Which made this woman, who called herself Cosmic Princess, the last person who interacted with him, someone Micah's mother barely knew. Cosmic Princess said they often texted each other in the middle of the night when they couldn't sleep, and they discussed their dreams. And he had seemed fine. He had texted that he was dreaming about finding abundance and joy. His employer called and said they hadn't heard from him, he hadn't shown up for work, and they didn't know how to reach his landlord or even what his latest address was. They asked if someone could check on him.

The next day Nick replied to Micah's mother's text, saying he'd stop by after work and see about Micah. That evening his landlord discovered his dead body behind his locked bedroom door, copious blood surrounding his upper torso. He was sprawled next to the bed, and it looked like he had hit his head on the way down. He had his keys and phone in his coat pocket as if he was preparing to leave, perhaps to where he worked in Sunnyvale. The coroner said the meth burst his aorta. Likely he felt a sudden stabbing, radiating pain to his chest and back before slipping into unconsciousness and dying from massive internal bleeding. Micah's mother called Matt, his former therapist, having remembered that Micah said that they had spoken. But she could not get through to his office and thought to call his lawyer, Michele, knowing they were friends. She wanted to tell Matt what happened, to connect with someone who knew him well, maybe for reassurance that her boy's life was not in vain. Michele explained why no one picked up Matt's line.

The last Michele heard, no one knew where Matt was. She learned that after his divorce was finalized, Matt drove up to Mount Rainier and parked his car in one of the parking lots near several trailheads but left it unlocked, with his phone and keys on the passenger seat prominently displayed. His family thought he had gone up one of the trails, but the various search parties could not find him. He simply vanished, never to be heard from again. His body, never found, remains missing to this day. Micah's mother read the internet articles from Matt's family requesting volunteers in the searches of multiple trails on the mountain, lasting several hours a few days apart, and then a month later, and up until then, nothing. No bodies even vaguely matching Matt's description had been found either dead or alive. His family kept his phone line open in the hope he'd show up someday.

Micah's mother asked Michele if she had told Micah about Matt's divorce and the lawyer said no that they had not spoken since the day he'd been released from jail. Micah's mother told Michele of her great sadness to think that Seth liked to ascribe his time on the Chemical as wondrous and magical, giving birth to dreams that he clutched as tightly as gems buried in the earth's core, and as hard to acquire. When Seth died, Micah had been the sole possessor of this knowledge. Micah's mother felt that part of her died with each of their deaths, but particularly with the death of Micah. He had suffered the most. In *Infinite Jest,* Gately takes Dilaudid to avoid "a terrible stomach-sinking dread that probably dates back to being alone in his XXL-Dentons and crib below Herman the Ceiling That Breathed." Gately hopes to lose the feeling that he's "under a storm-cloudy sky that bulged and receded like a big gray lung." This is what he needed the drug for. Once the drug kicks in, "the sky stopped breathing and turned blue."

■

I said to myself, Micah had to pull himself together with a steely strength to get up every single day and try to make a go of it. He lasted seven years without his brother. Much longer than I expected, as he seemed overly dependent on Seth. At worse, I expected him to cave like a depleted balloon, though I hoped Micah would rise to the task and work hard to accomplish the things they planned to do together, maybe in partnerships with other people. I hoped that he'd make a go of it and perhaps outlast me, but it was not to be.

I went to the last place my son had lived, a rental in a house filled with an odd assortment of people, run by two sisters from the Philippines who could barely speak English. We spoke haltingly and make sense of our different ways of speaking. They both said what a nice man he was and apologized for not finding his body until a few days had past and the whole house smelled of death. The smell was overpowering, clinging to all his things. I found a letter he had written to his brother before he died, handwritten in a notebook, and left on his bed, as if it was a farewell note.

He wrote:

"You left me when I needed you most. The last thing I'll remember is your face—you between worlds. Do I feel guilty? Yes, I'm here and you're not. Everything was going great, your plans for the future. So much left unsaid, nothing compared to what's left undone. We were going to change the world, you and me, remember? All those years spent laughing and crying together. We were supposed to complete each other, and now here I am with not much more than a distant memory. I forget what you feel like, what your energy means to me. Now you'll never age. Ironic that death can be the fountain of youth. I'll take what you've given me, great secrets of value and truth, and rejection by God herself. I'd trade it all for another look at your face, and yet...all I have to do is look in the mirror.

Speaking of mirrors, I might have well been talking to one. I haven't changed, but my energy has. The only difference now is I know what it means to die. I'll always be afraid, and lonelier than ever, I need to accept it. I've been left to suffer alone.

What it felt to touch your body. The secret of death. Your cold clammy skin. The fucking rigor mortis. You pulled back but you were DEAD. Defeated and you fought me...I didn't do this buddy, you did it to yourself. You're fucking face sullen defeated. No more fight. No more fight, no more life. Blotchy fucking stomach. Leaving me cold, afraid, alone. I fucking hate you. You miserable piece of shit. Come back to me, please, I can't live without you.

I'm having quite an emotional upheaval, huh? I've always felt something was wrong with me. Like something didn't sit right in my soul. Sort of a spiritual cancer. It's affected my confidence, my communication skills, and my desire to live. I can't quite put my finger on it. Something I hate to confess. I wish I could blame my brother's death on my misery, but it started when I hit puberty. I didn't feel human or connected. I felt lost and afraid. I sought many different channels to complete me, vices upon vices. Hard drugs, from heroin to fentanyl to LSD, hoping to find truth, but the truth is subjective, it's always changing. How can I trust something that always changes—something that would last and would be there in the morning when I wake? Objects come and go, and so do people. As badly as I wish a relationship or sex could save me, it can't. I am here, knowing I will die alone, despite the fact that I was born literally a few minutes apart from another person, someone I shared the womb with. I always come back to passion, yet I feel confused. I express through the guitar and piano a very sensual expression through my fingertips: My greatest love, loss, and adoration of life. And I can thank my brother for teaching it to me, something I'll be forever grateful. And knowing he'll never leave me, at least not for long. He gives me reason to live because my experiences are to be shared. I feel most alive when we all live as one. Namaste."

=

I wish I could talk with both my boys right now and tell them how much I miss them.

HORNING'S HIDEOUT

Mentally prepared for the work of taking all our camping gear out of our car and carrying things piecemeal, arms straining with the heaviest items, the temperature hovering close to ninety degrees but not humid, back braced holding the weight low on my hip, transferring weight to my core as much as I could manage, feeling heartened that the blue-grass concert in the coastal Oregon hills was going to be fantastic from various friends I met on the way. I knew I had to suck up the discomfort of hiking. There was going to be magic in *them there hills*, to coin an old saying. The concert started Friday and ended Sunday night, really an old-fashioned camping concert with most people living in tents with no running water or other amenities except for portables in designated areas.

We were not the only ones who had gone to Horning's to mourn a loved one. Among the friends who had done the same, I learned that Ben Kaufman, one of the founding members of Yonder Mountain String Band, buried his father's ashes on the hillside at Horning's. While I could not do the same; I was doing the next best thing. When my first boy died, the other son specifically requested that we follow the ancient Judaic tradition which calls for the unmutilated body to be buried in a simple shroud in an unpainted pine box and buried in a conservative Jewish cemetery. I had come to honor the individual and totally different spirits of my twin sons, both who loved raves above all else. That was the one thing they shared together, the essential thing they loved. The bouts of sobriety made the body less able to deal when indulging again, probably made it easier to overdose. And of course, I think about them a lot, imagining what they would be doing now: Would Micah have realized his dreams of being a DJ, and Seth a screenwriter? My babies. I was so proud of their achievements, so ambitious for them to succeed.

But then I remembered where I was, and the tasks I had yet to do. I had to stop my mental whirring while standing motionless staring off into trees, as beautifully hued as the bountiful leaves were, a rich emerald, my favorite color. Some things could go into backpacks, other things would fit in the wagon, and I'd cinch the whole mess up with pulley cables. I was happy that I had been working out at the gym for years doing lunges and bicep curls so I could concentrate on climbing uphill on wonderfully soft dirt trails without pain, the uneven surfaces necessitating proper placement of feet in rapid succession, taking account the weight of my load and in places rocky, with my eyes on the killer views of old growth forest lining the trail, knowing in my heart that the greatest beauty is in nature. Manmade engineering feats can be beautiful, but rarely make me fall on my knees in silent supplication.

I was familiar with camping in remote areas of the west coast, though I did not know the difference between so-called 'car camping' and the practice of parking the car in a designated area that necessitated traveling by foot a far distance, at least two miles, to reach the camping area where we were allowed to pitch our tent. Part of the way, we took the shuttle over the three steepest of hills in a vehicle that turned out to be a crazy mud-caked jeep that looked as if it barely survived Afghanistan, and the driver too, as if he had been raised like a sapling in a remote part of the country, looking sturdy as an oak, all gnarled and baked to a fine crisp by the sun, and as pleasant and happy to help us as we could wish for, and very much at home with knots and ropes and ready to handle whatever the situation called for.

Stretch and I borrowed a wagon that first time, when we took the boys, and piled the tent and the camping chairs, and bags of clothing, tied with twine up steep hills searching for a suitable site for our two tents. The second time we brought our own wagon, so we did not have to borrow, which saved us some steps and made things easier, having parked on the same hill near the entrance with thousands of other people who had arrived that day and many the day before in an effort to get a nice space for our tents, so friends could be close enough to join chairs in a communal area in the middle and share drinks, snacks, and tell scary stories around a camp stove, campfires not allowed. A lot of other people were doing the same thing, lugging their gear in wagons. It was an interesting look, to see the parade of people with their belongings piled in wagons, somewhat medieval. My feeling that we were getting a sense of how easy our modern lives are, and how much we would miss technology and how difficult it truly would be to lose all sources of electricity, say we were visited with a cataclysmic event, how paralyzed without our phones. I remembered my boys had been unhappy about the scant cell coverage, but then they got into the spirit of the festival. As things stood, open fires were not happening; this was Oregon after all, and the threat of wildfires high, so we would have to do without that sort of ancient comfort, the kind that our ancestors reached for. I could not truly imagine what it was like to be transported back to the time of the settlers, but I thought I could, and felt I did in flashes, like when we were hauling our camping gear in wagons. I remember my father taking us children on extended multi week camping trips in Montana and California, always involving campfires near lakes or rivers away from civilization, and away from designated camping areas, and that was one of the pleasures of camping, existing far away from stores, the closest 25 miles away. We kids slept under trees, eschewing tents, we had no sense of danger. My sons liked tents; they could not imagine sleeping without one, and told me it was impossible, and they had to have air mattresses.

As a child I thought it was the most fun thing in the world to suffer that sort of deprivation, the kind of physical discomfort that stings momentarily, but at the end of the day would be forgotten. I looked forward to sitting in front of a campfire, roasting marshmallows, still shivering from having dunked myself in snowmelt during the day. But in this modern reliving of this paradigm, we had no marshmallows, just multigrain chips and crackers, and chunky peanut butter. As we could use the hookups at an artist friend's RV down the hill when our cell phones needed charging, we were not completely cut off from the world, and though there was no Wi-Fi on the hill around our tent, we knew in the valley where the amphitheater and vending area were located, we would find coverage. Other tent dwellers said they were hiking back to the hill where their cars were parked and using their car batteries to keep the charge going in their cellphones, so it made us happy to know someone in the artists camp that we could mooch from. And of course, we knew if we had an emergency, we could hike up to our car, but I hoped we would not have to go there; it had been an arduous climb. In any case, there was a cooperative spirit around us, a friendly vibe not typical of most concert-going crowds; it seemed people thought if you were so eager to get there and do the climb, you were golden. Nobody complained except me about cellphones going dead. But then I saw a table near the trucks serving hot food near the amphitheater that offered to charge phones free from a battery that stored solar energy, and I felt heartened.

This time we came to mourn our sons, and everything felt different. I did not sleep that well that first night and woke up early. No one else was stirring; we had risen with the first evidence of the sun's rays peeking through the trees. The honey buckets down the hill were primitive, the kind you see at construction sites but serviceable, and we made sure we had extra napkins in our day packs, a stash just in case they ran out of toilet paper, which happened occasionally. There was no way to wash the face except for a crazy looking porta sink with a dribble of a flow that sort of worked, but not the way I would have wished, so not serviceable. Face washing would likely not happen and if that seemed too draconian, I could simply jump in the lake. There was one a mile or so away from us down the hill, and it looked clean enough.

We waited until early in the morning, around 7:30 by our cell phones and hiked down about a half a mile to one of the smaller stages with a barista setup, serving lattes and baked goodies in a makeshift unpainted planked hut, with forest all around. This improved our sense that we could overcome the drawbacks of living with scant sanitation back at base camp. I stayed away from the baked treats and did not allow myself to look at them as anything but idle curiosities, something I might see in a museum, though I did succumb to the latte, as did my boyfriend. Coffee is one of the best vehicles for supercharging a keto diet, further encouraging fat burning and weight loss, so I was happy to have that one treat. We both love it with hot foamed coconut cream.

Coffees in hand, we went to the top of the empty amphitheater—literally a gentling sloping hill with the stage wedged at the end of the flat area with the lake in view of the stage—to sit in the shadow of the trees that ring the amphitheater and watch the early risers set their blankets on the slope in preparation for what they call "ranching", having staked their spot during the day's events planned for that afternoon. We watched as the ancient water truck laid down a spray of water on the surface of the area where the serious dancers congregated, basically a large patch of dirt where the grass had been worn away to prevent it from becoming a dustbowl when the bands played their boogie music.

When we tired of that, we headed back along a series of roundabout pathways, since nothing provided a straight shot to our tent. On the way, we met a few of the families who brought toddlers, and several of these little ones were playing in the dirt near the path leading to our tent with evident enjoyment. The dirt was soft and malleable, and the kids were absorbed in their play, laughing and cooing in unison. We made a detour around them, happy to see their joy. Seeing these babies with dirty hands and faces brought back memories of times my children used to play in the dirt as youngsters. In my early days I also loved dirt. Stretch said he had the same reaction. Both of us had early childhood memories of playing in the dirt and knowing that dirt was not to be shunned, but a potential source of delight. My parents thought dirt was a wonderful low-cost way for kids to amuse themselves since we lived in a rural area that did not have many toys. We kids would cut up heavy-duty moving boxes and slide downhill on them until the cardboard wore out. And when no more boxes could be found, my brothers made roads and built dirt houses with their hands, while I used to pretend bake mud pies. But none of these kids had access to water. At this festival, there was a sense of conservation in the air. Alas, it was a different era.

In the communal area, chairs were set up around a table with food that reflected a healthy sensibility, homemade sourdough, and strawberry jam, all locally sourced. Our friends' young boys, Depree, 9, and Quinn 6, were scarfing bowls of cereal, leaving their sourdough sandwiches for later. They looked content until a girl about Depree's age appeared, slender and beautiful, tossing her abundant shoulder-length-dark hair, reminding me of my own early self, the way I looked in pictures, my wild hair cropped well below my ears. This girl took the sagebrush broom from the table and held it in her arms like it was a baby. Depree said he wanted it. The girl refused, said she had it first. The girl's father issued forth from his tent on the other side of the path across from the communal area like an oracle. "Nicole, why don't you share it," he said. "Bring peace and tranquilly to the world."

"No, I don't want to," Nicole said.

I told Nicole that I was the same way when I was young—I didn't trust any boy to return something I gave up, even with adults around. Then I thought about my boys when they were at that age, and Seth would outlast Micah, and make it physical, and one would slug the other, and they would trade slugs until Micah gave in, the peacemaker. And I could see that Seth reveled in his ability to outlast Micah. Frequently I had to force myself to stand back, not interfere until someone was choking the other, and not step in at all if they seemed to resolve their differences on their own. That rarely happened, but I tried to encourage them to seek their own solutions. If the boys seemed out of sorts, I would ask if we could talk about what happened to cause their initial skirmish so we could cobble together a solution.

Her father threw up his hands, "Nicole has her own mind," he said wryly.

We fell to talking. Turned out they lived a couple towns north of us near Seattle. We were joined by his wife, Nicole's mother, whom the daughter obviously took after, who said without preamble that her daughter liked to be in charge.

"She's constantly bossing us around," Nicole's mother said, with a petulant look on her pretty face.

"She'll slay them with her looks," Stretch said. "She'll get away with murder."

"I made jam from the strawberries in our yard," Tobi, Depree's mother, said, having come out of her tent and offering everyone sourdough slices with jam.

"We are both intermittent fasting so no food until 4 pm," I said. "Maybe later tonight we'll have some. We love homemade bread."

"I'm finally losing weight," Stretch said.

"I have a problem gaining weight," Brent, Depree's father, said. "I can't eat enough to make it stick. I eat all day long and nada. Speaking of which, I'll take some of that bread."

Tobi held out a couple of slices on a plate for him, her bulging thighs attesting to her love of sourdough. Brent took the plate and sat down and commenced munching, his cheeks squirrelly full.

The level of sharing reminded me of the time we went to a family reunion in Jackson Hole, with family that had come far and wide, not something I got to see very often. You had to love bluegrass and be willing to extend yourself for the privilege of being surrounded by old growth forest and a lake, with only a couple of barns and houses visible for miles and with cars tucked away. A beautiful illusion emerged each time we went to Horning's to see a weekend music festival featuring bluegrass or similarly inclined bands such as the gospel tinged Toots and the Maytals and bluegrass with more of a progressive acoustic vibe like the Infamous Stringdusters, the Motet, the Polish Ambassador, and Polyrhythmics, with The String Cheese Incident headlining. They played every night to rapturous crowds dressed in tie dye and fanciful clothing, girls in short shorts, and some in fairy costumes. I felt like I had come home to the family farm to witness this incredible spontaneous event.

The Cheese played crowd pleasures like "She Don't Say," and "Roll Over," and wound down the "Glory" jam, "Round the Wheel," and "Mrs. Brown's." Each time the headliner came out, huge balloons were tossed around, and I felt I transported to a spiritual place, and I knew that my boys felt the same way, their faces joyful as if we had ascended to the top of Mount Olympus. As if we were feasting with the gods of old, and dancing with my friends and family around me, everything felt transcendent, I saw the divine in everything, the gods everywhere. I could understand why, when Achilles scaled the walls of Troy and was about to sack the city, he was killed by an arrow, shot by the Trojan prince Paris. I could understand why the Greek warriors that day thought that the god Apollo guided the arrow into his most vulnerable spot, his heel—it makes complete sense when you realize that the ancient Greeks feared snakes most of all—many of their loved ones had been killed or bitten by snake venom, and their heels vulnerable when walking through fields as we were doing that weekend. But luckily we saw no snakes. The only creatures we had to watch for were the dozen peacocks that liked to hang around the lake front, looking for insects and plants to eat.

There were a lot of hugs and kisses going around. Dancing through the crowd, there were several horses on a stick. First there was just the brown horse, but then a white horse joined it. They ganged up to attack a jellyfish on a stick. And these windsock people props, huge stick figures made out of cloth that seemed to dance like oversized puppets as they made their way through the crowd, and then the statue of the fatted calf on a pole added to the gaiety. It felt like the gods were smiling, happy with humans for the moment. And while there were plenty of semi-naked people at this event, Horning's would not be complete without the completely naked hula hooper. I suppose he thought to have all appendages available if he needed to stop his hoop if it started to fall.

The next time we went, Yonder Mountain String Band headlined in the spirit of the Cheese and assorted other great bluegrass bands played that weekend like the Del McCoury Band and the Kitchen Dwellers.

We came to learn about Yonder Mountain when they moved to Horning's Hideout, where The String Cheese Incident and Leftover Salmon used to continuously host concerts. But it took Yonder Mountain String Band a while to get there. They started playing the summit in 1999 from their home in Boulder, Colorado and then added an Oregon show they called Dexter Lake Music Festival for their West Coast adherents, which they outgrew in a couple years. They are that good.

Yonder String kept the Grateful Dead energy alive with fast, rollicking bluegrass to country ballads to experiments with other genres like the soul/funk-tinged "Broken Records," and their dedication to keeping things almost entirely acoustic (and without drums) makes their sound totally authentic and not tied to any specific trend or era.

The tears from my heart spilled out through my eyes, expressing the grief that I lived every day listening to the finger picking skills of the clever musicians creating a powerfully told story of the deaths of loved ones forever gone. I mourned them—not so much my father as my sons. My father lived a full life, but my sons were just preparing their launch. Seth was writing a screenplay that had promise. He was a good writer, and his stories were getting published in literary journals. He was making a lot of friends, connecting with people, and in the words of Nietzsche, "and that is why when we are near them we felt human and natural for once and would like to cry out." With Goethe: "How magnificent and precious every living thing is! How suited to its condition, how true, how full of being." Ditto with Micah, the beautiful old soul, the magnificent friend.

For what reason I can't say, but I started thinking about Matt G. and wondered if he'd ever turned up. While in line for the bathroom, I looked on my phone to see if anything new popped up. I came up empty, the only mention was when I inserted this line: "Matthew Gittleman is a therapist who works with kids and families." That line was in an article displayed in MyNorthwest.com which aired on 97.3 KIRO News Radio on Apr 15, 2011, at 5:35 PM about kids as young as seven getting plastic surgery. I listened to the story narrated by Rachel Belle. Otherwise, the internet was scrubbed clean of Matt's name. Unlike the previous times I've checked, when the internet was packed with references to his 'gone girl' status. There were other Matthew Gittleman's with different middle names and different pictures. But then I remembered Matt's ex-wife was a top rated lawyer specializing in immigration law and working for an internationally recognized law firm. Matt and his former wife had moved to Seattle so she could pursue her law degree, and he kept a cozy home office overlooking a beautiful garden which I had visited many times to talk about my sons while he served me tea. He told me that he and his then wife adopted two children, and he spoke to me often in those days about them. He thought he was the glue that kept the family together; he was the emphatic one.

I began to speculate about his state of mind when he fell apart and she asked for a divorce. Perhaps he felt doubly betrayed, once by Micah and then by his wife. Perhaps for her it was bad for business to be intimately connected to a missing person case. This, at the bleeding heart of Matt's darkness, I stopped myself and decided not to probe. Was it really my business to rip open this painful memory and ask the ex anything about Matt? To ask anything of a woman I'd never met, considering my son could have been instrumental in triggering her ex-husband's mental breakdown. Even at my rudest, I never could stomach wanting to grind into wounds that barely had a chance to heal to appease my idle curiosity.

Late afternoon, we were all gathered in the communal area, no campfire, but still cozily sitting in a circle of camp chairs, the sun's brightness blunted by the thin polyester shield of the wide awning with the trees all around, leaving spindly shadows on the elevated fabric high above our heads. Sitting smugly in a chair in the middle of the communal space, with all of us around, Tabi pulled her dark curly hair away from her face and said that she'd heard Northwest String Summer would be no more; the producer decided he was finished promoting it after a run of fifteen years or so. Tabi's voice sounded a note of dreadful finality. Everyone around her looked stricken as well, as if they had heard the world was soon to cave in, and there would be no music forevermore.

Just then Depree went up to Nicole and smite the sagebrush broom out of her hands with a slap of his hand. Hers was a loose hold, but she made up for it by crying shrilly with a voice that did not seem to have issued out of a young girl and immediately pulled at the broom now lodged in Depree's fist with both hands, shaped now like the long talons of a harpy eagle. She pulled with all her might, and continued screaming as if she were fighting for her life. They wrestled with the handle, like arm wrestlers sometimes buckling, other times pushing the other arm down, with neither one giving much that could not be taken back. The children were roughly about the same size, though the girl was taller, slender, and willowy like a model with no muscles to speak of. Then Nicole seemed to tire noticeably, her arm giving way.

"It's mine now," Depree growled, yanking at it so hard it fell to the ground.

Tabi rushed over, her ample behind shaking, and clucked over her son with the anxiety of a mother hen whose chickee is misbehaving. She sternly commanded him to give it back. When he hesitated, she waved him off and said, "Get out of my sight, I'm so angry at you."

Depree went running along a path leading away from our general area and disappeared into a grove of trees. I found it hard to watch, thinking he would surely get lost on a mountain with a lot of crevices, trails with dead ends, and strangers milling about. Amid haunting images of my boys as they looked the last time we were together at Horning's peopling my mind's eye: Two tall rangy boys, Seth with his beautiful smile, his arms spread, that special smile that everyone who have ever met him mentions, and Micah looking solemnly at his brother with rapt attention as if he was in the present of a god, and simply happy to be in his orbit. It's the same look I have on my face.

ACKNOWLEDGEMENTS

"Anatomy of a Firefighter" was published in *Potato Soup Journal*, "The Hick and his Wife" in *Quail Bell Literary Magazine*, "Betrayal" in *Citron Review*, "Terminal" in *Cultured Vultures*, "Grandpa" in *Crack the Spine*, and "Fourth Child" in *Urban Arts*, "Family Dinner" was an honorable mention in Glimmer Train's Fiction Contest for Emerging Writers in 2015 and never published. "Jail" was published *in Logophile Magazine* in April 2015 and "Zero Evidence" appeared in *Juked* in 2020, "Ice Dunking" in May 2019 issue of *The Catamaran Literary Review*, and "Breastfeeding Blues" in the June 2019 issue of *Adelaide Literary Magazine*. "The Sky Stopped Breathing" won first place for creative nonfiction in the Adelaide Literary Award 2019 Contest. An anthology by Riverfeet Press titled *Awake in the World, V.2* published my essay "Calamity Jane" in August 2019.

I thank my teachers at Bennington Writing Seminars, chiefly Askold Melnyczuk, and Brian Morton, who guided me on my path of learning how to inject the self into essays, which I had never done in all my years of freelance reporting for business journals, and it was difficult journey for me. I was finally able to cough out some semblance of stories, disjointed at best, and these wonderful writers at Bennington were encouraging and able guides, helping me learn how to craft creative nonfiction and fiction in way I had never been able to achieve.

I thank the people at Vine Leaves Press, in particular Elaina Parsons and Heather Marshall for their wonderful editing, and publisher Jessica Bell for providing a nurturing, inclusive environment.

For my story "Anatomy of a Firefighter", I found information about fires and how they behave on Britannica.com and the particulars of the canyon fire of 1968 on www//fire.lacounty.gov/51-years-later. In "Calamity Jane", I interviewed Daryl McElroy, president of the Texas Bronc Riders Association, read *Rodeo News* and wranglernetwork.com as well as Wikipedia. In "Ice Dunking", I used information from Lonely Planet.com, Skarksider.com, Wikipedia, the wildswimmingbrothers.com, and the washingtonpost.com.>history>2023/03/05.

In "Michael and Amy", I relied on *Psychology Today* and Harvard.edu.com for information and statistics about infidelity and partner swapping. In "Therapy for Dogs", academyofanimatedart.com/color-symbolism. In "Zero Evidence", I found "The Gambler's Lament" in Wikipedia, and information about lawsuits in NYPost.com>2016/02/27, and atlaobscura.com/articles/monte-carlo-suicides, onlinebooks-library.upenn.edu/cassellsweekly; nytimes.com/216/06/15/books.review/making-monte-carlo-by-mark-braude.html.

VINE LEAVES PRESS

Enjoyed this book?
Go to *vineleavespress.com* to find more.
Subscribe to our newsletter: